MW00987886

THE BOOK OF plans FOR smallgardens

MITCHELL BEAZLEY

THE BOOK OF plans FOR

smallgardens

General Editor
Andrew Wilson

The Book of Plans for Small Gardens

General Editor **Andrew Wilson**

First published in Great Britain in 2007 by
Mitchell Beazley, an imprint of Octopus Publishing
Group Limited, 2–4 Heron Quays, London E14 4JP.

Copyright © Octopus Publishing Group 2007

All rights reserved. No part of this work may be reproduced
or utilized in any form or by any means, electronic or
mechanical, including photocopying, recording or by any
information storage and retrieval system, without the prior
written permission of the publisher.

A CIP catalogue record for this book is available from the
British Library.

ISBN-10: 1 84533 206 7
ISBN-13: 978 1 84533 206 8

Commissioning Editor **Michèle Byam**
Art Director **Tim Foster**
Executive Art Editor **Rhonda Summerbell**
Senior Editor **Suzanne Arnold**
Editor **Susanna Edwards**
Designer **Colin Goody**
Picture Research Manager **Giulia Hetherington**
Picture Researcher **Jenny Faithfull**
Indexer **Sue Farr**
Production Controller **Angela Young**

Set in Frutiger

Colour reproduction by Sang Choy, Singapore
Printed and bound by Toppan, China

CONTENTS

How To Use This Book

Some designs are given an individual page. Others are displayed across two pages in order to clarify the message or to include additional supporting information. For example, the work of those designers who open each section is illustrated in this way.

The chapters are designed for ease of reference, determined by garden type and the challenges posed. Initially, it may be most appropriate to refer to the section or sections that most closely reflect one's own garden. However, many designs in other sections may well contain ideas that can be easily interpreted or transferred to another scale or garden type. It is important to look at a range of design ideas with an open mind rather than to look for a specific garden because it resembles one's own.

Each design is shown as a plan with some additional visual support. Often, if the garden is not yet built, this support will be in the form of one or more of the drawings identified in the introduction. Where the gardens have been realized, photographs of the completed scheme are used. In some cases photographs from existing gardens showing planting or construction of a similar vein have been used to support or explain the design ideas.

The individual designers responsible for the work shown have been invited to explain briefly their gardens, providing information on their inspirational sources, briefs from the garden owners, or the character and context of the sites on which they have worked. Additional information, in bullet point form, helps to clarify why gardens have been created in a particular way, providing insight into the design process and into the final proposals. A typical page layout is shown here to help the reader navigate the book.

Garden designer's name and / or name of design practice

The main details of the garden, showing approximate size, soil type, aspect (orientation), and any key features within the garden. All gardens, except where noted, are in the northern hemisphere

Plantsman's Garden

KEITH PULLAN GARDEN DESIGN
DIMENSIONS 15 x 12m (50 x 40ft)
SOIL alkaline
ASPECT south-facing but on a north-facing incline
KEY FEATURES different planting areas for a wide variety of plant types

This was a very steep garden with a slope rising away from the house and almost no view out from the house from the ground floor. The owner wanted spaces for sitting, a pond, and a purpose-built orchid house, as well as a big area for planting a large variety of different plant types.

From the house several interconnected levels are used to create seating and planting areas and water features within a confined space. A rectangular grid forms the basis of the design, providing consistent shapes in both plan and elevation. Against a backdrop of a dense conifer hedge at the back of the garden raised beds of very dense planting are at a higher level than the rest of the garden. Within this shelter, a small, intimate sitting area is constructed with an overflowing basin water feature as a focal point. Leading back to the house, rockwork is built into a slope as a habitat for rock and scree planting. Stepping stones lead back to the house as an informal path.

In the centre of the garden a formal pond, planted with waterlilies, is fed by a water spill and this borders a larger terrace for dining near the house. A pergola screens the garage at the side of the garden and provides an opportunity for the owner to grow a variety of climbers.

water feature

dining area

water spill

rockwork slope for rock and scree planting

formal pool feature

A brief description of the design, usually including the client brief or requirements, and any particular issues or problems with the original site

Additional view to support the plan; in this case, a perspective

above *This sketch shows how the different levels and planting types work together, with a water feature as a focal point.*

88 INFORMAL GARDENS

Garden plan, showing the
layout or design of the garden,
often in relation to the house,
and the shape of the site

Directional pointing to
north, when possible

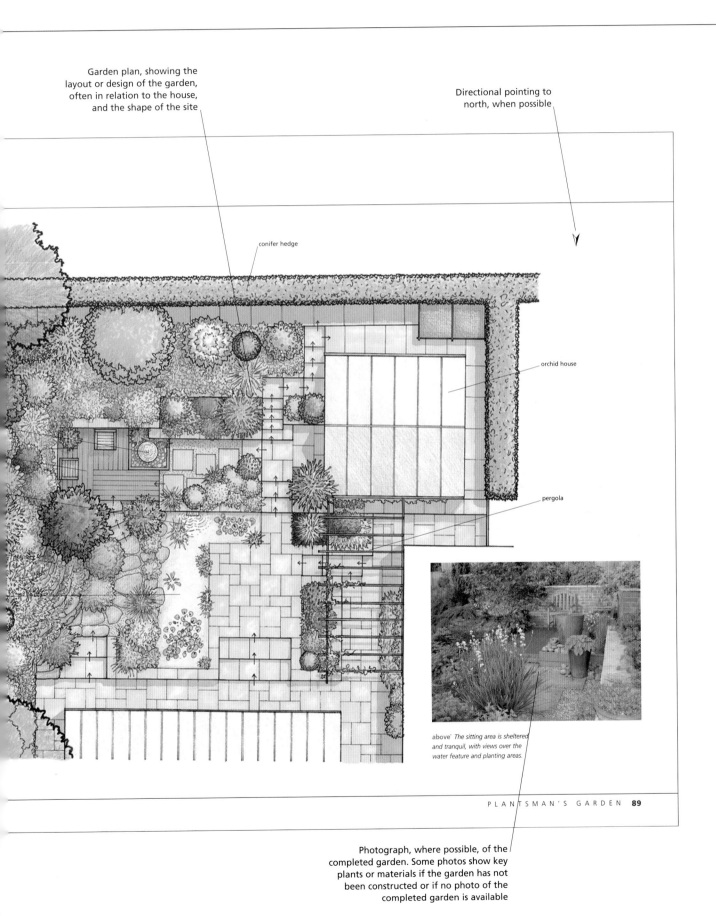

conifer hedge

orchid house

pergola

above: *The sitting area is sheltered
and tranquil, with views over the
water feature and planting areas.*

Photograph, where possible, of the
completed garden. Some photos show key
plants or materials if the garden has not
been constructed or if no photo of the
completed garden is available

INTRODUCTION

The Book of Plans for Small Gardens is dedicated to the design of small spaces, whether self-contained gardens or solutions for a part of a larger area. There are approximately 140 gardens within this book, produced by a wide range of designers. What they have in common is the scale of garden space, which ranges from the modest to the positively tiny. Although the spaces may be small, the ideas and approaches are wide-ranging and imaginative.

The designs are always shown in plan form because this enables the complete layout to be understood. Additional supporting drawings are included to provide a better sense of scale; or they may concentrate on a specific detail of particular interest. It is often the photographs and the designer descriptions that bring the gardens to life – the former showing the reality and the latter explaining the thinking behind the design and the problems solved. This provides an insight into the work of the designer and the process of design.

The range of possibilities and options for difficult, challenging, or restricted spaces is clearly communicated through the wide variety of designer responses, producing in the process an inspirational and rewarding collection of ideas.

Small Garden Design

For many of us, the reality of the gardens that we own can best be described as limited, small, or modest in scale. But, these descriptors themselves are relative terms.

A suburban plot may typically stretch to 30 x 6m (100 by 20ft) for example; small by the standards of revered British houses Sissinghurst or Hidcote Manor but positively gigantic by comparison with a balcony or courtyard that might be considered generous at 2 x 3m (6 x 10 ft). Yet a long, narrow plot creates design problems that require clever and specific solutions just as tiny spaces restrict options and demand a flexibility of use.

In dense, urban areas, garden spaces will not only be small but also lacking in privacy, shaded by surrounding walls and buildings, and open to pollution; these are harsh environments that need to work hard in providing relief and refreshment, privacy and escape.

The value of even the smallest garden space should never be underestimated, whether it is a plant-filled paradise or a minimalist oasis. The proof of this lies within the pages of this book, in which a huge range of small spaces has been given a new lease of life,

rejuvenated by designers answering the needs of their clients and resolving issues, surmounting difficulties, and inventing solutions to the demands of small spaces.

Small garden spaces have their own difficulties and special requirements. Many designers will charge a higher fee per square metre (yard) for the resolution of small-space design than for larger schemes. This allows for the detailed level of planning and often for the sheer logistics of clearing a garden and introducing new elements within a restricted or inaccessible space. With small gardens, considering costs and budgets simply based upon the size of a space is limited and unrealistic.

DESIGN CONSIDERATIONS

What all small gardens have in common is limited space. For small-garden owners this means that the plot must work hard for the investment made, in time or finance, in creating a workable garden. The combination of interesting planting, perhaps water or sculpture, and a space in which one can relax is certainly possible, as many of the examples in this book show. However, these activities and elements must all be contained within the same space, creating the need for great flexibility.

For the basic design, it can be difficult to come to terms with the fact that a table accommodating four or six people will need the same amount of space whether a garden is small or large. It is often tempting to make everything in a small space effectively smaller in scale in order to fit more in. This leads to a visual and functional overcrowding, together with an awkward sense of scale that can be visually uncomfortable and physically restrictive.

To create visual impact and to allow the space to be used successfully, it is often better to approach design from the opposite direction, making big statements in small spaces. This creates the need to simplify and limit one's options, perhaps the most important aspect of good design. This rule applies not only to furniture, the palette of hard materials, or the use of sculpture and ornament, but also to planting design and the selection of the range of species that will create atmosphere, drama, and change within the garden.

In recent years, garden design – or, more specifically, planting design – has changed and evolved dramatically from a rich and diverse plant collection often described as "the English style", which devoted space to a few each of just about every species available, to a more restricted palette in which the fewer species chosen work much harder to deliver a clear and structured design message; one that is often more spatial or sculptural than purely decorative. Even in smaller spaces, this refined and considered approach will pay dividends in creating stylish and sophisticated outdoor spaces. Much of the effort lies in choosing the selection of species that will create the garden character and then making those species work hard. The use of inter-planting – allowing plants to grow together amicably, effectively in the same space or area – allows planting to be enriched without becoming cluttered or choked. Bulbs planted through ornamental grasses provide a good example of this approach, although many perennials – such as salvia, centranthus, knautia, and astrantia – can be combined in this way.

opposite *This space is divided by an architectural pergola that provides a central focus and relates to the strong architectural backdrop.*

below *This isometric view shows the intricate form of the box hedges, laid out like a parterre, to provide a three-dimensional picture of the proposed design.*

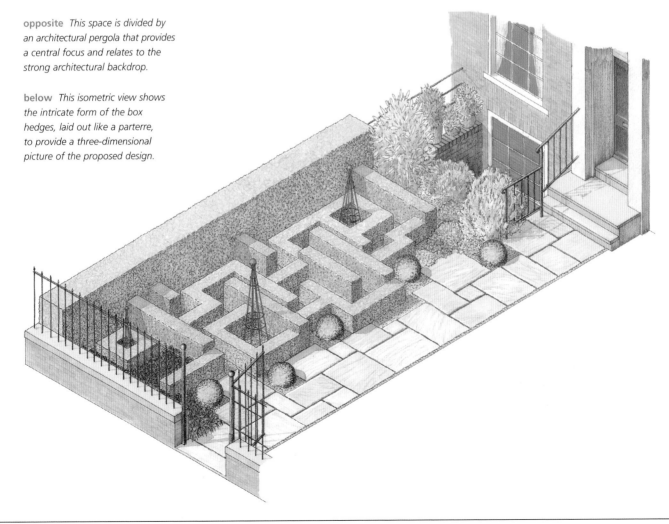

What many garden owners are looking for is a utopian paradise in which planting is colourful and active all year round. Potential clients frequently ask for year-round interest when discussing their needs. In many ways this is both difficult to achieve and not necessarily a desirable outcome, especially within a restricted space. To maximize year-round interest, one has to spread species selection wide in order to cover the four different seasons with some sense of variety. In smaller spaces, this will lead to one or two examples of each species, a complex palette, and a visual impact that is watered down as a result.

By selecting the seasons of greatest interest and accepting that, for example, winter will be a quieter period in the garden, much greater rewards and results can be gained in the periods when the garden can be most enjoyed. One successful method if colour and interest are required through the year is to create permanent planting in the garden as a whole but to top up and refresh the planting with annuals and bedding that could be restricted to pots and containers. This can introduce dynamic change, bold colour against a more neutral, permanent, planting backdrop, and the concept of colour changes that could affect mood and atmosphere.

As climate change becomes more a fact of life than a possibility, restrictions on our planting palettes may become enforced rather than optional. Gardeners across the world will have to review and evolve their planting styles and habits to accommodate these changes. A wider awareness of habitats and successful but flexible planting associations appropriate to regional weather patterns will be required if gardens, whatever their size, are to succeed.

Individuals want different things from their gardens but the following extremes in aesthetic presentation and use of a garden may help you to consider a direction for the satisfactory and successful resolution of your own small-garden planning.

THE PLANTAHOLIC GARDENER

For many small-garden owners, even the tiniest space represents an opportunity to collect, grow, nurture, and observe as wide a range of plant material as possible. For the plantaholic, one of everything is the rule and there is certainly a charming fascination in the discovery of previously unseen or literally hidden treasures. The sheer diversity of plant life that can be crammed into smaller spaces is amazing and seems to be something of a challenge.

However, design is in part about coherence and structure, organization, and visual legibility. In this kind of garden, it is the hard materials, furnishings, and ornaments that need this treatment, allowing the planting cornucopia to be displayed to its best advantage. A single material for all pots and containers in the garden would begin this method of coordination. Simple paving patterns using one or two types of paving at the most would also produce a successful foil or contrast to the varied leaf patterns or flower colour. By choosing darker materials such as slate, you can emphasize and enrich the greens of foliage. In this way, a much more evocative and intriguing atmosphere can be created, which also has the potential to make the garden space seem bigger.

Disguising or screening walls or fences with foliage will contribute to this quality. By losing the defining boundaries in this way, you make it more difficult to judge exactly where the garden ends. Darker materials introduce deeper, more intriguing shadows, and the use of dark-stained trellis, fencing, or wall coverings will intensify this sense of expanded space. Use larger foliage plants and dramatic forms to the foreground with smaller-leafed planting towards the boundaries. This creates a sense of increased depth and plays up the excitement of the garden.

Space for sitting and socializing is likely to be a subservient requirement to the worship of the plant, although the introduction of chairs or benches will allow the plantaholic to feel at one with the all-enveloping flora. That sense of nature growing all around, nurtured and lovingly tended, can be savoured and absorbed with delectable pleasure.

left *Planting is one of the elements in this stylish and sophisticated city garden. Finishes and surfaces provide social spaces.*

opposite *Huge drifts of astilbe soften paving and produce a carpet of colour. The light woodland edge provides niches for varied planting.*

THE SOCIAL GARDENER

For some garden owners, plants are a necessary burden requiring maintenance, pruning, tidying, and trimming. This garden owner is more interested in relaxation and the pleasure of the great outdoors, shared with friends and family. For them, the small garden represents a social opportunity; a place for food and drink, to watch the sunset and the city lights glow over a gin and tonic or a beer. Whereas the plantaholic will work in the garden, the socialite works elsewhere. The garden becomes a setting for outdoor recreation rather than a gardened space.

In this small space, the focus will be on paved surfaces designed to take tables and chairs, a barbecue, and perhaps a parasol or pergola for shade and privacy. Water will be included to create sound and movement, perhaps to counter the urban noise. Lighting for entertainment and drama after dark will be an essential, and, finally, the planting will be simple and easy to maintain. Some people may even entertain plant-free spaces, treating the garden literally as an outdoor room, maximizing the usable area.

Whereas the plantaholic could disguise boundaries and create visual depth, the socialite gardener revels in the architecture of the space. This simplicity or more minimal quality means that attention must be paid to the hard materials used, to their qualities and to the finish or detail of the paving and construction. In a small space, all of the connections, joints, and surfaces will be easily seen, leaving little room for cost cutting or disguise.

By comparison, these are more expensive gardens. Planting is always cheaper than paving and constructed elements. It is also much easier to deal with as an amateur, whereas higher-quality paving and construction often need skilled labour and experience.

Light surfaces such as limestone are often used, creating a sense of space by simplifying and expanding areas of paving. Simple decks using the long, horizontal lines of the thin decking timbers to widen the space or apparently increase length are typical.

For planting, bold blocks of texture such as grasses or taller bamboo create light-reflecting or light-filtering qualities, and climbers can be used to create green walls without occupying too much of the ground surface.

COMMON CONCERNS

For designers, it is important to understand these different characteristics in the people who come to them as clients. It is also necessary to understand the functional needs of the garden: gardening or entertainment, children's play, or sun worship. If you are undertaking a garden-planning exercise for yourself, take the time initially to assess your needs and your way of life. Be objective and plan your approach carefully, because the whole character and quality of the garden will depend upon this early direction.

Each garden will be different, but there are several common issues and concerns that can be resolved easily. Unless the idea is to create a minimalist space, planting beds or areas need to

be as large as possible. This creates a good sense of depth, allowing plants to be layered and allowing light to fall or penetrate between the different forms. Planting in simple but large masses allows plants to move in the breeze as a whole entity and to reflect light in the same way, creating different qualities from those given by a more mixed or varied range. This approach needs generous amounts of space to create the necessary impact.

Generous planting will also help to disguise unsightly views or boundaries. One problem in smaller, urban spaces is that only one or two of the boundary fences or walls will be in your possession. This makes a uniform treatment with hard materials or finishes very difficult, unless neighbours are willing to change their boundaries, too. Planting, and specifically climbers and wall shrubs, can be used as a way of harmonizing the space or creating a more coherent design approach. In this way, a regular rectangular or square plot can be transformed into a completely different spatial experience. Taller plants will provide vertical emphasis within the space, although planting larger specimens or tall hedges close to boundaries can cause disputes with neighbours. There are planning rules and legislation that cover these issues.

Changes of level in the form of steps will always create visual interest in a garden, but in restricted spaces they can be difficult to incorporate and potentially dangerous. As a rule, it is always

above *It is important to emphasize steps and changes in level to make the transition as safe and clear as possible.*

below *This plan shows an early indication of plant species as a precursor to more detailed planting plans.*

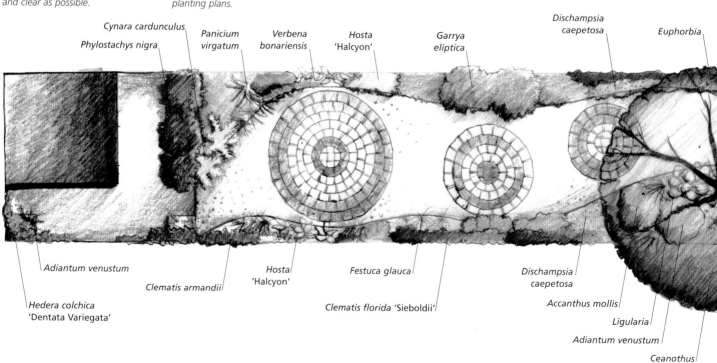

Cynara cardunculus
Phylostachys nigra
Panicium virgatum
Verbena bonariensis
Hosta 'Halcyon'
Garrya eliptica
Dischampsia caepetosa
Euphorbia

Adiantum venustum
Clematis armandii
Hedera colchica 'Dentata Variegata'
Hosta 'Halcyon'
Festuca glauca
Clematis florida 'Sieboldii'
Dischampsia caepetosa
Accanthus mollis
Ligularia
Adiantum venustum
Ceanothus

best to allow for more than one step in any level change, on the basis that a single step is often missed or easily ignored. This can often happen in summer, when light is stronger and shadows shorter. Having two or more steps makes the difference between the higher and lower paved surfaces much more obvious.

Where space is tight, such a level change, which would be 300mm (11⅞in) or so, is often not possible. It becomes important, therefore, to draw attention to the steps in other ways, perhaps with a change of material for the actual steps or a different material used for one of the levels. Lighting can also be used to draw attention to the level change after dark, when potentially the danger increases. Recessed lighting in the steps themselves can be used to floodlight across the steps and the lower level. This creates excitement and drama but also deals with the issues of safety.

Raised planting beds and containers are often associated with small garden spaces. They provide an architectural quality to the space and can often help in retaining or tidying plant material away from usable surfaces. A wall height of 450mm (17¾in) will also provide useful extra seating. Conversely, raised beds are by nature urban in quality and can create problems of droughting, because they dry out more quickly due to the effects of wind and evaporation. The materials used in construction can also absorb moisture from the soil or growing medium. As a result plants will

struggle and never really achieve full height or health. Once again, it is a case of big being beautiful. By maximizing the surface area of raised planters, you allow more rainwater to penetrate into the bed. Irrigation can help, although this cost must be considered at the design and construction stage as an extra. It is best planned into the original design, rather than added later. Some systems rely on refillable water tanks within each bed or container, a better solution than piped irrigation, which results in a series of link pipes between different beds.

The urban quality of raised planting is appropriate for town or city gardens, but it is important to take care of the boundary walls and when using it against a house or apartment wall. Raising structures against existing walls will create damp penetration. With a free-standing boundary wall, this is not usually a problem, but against a building it will breach the damp-proofing course and allow moisture to penetrate the structure. It is important to remember that gardens are not islands but are linked into the surrounding neighbourhood. Actions within your space can have ramifications for others.

It is always useful to consider that planting itself can be selected for a range of heights and forms, meaning that the additional height provided by raised containers becomes unnecessary. If budgets are tight, this approach can also save a great deal of

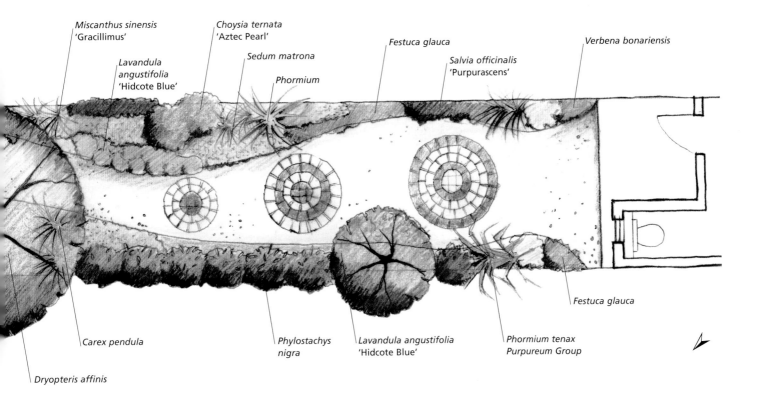

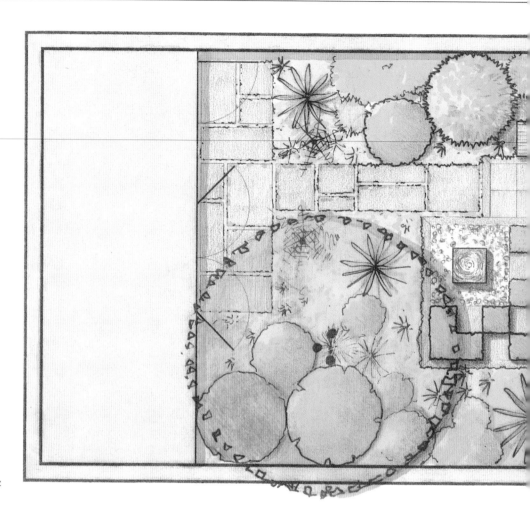

above *Lighting can alter our perception of a garden. Here, light is thrown onto a wall to produce interesting reflections.*

right *A clearly drawn and coloured plan can explain layout and level changes, planting types, and hard materials with great efficiency.*

money. Small urban spaces will always cost more to build per square metre (yard) than their suburban or rural counterparts. For the garden contractor, access and storage are the main issues, because many urban gardens are remote and isolated from the road, with no space for dedicated parking. In addition, many people deal with the needs of their houses first and then turn to the gardens, meaning that excavations and unwanted materials have to be taken out, and new materials and artifacts brought in, through a pristine interior. Few people start with the garden.

ROOF GARDENS

Nowhere is this more emphasized than in the creation of roof gardens. Access is frequently via a lift or tight stairwells, and materials have to be manhandled from street level. Crane hire is possible but is often prohibitively expensive for smaller spaces.

Roof spaces also have specific issues and requirements, and safety is of paramount importance. The opportunity to enjoy panoramic views has to be balanced with the need for balustrades

at a safe height and for the protection of planting from exposure to winds, which can desiccate foliage and eventually kill all but the hardiest species. It is often better to consider plants that do well in seaside conditions and are more tolerant of wind, although drought and temperature extremes are also prevalent. Protection from the wind is also an important factor in using the space, which may mean that certain views are sacrificed in order to provide sufficient shelter. Glass is a popular choice of material, although it needs regular cleaning unless the more expensive self-cleaning glass is used.

Weight restrictions provide another area of concern in creating successful roof gardens. In new or purpose-built developments, roof-garden spaces will be designed to accept certain loadings, which should also be easily researched. In older properties, these loadings may be inadequate or may not have been considered at all and, before any work is done or plant material and artifacts are introduced, it is essential that you consult a structural engineer for advice on the limits. In apartment blocks, the likelihood is that the

roof or what lies underneath will not be your property. The potential for damage, injury, and legal proceedings is plain to see.

Even in purpose-built roof-garden spaces, loadings may be limited. Planting may therefore be restricted to a lawn, low groundcover, or low shrub and perennial species. These smaller plants require shallower depths of soil or growing media, with lawn and groundcover succeeding well in depths of only 150mm (5⅞in). Drainage layers will be required to prevent beds from becoming waterlogged, and excess water must be stored or drained effectively.

Recently, absorbent planted-roof surfaces have become popular in the search for more sustainable urban systems. Sedum matting fits neatly into the category of low groundcover planting and is now easily available. Larger plants, important for structure and scale, need depths of 600mm (23¾in) to 1.2m (4ft), putting much greater loadings on the roof structure. Trees often need to be located in specific positions relating to the supporting framework below, and lightweight materials such as polystyrene can be used to reduce excessive weight loads in planting areas.

Paving needs to be light in weight, or can be supported off the side walls rather than laid onto the roof itself. Decking is a popular roof-garden material for these reasons, with deck boards supported on joists similar in design to those in internal suspended floors. Drainage and waterproofing must be considered as a fundamental aspect of good roof garden design and, although decking will cover up unsightly services and structural elements, it is essential to ensure that water will not puddle or collect to any depth in the space below. The expansion of the water as it freezes would cause damage that would remain unseen, allowing moisture to penetrate the fabric of the building.

AWKWARD SPACES

Some gardens are classified as small because, although they are long, their width is restricted. There are two basic approaches to this problem: to divide the garden into a series of small compartments, or to exaggerate the width. The former relies on the element of surprise in that a succession of small and different spaces will lose the sense that the garden space is tight. The connection with the house is lost as one moves through the spaces, and the sense of detachment and privacy potentially increases. The garden "rooms" can be defined by walls or fences, which occupy the least amount of space. Hedges will provide a solid structure and an architectural quality while retaining the softness of planting, and loose but structural planting such as bamboos and shrubs will create a much more relaxed, possibly jungle-like, atmosphere. Each type of compartmentalization can be used in the same garden, perhaps increasing the sense of informality as one explores further into the garden.

Exaggerating the width relies on emphasizing it, running lines of paving across the garden, or steps that stretch across the entire space rather than following a narrow pathway. Water rills or narrow, canal-like features can be used in the same way, perhaps with stepping stones to provide a crossing point. Walls or hedges and other barriers may still be used, perhaps to disguise the length of the space; but emphasis should always be placed on the horizontal width of the plot.

A third option may be to clear the entire length of the garden and to use this as a single space, perhaps with a sculpture or plant specimen at the end working as a focal point. With this scenario, the boundary treatment, whether hard or soft, would need to be consistent and considered for privacy and containment, so as not to distract the eye.

Many small gardens fall into the category of awkward in almost every sense, being uneven, irregular, polygonal-shaped plots that seem to defy any kind of order and structure. In these situations, many people make the mistake of following the boundaries and reflecting their pattern in the general layout of the garden. In fact, a more successful solution is to work in the opposite direction, forgetting the influence of the boundaries and creating a completely new design within the space available. For some people, the worry is that valuable space will be lost. However, if you identify the usable or functional space that you need, and use planting to fill the rest of the awkward spaces, you will lose the impact of the boundaries and soften the garden dramatically. It is much cheaper and more effective to allow plants to fill awkward spaces than to cut and lay more expensive hard materials into complex angles and shapes.

All of these solutions to difficult sites and tight spaces are embodied in the designs to be found within this book. As much as possible, designers have emphasized their specific solutions in the descriptions that accompany the design plans. Even if you do not find a mirror image of your space, it is useful to read their

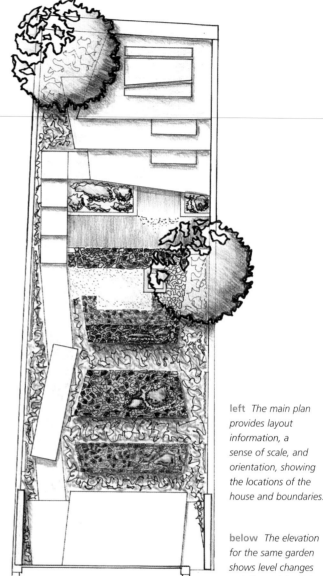

left The main plan provides layout information, a sense of scale, and orientation, showing the locations of the house and boundaries.

below The elevation for the same garden shows level changes and the anticipated heights of vegetation, walls, and structures.

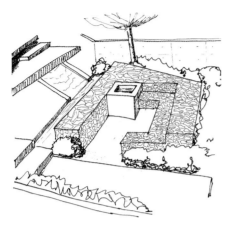

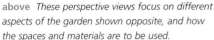
above *These perspective views focus on different aspects of the garden shown opposite, and how the spaces and materials are to be used.*

ideas and responses in order to understand their approach. This may inspire you to apply your own ideas or to consider employing a designer to help solve your particular problems.

THE PLANS IN THIS BOOK

Each design will include a plan drawing, which is used to show the layout or geometric pattern of the garden. Normally these drawings are produced to a scale so that measurements can still be recorded accurately. Designers use colour or different line types and thicknesses in order to give these two-dimensional drawings depth and atmosphere. This makes the drawings more accessible to the layperson.

In addition, supporting visuals may be used, such as elevations, to indicate heights; axonometrics, to give a measured, three-dimensional view; or perspectives, to show how it feels to stand within the garden. Elevations or axonometrics can be produced to an accurate scale, but perspectives, although measurable in

relative terms, are often drawn as freehand sketches to provide a feeling for the garden rather than an accurate image.

Each of these images is an attempt to show the form that the garden will eventually take. Computer-based drawing is now rapidly taking over from hand-drawn images. Although in some cases these drawings still seem engineered, there are many techniques such as montage and photo-realistic collage that produce convincing and dynamic visuals that can't be produced by hand. The book contains a wide range of design approaches and expressive graphic techniques that are often selected to complement the design idea, from the sumptuous to the sketchy, the detailed to the minimal.

Whatever the reason you had for selecting this book, I hope you enjoy the richness and invention of the designs within and that you feel inspired to join the army of garden owners working their magic on small, possibly awkward, but treasured spaces.

Andrew Wilson

below *This long sectional elevation shows the relationship of the house and its garden "room" to the rest of the garden space. It concentrates particularly on the stepped terraces and the boundary treatments.*

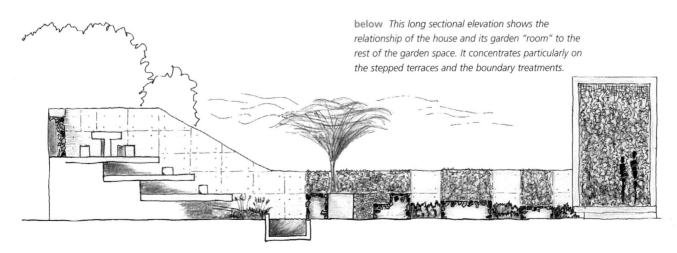

INFORMALGARDENS

Informal gardens are typified by soft, unequal curves, irregular combinations of rectangles, or a composition of different shapes and forms. Although they may be designed on a regular grid, their appearance suggests a casual informality that seems to match the contemporary lifestyle and produces drama and an element of surprise. Large, simple areas of paving may be balanced by smaller but highly textured or coloured surfaces. The aim is to create a visual balance without repetition.

In truth, many informal compositions are a subtle blend of formal elements combined in an irregular way. The rectangle can be easily identified as a formal shape with a central axis splitting it into halves. By combining these shapes in an irregular way, perhaps interlocking or overlapping them, new shapes and forms can be created. Focal points can still be introduced, either as incidents to be discovered or as centrally placed sculptures or ornaments that produce a dynamic interplay between symmetry and asymmetry. If curves are used, they should be clearly defined and measured. "Natural" curves, produced randomly, will create a level of complexity that is confusing and fussy in a small space. The combination of a clearly defined geometry and loose or irregular plant forms will always create exciting visual interest.

Garden for Mothers and Babies

ROBERT MYERS – ELIZABETH BANKS ASSOCIATES

DIMENSIONS 36 x 15m (120 x 50ft)

SOIL imported loam

ASPECT south facing

KEY FEATURES long canal with water jets

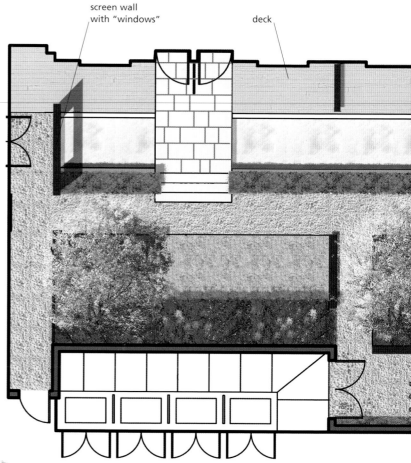

screen wall
with "windows"

deck

above *Groups of Indian bean trees
(Catalpa bignonoides, above) and
birch trees were chosen to create
sub spaces within the garden.*

left *A computerized montage
provides visualization for the space.
The water jets in the long canal
give a calm focus for the garden.*

Ramp up

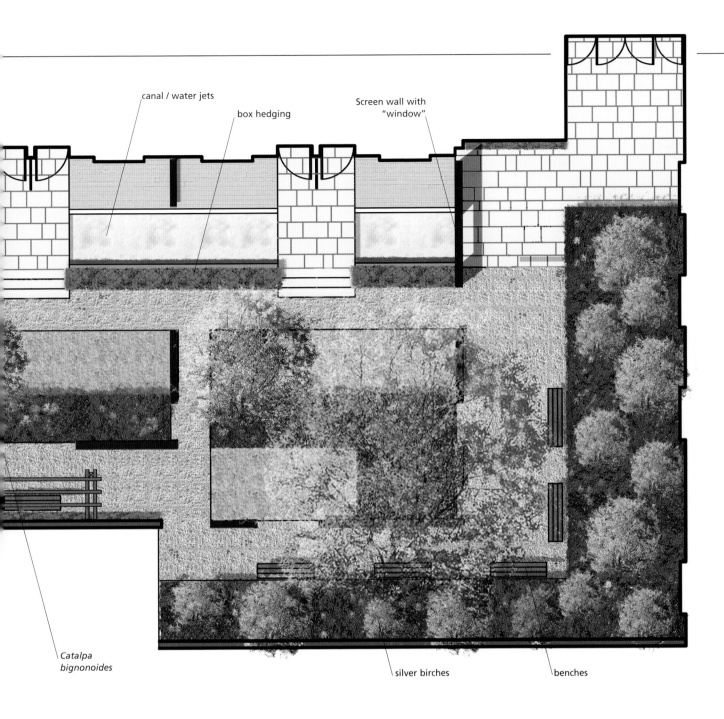

canal / water jets

box hedging

Screen wall with "window"

Catalpa bignonoides

silver birches

benches

This courtyard garden forms the focal point of a midwife-led birthing unit at a large hospital. The garden aims to provide relaxation and reflection for mothers and families, and also to provide privacy for the birthing rooms and a small amount of private terrace space.

The resulting design divides the space lengthwise with a long canal, crossed by stone paths, along the face of the building. Within the canal, water jets give movement and a calming sound. Outside each room is a small private deck, and a low box hedge along the pool creates a sense of enclosure for the birthing rooms. At either end of the canal are screen walls with "windows" through

them. Low walls (1m/1yd high) are used around the planting beds to increase the sense of enclosure and interest, giving different textures and contrasts at every viewpoint.

To divide the space further and to provide different private sitting areas within the garden groups of multi-stemmed white birch trees and three multi-stemmed *Catalpa bignonoides* create sub-spaces. One *Robinia pseudoacacia* is used as a focal tree in the garden. Seasonal interest and colour is provided by mixed shrub and herbaceous planting with a particular emphasis on scented plants. Benches are provided around the garden set against plain rendered walls.

Surprising Secret Garden

IAN SMITH – ACRES WILD

DIMENSIONS 16 x 6.5m (53 x 22ft)

SOIL clay

ASPECT south facing

KEY FEATURES comfortable contemporary space

The owners wanted a surprising and secret garden to complement a new extension to their Victorian terraced house. They needed space for dining, as well as a separate hidden space for reading and contemplation. The garden suffered from overlooking neighbours, and screening was also needed for a large shed and an air-conditioning unit.

In the resulting design, which uses limited colours and material to unify the space, the garden is partially divided to create a sense of intrigue: not all of the garden can be seen at once. Focal points are placed at the end of vistas to lead the visitor through the garden. An open, sunny dining space near the house contrasts with a smaller, shady, and secluded area toward the middle of the garden and the work area at the end of the garden, which is well screened with trellis. The paving materials also provide textural contrast but unifying colour with smooth-finished concrete slabs set against "flame-textured" granite setts.

Planting in the garden has a theme of complementary textures and shades of green. Pleached lime trees provide screening from overlooking neighbours, *Betula utilis* var. *jacquemontii* and *Robinia pseudoacacia* 'Umbraculifera' give height and privacy, while miscanthus, fatsia, hostas, and *Rheum palmatum* provide texture.

house   dining area   shady, secluded area

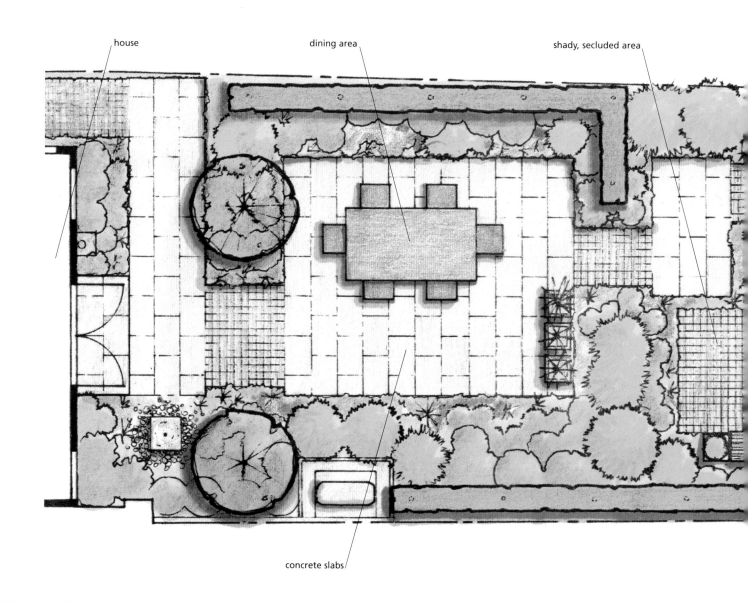

concrete slabs

above *A perspective helps to show the open dining space and how surrounding pleached lime trees act as an effective screen.*

above *This shady private area of the garden, screened with trellis, is ideal either for reading or for contemplation.*

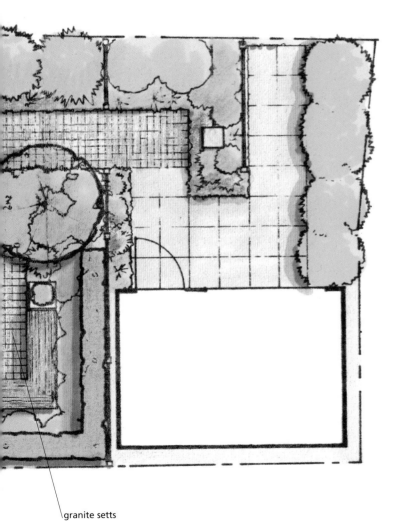

granite setts

Abstract Vegetable Garden

ANDREW DUFF

DIMENSIONS 200sq m (2,154sq ft); part of a much larger garden
SOIL fine loam
ASPECT south-west facing
KEY FEATURES abstract shapes in gravel and grass

The concept for this vegetable and fruit garden is taken from an abstraction of the surrounding hill shapes and textures from plant leaves, throwing bold shapes across the space, far removed from the typical traditional vegetable garden or orchard. For this total garden renovation, the owners' brief was to create "a country garden" with strong structure punctuated by "fluffy" planting schemes. They envisaged long walks through the surrounding landscape with their children.

The dramatic shapes are inspired by the celebrated landscape designer Burle Marx's dynamic gestures to a garden's surroundings. Gravel paths wind through the space with wider areas and constricted points, giving movement and dynamism to the journey. Large sweeps of mown grass juxtapose shapes of rough grass and bulbs. These are interplanted with fruit trees, and planes of single-species planting cut through each other in turn, creating the abstract vegetable beds. The whole design forms a picture of generosity of space and informality. Crossing the path at random intervals, pergola beams give height and increase the sense of movement through the space.

At the centre, a modern hedged secret garden with a sun terrace is enhanced by the gentle sound of water in the pool.

secret garden

pergola beams

below *The dramatic shapes and textures of the planting in this garden are well illustrated by this area of the vegetable garden.*

Completely Minimal

JAMES ALDRIDGE GARDENS

DIMENSIONS 22.5 x 17.5m (70 x 57ft), including the house

SOIL clay

ASPECT west facing

KEY FEATURES green walls

This minimalist house required an equally minimal garden, and relating the garden back to the house in terms of scale and detail was important. The clients owned the portion of the garden behind the house, but only leased the area to the north east, so were unwilling to spend much money on that area. The interior floors were already laid with limestone slabs.

The back wall of the house is divided into four large panels of glass; the middle two panels slide open to form doors leading out into the garden. The wall facing these doors is clothed in a series of "green walls" that are sized to match the doors on the house. They are fabricated from galvanized box-section steel with a 150 x 150mm (5⅞ x 5⅞in) galvanized wire mesh attached to the rear of the framework. This in turn is covered in *Trachelospermum jasminoides* for evergreen covering and its white scented flowers.

Within the paving, a planting square contains a multi-stemmed *Cornus kousa* var. *chinensis* underplanted with a mass of *Ophiopogon planiscarpus*. To the side of the garden, on the leased land, a lawn is laid with a second cornus planted through.

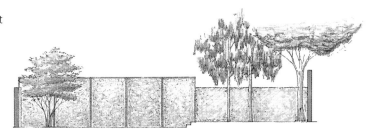

right Two elevations showing screen walls made from box section galvanized steel.

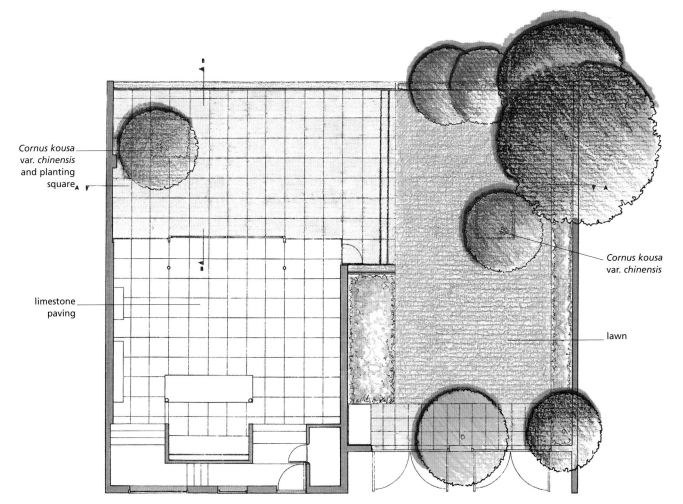

Cornus kousa var. *chinensis* and planting square

limestone paving

Cornus kousa var. *chinensis*

lawn

Grown-up Garden

TERENCE McGLADE – PERENNIAL GARDENS CORPORATION

DIMENSIONS 20 x 5m (60 x 16ft)

SOIL loam

ASPECT south facing

KEY FEATURES deck and woodland area

As a reincarnation after its use by children – having included a large play structure – this garden was to become a more adult space for relaxing, dining, and, especially, gardening. The owner was very keen on collecting plants and wanted an "oasis" from city life. Access to the garage at the bottom of the garden and a side entrance to a relative's garden also needed to be maintained.

Set on three levels, the deck leads directly from the house and provides a sunny spot for dining, with shade available from an umbrella or screen above. A sunken paved terrace has a more private feel with dense planting into stone, raised beds on either side. Paving is of Colorado red sandstone inset into brick pavers. Against the boundary and up a step is a large, built-in stone barbecue. Farther down, a step leads through a yew hedge into a densely planted woodland garden. A copper beech tree is surrounded by low, woodland planting and the narrow path zigzags through the space to the garage.

Planting is lush and varied, including a collection of hostas, bamboos, roses, and hydrangeas.

above *In this section of the garden decking leads to a sunken paved terrace suitable for relaxing. On either side of the terrace are planted raised stone beds.*

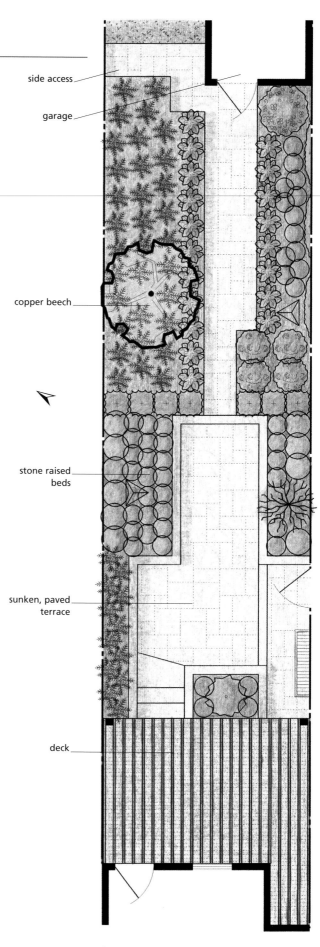

side access

garage

copper beech

stone raised beds

sunken, paved terrace

deck

Sensational Lighting

PHILIP NASH DESIGN

DIMENSIONS 9 x 4.6m (30 x 24ft)

SOIL neutral

ASPECT east facing

KEY FEATURES lighting and a flame feature in pool

above *Set in the corner of the main terrace, an important feature of this courtyard garden is the bespoke bench seating and a table.*

The aim for this client was to create a highly individual, contemporary courtyard garden to complement the interior of the house. The resulting design has raised plinths and a raised terrace. Each of these elements is built with a frame of C section steels supporting limestone. The edges of the plinths are lit with LED flexilights at night to give an appearance of "floating". On the main terrace bespoke bench seating, constructed from marine ply set on steel supports, and a table are set into the corner of the garden. Shade loving ferns are planted under the benches maximizing the available space in the garden and increasing the feeling of being "connected" with the plants.

Towards the back of the garden a steel pool has stepping stones across giving access to the back entrance. A glass water wall is fixed to the rendered back wall of the garden with water cascading into the pool below. A naked gas flame burner is also set within the pool bringing another wonderful and exciting element to the design. The flames are reflected in the water and these reflections then ripple up the walls and over the glass.

Lighting is an integral feature in this garden with the LED lit plinths and terrace and further feature spotlights all controlled by remote control to alter light levels and effects. There is also a sound system incorporated to introduce ambient relaxing sound into the space. Planting is highly architectural and exotic in style.

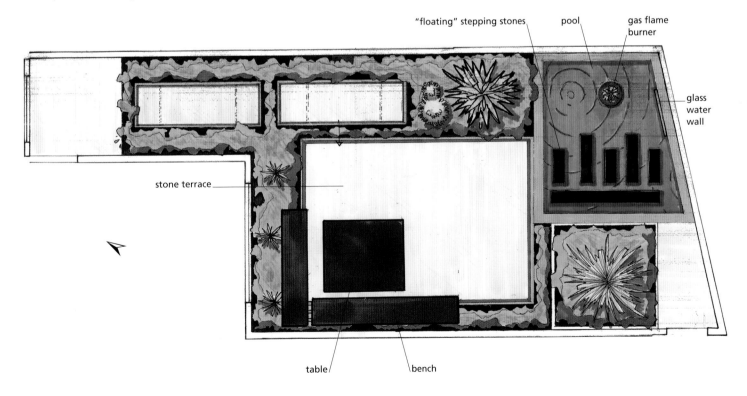

Tropical Courtyard

OLIN PARTNERSHIP

DIMENSIONS 20 x 20m (60 x 60ft); part of a much larger area

SOIL sandy loam

ASPECT south facing

KEY FEATURES palm trees and acrylic "bubbles"

An urban courtyard within a new residential development, this area is heavily used throughout the day and after dark. The designers therefore needed to create excitement and interest, but also had to work within climatic constraints: the property is in a region that experiences considerable heat and occasional hurricanes.

Pebble paving is in large, textured, ripple-like swirls for the effect of movement and interest, and to divide visually the large space. Overlaid are "islands" of planting of varying size and height, giving a choice of paths; in this way the magnitude of the space is brought down to human scale. Planting is dominated by palms, including the *Caryota urens* (Toddy palm) and *Caryota mitis* (Fishtail palm). At the lower level, a wide range of planting emphasizes fragrance and white flowers (*Trachelospermum jasminoides, Gardenia thunbergia,* and *Thunbergia grandiflora* 'Alba'), which remain visible after sunset. Large acrylic "bubbles" placed randomly around the courtyard add colour and humour, and acrylic bubble benches that glow after dark are positioned around the courtyard. Overhead, a fabric tensile structure provides shade, and it can easily be removed in the event of a hurricane.

above *A computer-generated image gives a clear idea of the proportions (as well as the proposed acrylic "bubbles") for this courtyard.*

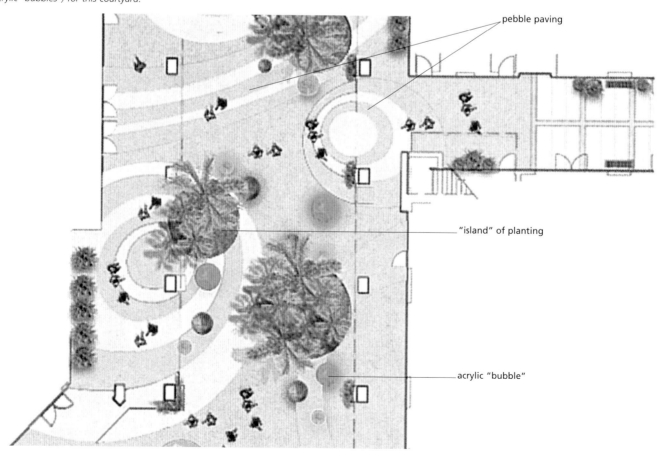

pebble paving

"island" of planting

acrylic "bubble"

Waves and Defences

DEBBIE ROBERTS – ACRES WILD

DIMENSIONS 16 x 22m (53 x 63ft); seaward part of a larger garden

SOIL shingle and pebbles

ASPECT north-facing slope with shingle beach to the south

KEY FEATURES curved retaining wall and angular timber benches

above *The illustration shows the sheltered swimming pool area, surrounded by planting suitable for a coastal garden.*

The owners of this property wanted to create a beach garden that responded to the local coastal landscape both functionally and aesthetically. They wanted to use the area for informal gatherings and barbecues, and to form a sheltered garden area within which a swimming pool and hot tub could be located.

In answer to this brief, the designer created wave-like curves on the ground to divide the garden areas and create the vertical divisions. A shingle swale on the seaward side of the curving retaining wall helps to direct any tidal overflow away from the swimming pool garden. Angular benches represent coastal defences and help to unify the squareness of the house and pool with the curving design. A boardwalk and verandah wrapping around the house allow for a stronger inside–outside connection. Evergreen hedging on top of the retaining wall provides some shelter and enclosure to the swimming pool garden, and a stone or concrete frieze provides additional vertical interest at the end of the pool. This is lit at night when viewed from the house.

Planting in the garden has to be incredibly tough and salt- and wind-tolerant, and includes tamarisk, salix, cistus, and rosemary.

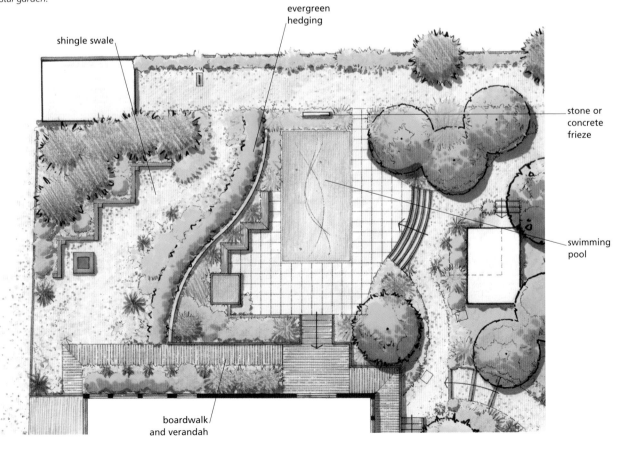

evergreen hedging

shingle swale

stone or concrete frieze

swimming pool

boardwalk and verandah

Garden on View

TERENCE McGLADE – PERENNIAL GARDENS CORPORATION

DIMENSIONS 20 x 8m (60 x 25ft)

SOIL sandy loam

ASPECT north facing

KEY FEATURES pergola and barbecue

Attached to a contemporary house with two storeys of glass at the back and a garage in daily use at the end of the garden, this space needed to look wonderful at all times. The garden is in shade for most of the day, with a maximum of four hours of sunshine, and the owners wanted a seating area for morning coffee, planting for a real garden feel, and a separate dining area with a barbecue set out of sight from the house.

Leading directly from the house, a pathway runs straight to the garage for maximum ease of use. The garden is laid out in a very formal rectangle bisected by a large pergola acting as a room divider between the path and the relaxation areas. Steps up near the house and again near the garage bring movement to the garden and help to delineate the different usages for the space.

The small terrace near the house has a formal stone wall with water cascading down into a stainless-steel trough providing an interesting focal point from the house and a relaxing space for

coffee. The rear of the water feature takes the same line as the step up into the garden and the raised bed edging of Wiarton *stone* continues the theme. A large stone barbecue is screened from the house by lilacs and low shrubs. At the end of the garden a Japanese maple (*Acer palmatum* 'Bloodgood') screens the garage and provides the visual contrast with other, mainly green, leaves.

above *A large pergola divides the pathway leading from the house from the areas of the garden intended for relaxation.*

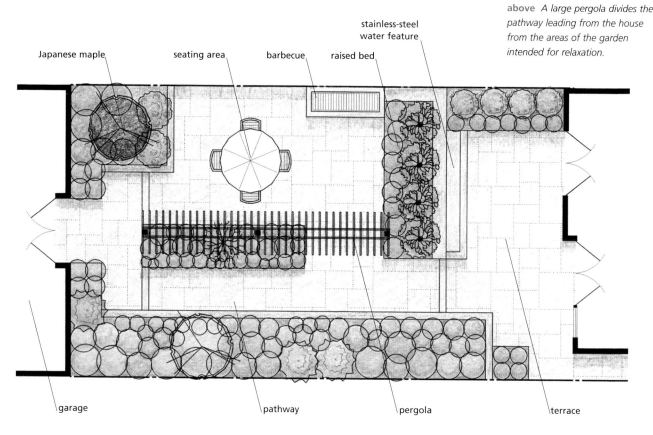

Japanese maple   seating area   barbecue   stainless-steel water feature   raised bed

garage   pathway   pergola   terrace

Wrap-Around Garden

TIM THOELECKE – AMERICAN
ACADEMY OF LANDSCAPE DESIGN LLC

DIMENSIONS 13.5 x 12m (45 x 40ft)

SOIL neutral

ASPECT north-east facing

KEY FEATURES wheelchair friendly arbour

above *In a garden that wraps around the house a narrow path in the front leads towards a terraced seating area.*

In this broadly square plot with the house at its centre, the garden wraps around the house and the owners wanted areas for sitting out in different parts of the space for different times of day and different moods. Views from the house over the garden were important, as was privacy from the street. A large area of lawn was also needed for children to play.

Elements of the house's architecture gave inspiration for the design of an arbour at the side of the building, linking the garden visually with the home. Narrow paths, passing through lush, dense planting, lead from the front of the house to the rear, and across the back of the house, giving interesting views and opening out into focal points from the windows. In this way, movement and interest are brought to the garden. Three terraced areas were incorporated in the design: one as a sitting spot beside the garage, a small terrace outside the kitchen for barbecuing, and a larger, main terrace for entertaining and dining. A curved lawn sweeps around the house, pulling the whole design together, and beds along the outside border provide depth and colour in the planting. River birch trees are planted at the focal points from the windows at the back of the house.

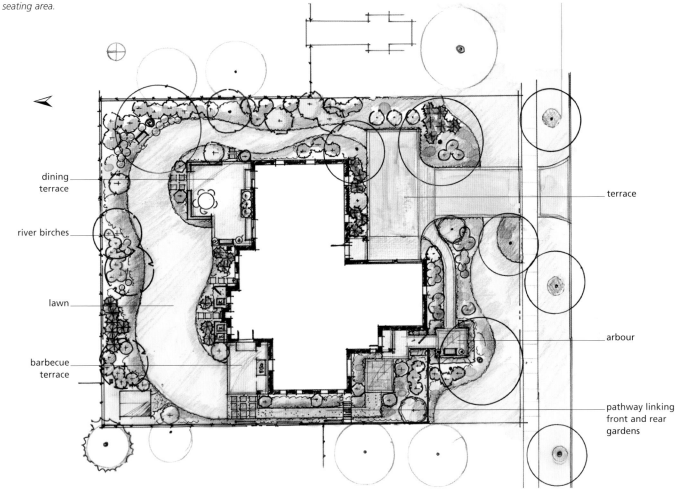

dining terrace

river birches

lawn

barbecue terrace

terrace

arbour

pathway linking front and rear gardens

Koi Pond Terrace

DEBBIE ROBERTS – ACRES WILD

DIMENSIONS 20 x 20m (60 x 60ft); part of a much larger garden

SOIL heavy clay

ASPECT east facing

KEY FEATURES contemporary koi courtyard

above *A more formal area of this generally informal garden incorporates the koi pond and sun bathing area.*

The owners of this barn conversion wanted a contemporary space in the most private area of their large garden. They wanted a koi pond, some shelter, and a space for sun bathing. The drive needed to be screened and the garden was to provide an enhanced view out from the the dining room.

To satisfy these requirements and to ensure that the garden fitted into its surroundings, a square motif was taken from the architecture and repeated in the shape of the koi pond, the box "tables", the gazebo, and the paving slabs. Brick, flint, oak, and tiles were used to reflect the prevailing architecture, and a pebble trim was used on the pond to reflect flint walling on the buildings.

Heavy clay soil produced drainage issues and a water pipe running diagonally across the site dictated the location of the pool. In addition, the pond filtration system was concealed beneath the decked gazebo floor for easy access.

Planting is focused on foliage and structure, with screens of *Pyrus calleryana* 'Chanticleer' and *Prunus lusitanica* "trees" along the boundaries of the garden. *Yucca gloriosa* marks the corners of the pond and *Phormium tenax* 'Purpureum Group' and *P. cookianum* 'Rubrum' are planted throughout. The box "tables" are of *Buxus sempervirens*. Background planting is of bamboos and grasses, with *Ophiopogon planiscarpus* 'Nigrescens' edging to reflect the barn's colour and *Acaena microphylla* edging to echo the brick colour.

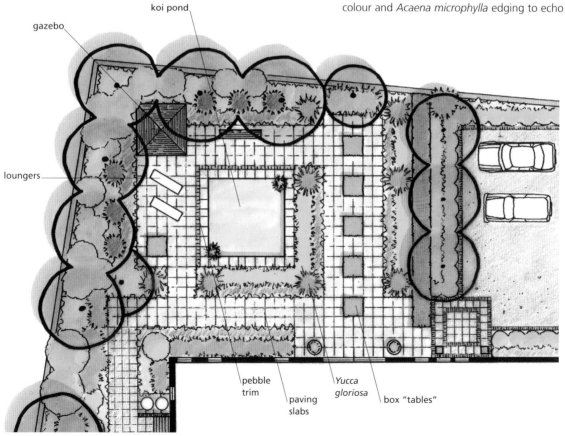

Family Fun

TIM THOELECKE – AMERICAN ACADEMY OF LANDSCAPE DESIGN LLC

DIMENSIONS 80 x 20m (260 x 60ft)

SOIL heavy clay

ASPECT south facing

KEY FEATURES hot tub

With six children under the age of 13, the owners of this house were keen to preserve a large lawn area for play and to incorporate a big hot tub for family relaxation. They were also very knowledgeable about plants, design, and construction.

A terraced area near the house is designed in bluestone, with a limestone seat-wall built in. Bluestone coping tops the walls to match the treads on the steps in the garden. The terrace is enclosed in some areas with planting and the open areas allow access for the children when they are playing.

The garden is not all visible at once from the house, lending an air of mystery. A pond is situated near the house so that it can be enjoyed all year round both visually and for the sounds it provides. The children also enjoy feeding the fish. A large hot tub is also incorporated into the design. It gets used throughout the year, so access is easy from the house but, to disguise the size, it is surrounded by dense, lush planting as well as a cedar enclosure to make it blend in with its surroundings. The balance of the garden forms a large curved lawn which is surrounded by trees and strong colourful planting, giving a play area for the children.

above *Appreciated by both adults and children a large spa or hot tub is a welcome feature in any medium- to large-sized garden.*

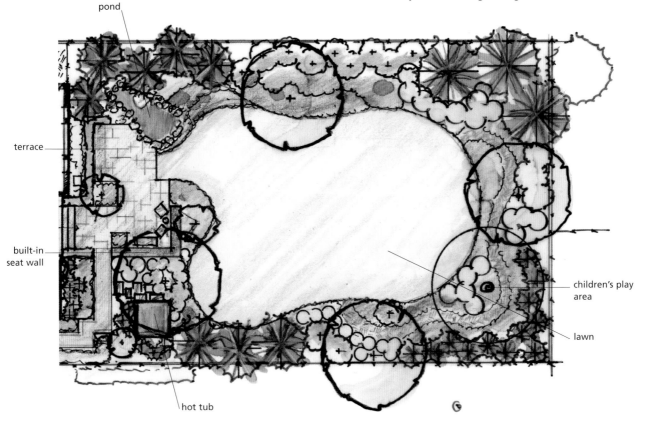

pond

terrace

built-in seat wall

hot tub

children's play area

lawn

Asymmetrical, Contemporary Garden

CLAIRE MEE DESIGNS

DIMENSIONS 9 x 8m (30 x 25ft)

SOIL clay

ASPECT south-west facing

KEY FEATURES different decked levels

Transformation from the appearance of a squash court – a square, flat, walled space – into a garden with varying levels and interesting year-round planting was the requirement here. The house's interior was very contemporary and the owners wished to echo that in the garden. They also wanted a covered area for entertaining with privacy from overlooking buildings.

To create more interest in the space, the garden is divided with raised deck areas. Leading out from the kitchen, a limestone terrace is punctuated by a small group of ornamental trees giving height and interest, and screening the two garden doors from each other. From ground level, steps lead up to a decked dining area, covered with a pergola, which is south-east-facing to catch the morning and midday sun. The back of the pergola is fenced in willow panels to increase the sense of enclosure and also to screen an unsightly bathroom window.

Outside the door from the living room another decked area forms a very large step on which a built-in bench is constructed. A raised rill brings the sight and sound of water, which falls into a large, ground-level pool. The rendered walls of the rill, and behind the pool, give form and structure to this part of the garden, and also obscure a barbecue behind it.

raised deck

ornamental trees

above *This raised deck dining or entertaining area is afforded a degree of privacy by a wooden pergola and willow panels.*

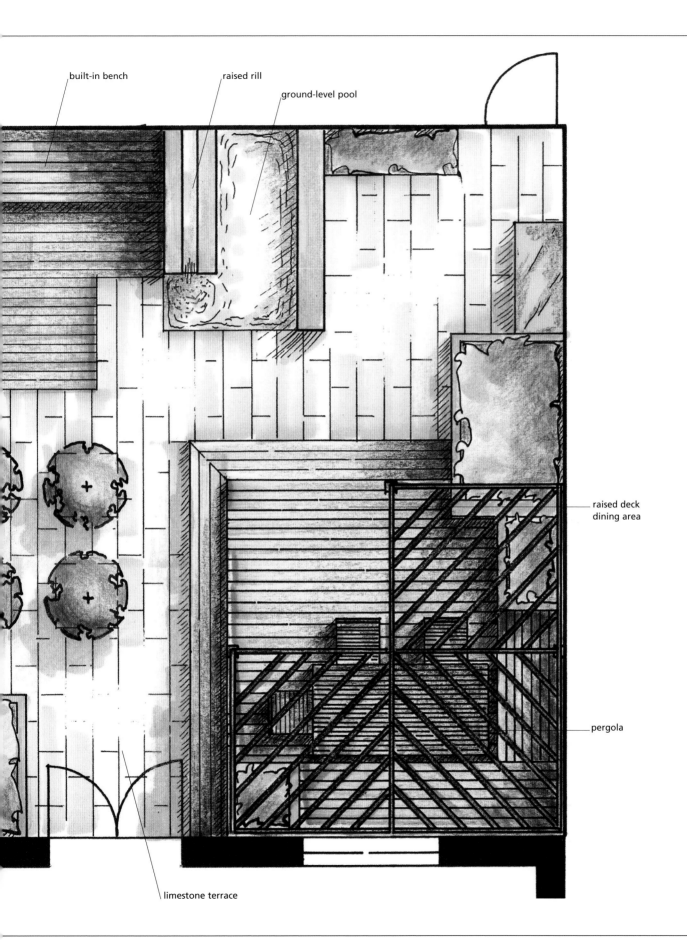

built-in bench

raised rill

ground-level pool

raised deck
dining area

pergola

limestone terrace

Timeless Elegance

CHARLOTTE ROWE

DIMENSIONS 8 x 7m (25 x 23ft)

SOIL clay

ASPECT north facing

KEY FEATURES raised rill

These owners were looking to upgrade the garden now that their children had left home. They wanted an elegant, peaceful space to enjoy from their new kitchen, with formal planting. A particular requirement was to provide screening from neighbours.

The main design element in the garden is the long water feature that can be seen from the back of the house. From the side passage of the house, a paved pathway leads through gravel formally planted with clipped box balls, and the eye is drawn out into the garden, toward the sound of falling water. From a small, upper pool the water falls through a key-hole shaped spout into a long, ground-level pool. Planting to this side of the garden is of shade-loving plants including bamboos and ferns. Two standard olive trees are planted alongside the pool and provide a border to the large terrace in the main garden. Paving is of smooth, cream, Indian sandstone edged in Cotswold buff gravel. Raised beds with formal planting provide structure to the side of the garden. Two facing benches are built into the retaining walls. At the end of the garden, a row of pleached hornbeams gives structure as well as privacy. An antique head set on a pedestal provides a focal point from the kitchen at the back of the house.

Lighting is used to pull the garden in around the house and to create the sense of an extra room at night.

side passage

kitchen and dining area

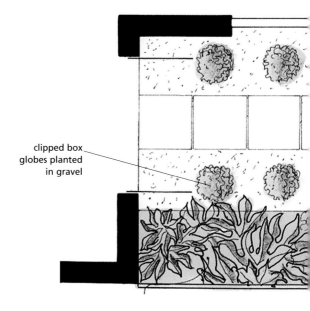

clipped box globes planted in gravel

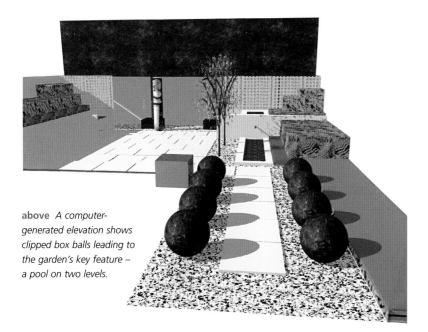

above *A computer-generated elevation shows clipped box balls leading to the garden's key feature – a pool on two levels.*

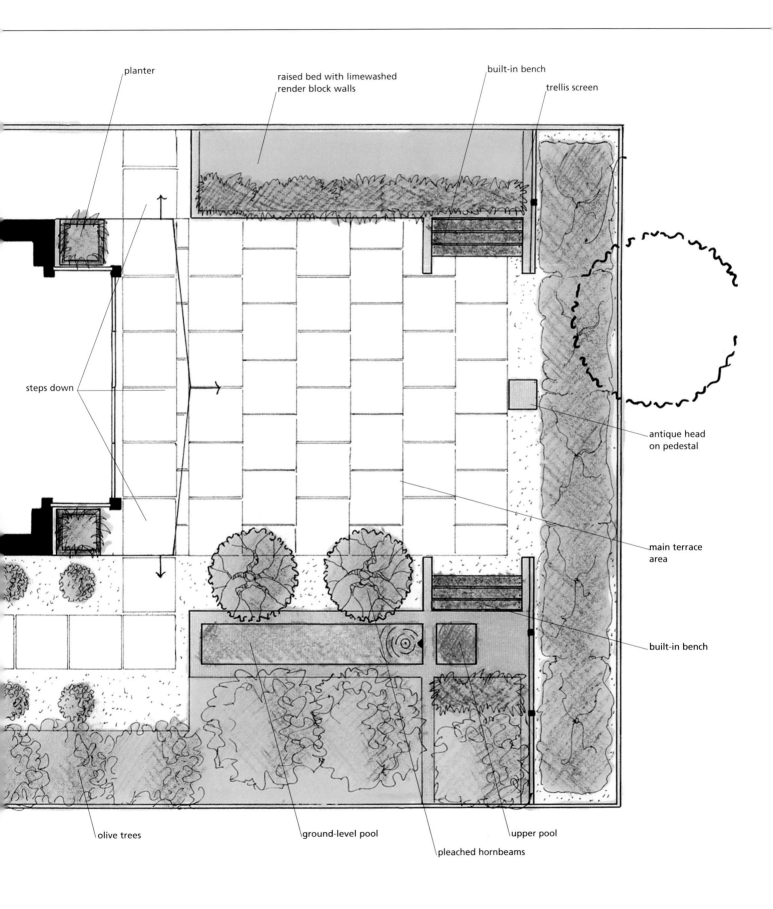

planter

raised bed with limewashed
render block walls

built-in bench

trellis screen

steps down

antique head
on pedestal

main terrace
area

built-in bench

olive trees

ground-level pool

upper pool

pleached hornbeams

Relaxing Workplace

ANDY STURGEON GARDEN DESIGN

DIMENSIONS 23 x 10m (70 x 33ft)

SOIL not known

ASPECT south facing

KEY FEATURES reflective pool with square voids

Designed as a setting for a home office, this garden provides a stimulating and thought-provoking space from which to work, but also a calm, tranquil area in which to unwind. The office space is at one end of the garden, and a path created from large, oak cubes leads to a square lawn at the far end. These oak cubes also form a sculptural feature whose shape is echoed in the dark, reflective water of the pool with square voids.

A water chute starts on the roof of the office and cascades down over the terrace, bringing movement and sound to the garden, in contrast with the dark stillness of the pool. Stone on the terrace is honed and sawn to create a crisp finish, again echoing the pool voids. River birches give areas of dappled shade, and evergreen structure is provided by *Ilex crenata*, clipped box balls, hebes, and *Pittosporum tobira*. Ornamental grasses and astelias provide a contrast of texture, which is then brought to life with the addition of colour using perennials and bulbs.

above *The black voids that cross the pool echo the architecture of the oak cubes leading from the office to the relaxation area.*

left *Dappled shade is supplied by the river birches, and the contrasting colours and textures are supplied by a variety of planting, to create a relaxing area.*

storage area

office area

rill

main patio

rill water falls to earth

above *This axonometric shows how the water plunging from the roof creates movement and sound near the office space.*

oak cubes

stone stepping stones

entrance path

second
seating
area

bench

Connecting Interior to Exterior

VLADIMIR SITTA / ROBERT FABER – TERRAGRAM PTY LTD

DIMENSIONS 9 x 5.5 m (30 x 18 ft)

SOIL sandy loam, very slightly acid

ASPECT south-east facing (in southern hemisphere)

KEY FEATURES sculptural gateway, water feature

With prime city land at a high premium, an extension to the house was built partially cantilevered over a swimming pool, creating an illusion of a much larger body of water. Conceptual work for the garden was carried out simultaneously with that for the house, to ensure a strong design link, and the resulting house opens completely at the back to allow the inside and outside spaces to flow together.

The rear garden is dedicated to an outdoors lifestyle, with much of it used for the swimming pool. A large, decked area provides an outdoor sitting space with the pool encroaching into it. Mandatory security fencing is incorporated using vertical, stainless-steel rods

left In this inner city garden a decked seating area leads to a large swimming pool, crossed at one end by a security fence made of stainless steel rods.

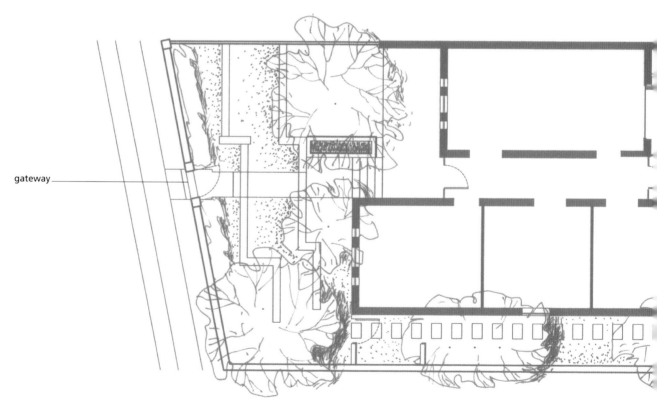

gateway

Front garden

to form a barrier. This has a removable section, through which temporary, unimpeded access to the pool can be achieved.

A grove of lemon-scented eucalyptus is planted to bring height, structure, and contrast to the flat, reflective surface of the water. On the opposite side of the pool, another terrace has storage lockers for garden accessories and toys to maintain the garden's pristine look when the pool is not in use.

The contemporary front garden is densely planted to screen noise from the street, and a pathway leads up to the house from a new gateway that is backlit at night to resemble a Chinese lantern. The clean, modern lines of the front garden extend through the house and out into the back, creating a strong visual link between the contemplative space at the front and the setting for a hedonistic lifestyle in the back garden.

above *A key feature of the front garden is a sculptural gateway – backlit at night to resemble a Chinese lantern.*

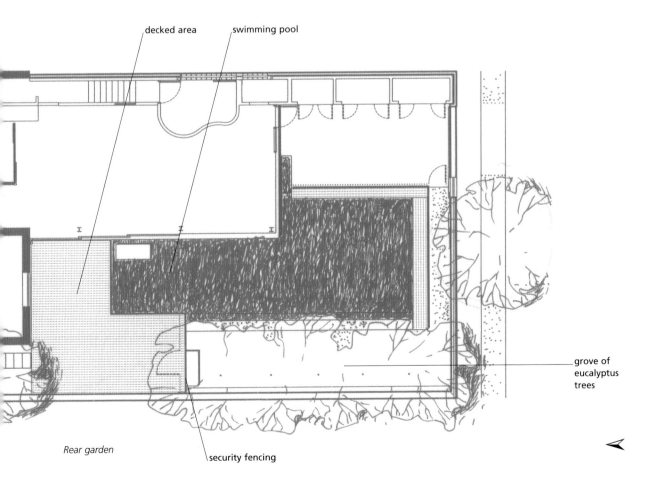

decked area   swimming pool

grove of eucalyptus trees

Rear garden   security fencing

Hot Tub Heaven

SARAH EBERLE – HILLIER LANDSCAPES / ANDREW HERRING – HERRING HOMES

DIMENSIONS 16 x 10m (53 x 33ft)

SOIL medium loam

ASPECT south facing

KEY FEATURES sunken sitting area and a hot tub

Within this larger country garden, the owners were keen to have a private area with a sitting space related to the drawing room of the house, and for a hot tub to be incorporated into the design. The courtyard space is overlooked from a shared boundary but had potential to be an interesting and secluded spot.

Immediately outside the house, a deck spans the width of the courtyard. A hot tub is set into this deck and integrated into the levels, with steps running around the circumference leading down to steps to a sunken terrace. This sunken area forms a secluded sitting area with walls retained by vertical timber poles and paving of informal, natural pebble mosaic.

Blousy planting of grasses and bamboos creates enclosure but not a visually heavy wall of planting. The bamboos *Phyllostachys aurea* and *Phyllostachys nigra* are used in staggered formation to provide a screen while allowing glimpses of the view to appear occasionally. Groundcover of liriope, dryopteris, tiarella, and leymus in large drifts provides lower-level interest and again emphasizes the effects of filtered sunlight.

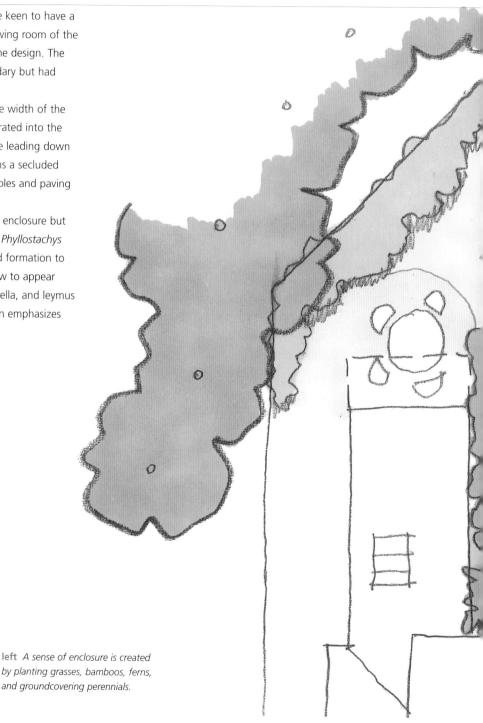

left *A sense of enclosure is created by planting grasses, bamboos, ferns, and groundcovering perennials.*

above *Set into a large deck, this hot tub has been integrated into the overall design; alongside it steps lead down to a sunken terrace.*

sunken area

deck

steps down

hot tub

City Refuge

TIM THOELECKE – AMERICAN
ACADEMY OF LANDSCAPE DESIGN LLC

DIMENSIONS 10 x 4m (33 x 13ft)

SOIL heavy clay

ASPECT east facing

KEY FEATURES attractive paving, water feature

The owners of this small back garden work very long hours and were looking for a garden to entertain in and to relax. They enjoy gardening but don't have much time available. Access to the back garden was limited.

The design incorporates a small area paved in New York bluestone with bricks used for the retaining walls, and a built-in seat to match the house. Copings and treads for the wall and steps are also in bluestone. A bespoke trellis was constructed to obscure the garage and this gives a strongly decorative pattern to the garden. A self-contained water feature was chosen by the owners and a barbecue is incorporated into the design. The planting is all low-maintenance and chosen to be as pest- and disease-free as possible and also not to need staking. A small dining table and chairs provide a welcome place to relax and pots of flowers make a colourful splash in the garden.

above If well designed even the smallest back garden can have clearly designated areas for dining and entertaining.

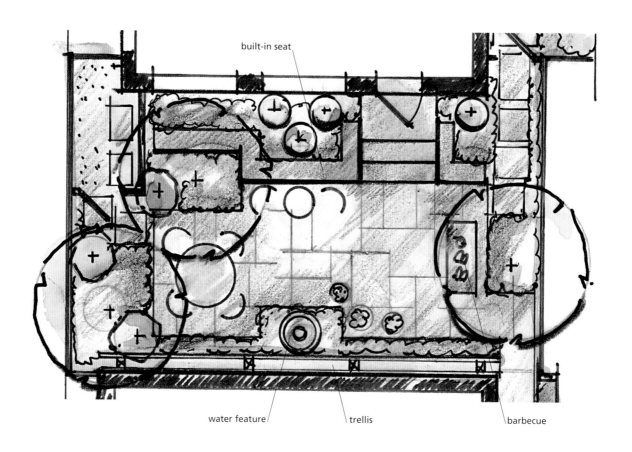

built-in seat

water feature

trellis

barbecue

Natural Garden for Wildlife

JULIE TOLL

DIMENSIONS 16 x 14m (53 x 47ft)

SOIL very heavy clay

ASPECT south facing

KEY FEATURES varied, dense planting

With owners who were keen gardeners and who wanted to increase their knowledge of plants, the brief for the design of this garden was to provide large areas of planting and the creation of several different plant habitats.

Offsetting the lines of the garden on the diagonal increases the sense of space, and the random paving slabs in the terrace are initially laid tightly together and then gradually spill onto a small, flowering lawn, enhancing the feeling of informality. A bench set onto the paving just outside the house provides a spot to sit beside a small, decorative pot from which water falls onto gravel. A curved pool with a gentle slope of pebbles provides an opportunity to enjoy water lilies and other pond planting, and a hazel-roofed shelter forms a sitting area from which to look across the lawn.

A bog garden is fed by water from the pool and a timber deck links the two together. A meandering path leads through a woodland area and back to the main terrace via an area of gravel with timber sleepers as stepping stones.

Planting is lush and complicated. The ability of each plant to attract wildlife is crucial, and the collection here requires a high level of maintenance to keep it at its best.

above *Water lilies can provide spectacular colour, scent, and texture as well as shading a pool and sheltering fish beneath.*

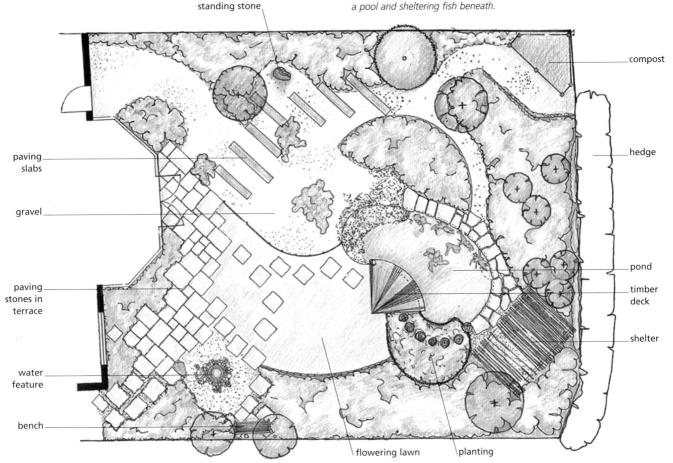

standing stone

paving slabs

gravel

paving stones in terrace

water feature

bench

compost

hedge

pond

timber deck

shelter

flowering lawn

planting

Simple Country Garden

MICHAEL DAY

DIMENSIONS 19 x 15m (57 x 50ft) maximum

SOIL well-drained alkaline

ASPECT south-facing

KEY FEATURES clipped box hedges to bring the design together

The garden of this pretty, Cotswold stone cottage was already partly established but additional seating areas were desired by the owners and they also wanted the garden to work together as a whole. Minimal hard landscape works were needed to complete the garden structure. The owners particularly wanted it to look good in the winter. There were several mature trees on the site already, as well as a mature beech hedge that gave structure and privacy from neighbouring buildings.

The garden is unified by the use of box and topiary in a variety of different forms. Low box hedging edges the lawn, with box cubes at the corners. Two box balls form sentries either side of an ornament at the end of the garden, which acts as a full stop to the vista. Either side of the new seating area to the east of the garden, two standard box trees provide vertical interest and add definition to the space. A small, woodland sitting area forms a restful and shady spot in which to linger among tall planting of ferns, *Digitalis ferruginea,* and *Helleborus argutifolius.* Two *Osmanthus delaveyi* flank the stepping-stone entrance to this area.

On the other side of the garden, a seating area features an old, stone table that was found on-site. Planting is of rows of *Calamagrostis* x *acutiflora* 'Overdam' and *Aster* x *frikartii* 'Monch', which lead to a short, paved path edged in *Iris* 'Jane Phillips'.

above *Clipped box forms act as sentries to the dominant ornament situated at the end of the garden.*

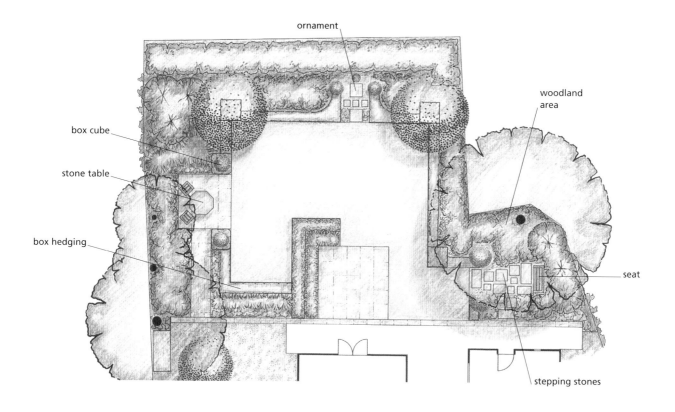

ornament

woodland area

box cube

stone table

box hedging

seat

stepping stones

Half for Adults, Half for Kids

SUSANNA EDWARDS

DIMENSIONS 30 x 10m (100 x 33ft)
SOIL clay
ASPECT south-west facing
KEY FEATURES deck, trampoline, and Astroturf lawn

For a family with three very active pre-teenagers, the brief for this design was to provide a large space for outside dining with a water feature to disguise ambient noise, and to incorporate a sunken trampoline and a large area suitable for children to play outdoor games. The owners also wanted to grow fruit and vegetables if a suitable space could be found. The level changes by 1m (3ft) from the house up to the middle of the garden.

Immediately outside the house, a large, hardwood deck provides a sunny and sheltered place to dine, surrounded on the garden side by a 50cm- (20in-) high, rendered retaining bed that is densely planted with scented perennials and grasses, and includes *Verbena*

bonariensis for height. Within this bed is a water feature of three granite blocks in diminishing sizes with water rising through and cascading over on to pebbles below.

From the lower terrace level, a brick ramp leads up into the garden, allowing the change in level to be effectively imperceptible to running children. The southern wall is densely planted with bamboos, and *Pittosporum tobira* and box (*Buxus*) spheres accentuate corners of the beds throughout the garden. A trampoline is set at ground height for maximum enjoyment and safety. Raised vegetable beds are incorporated into the planting behind the trampoline.

Dividing the garden is a hornbeam hedge, which allows the children freedom to kick balls on the Astroturf lawn behind without fear of damaging the planting or vegetables.

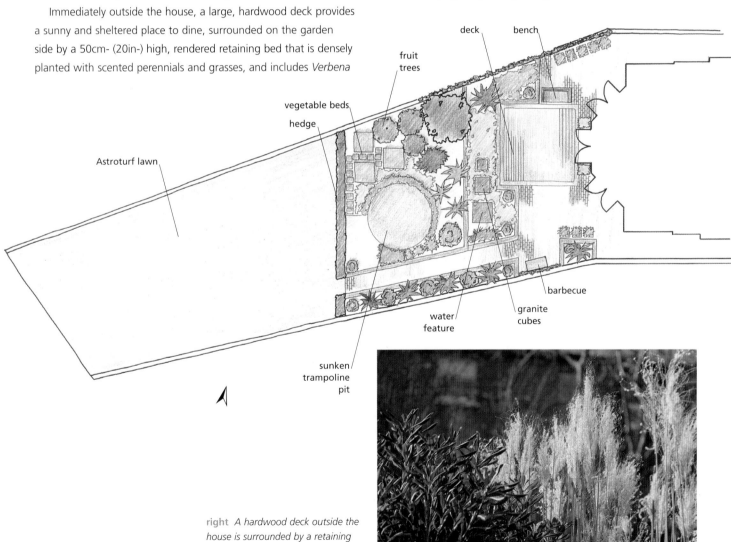

deck   bench

fruit
trees

vegetable beds

hedge

Astroturf lawn

barbecue

water
feature

granite
cubes

sunken
trampoline
pit

right A hardwood deck outside the house is surrounded by a retaining bed densely planted with scented perennials and grasses.

Simple Family Garden

CLAIRE MEE DESIGNS

DIMENSIONS 16 x 7m (53 x 23ft)

SOIL clay

ASPECT north-west facing

KEY FEATURES pergola for dining

The owners' brief for this garden was to create a simple family space with pretty planting and somewhere for the children to play. A large seating area for dining was required and a new glass extension to the rear of the house made the indoor and outdoor space seamless.

In order to maximize the sun in this garden, the main sitting area is at the far end from the house, with a light pergola shading the diners and providing supports for planting of wisterias. From the house, the main view is of a long, rectangular lawn, giving a formal air. Standard olive trees and box balls are planted at regular intervals among lush and exuberant planting of herbaceous perennials to bring structure, scent, and colour to the borders. A bench is set into the planting on one side of the garden, providing a place to catch the last of the evening sun and to watch the children play. A small border of lavenders and box screens a bark-covered play area in

which a swing has been incorporated. Surrounding the garden, a high, battened trellis gives privacy and intimacy to the space. Against the back wall, under the pergola, mirrors are inset to increase the impression of space. Also under the pergola, a bench seat is built into the corner, around the base of a tree.

above *The bench set into the planting on one side of the garden has been positioned so that it catches the late evening sun.*

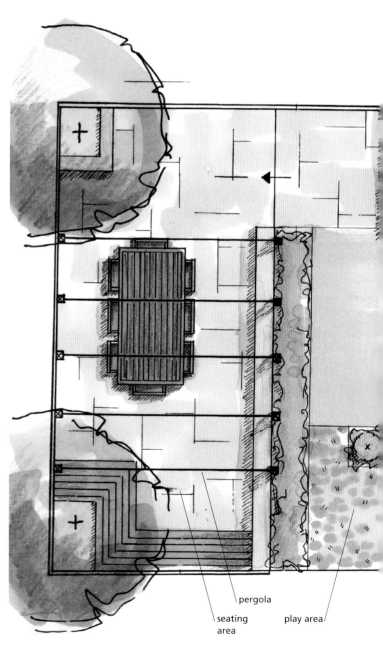

pergola

seating area

play area

right This picture shows the glass extension to the rear of the house, while a pergola shades the main sitting area (in the foreground).

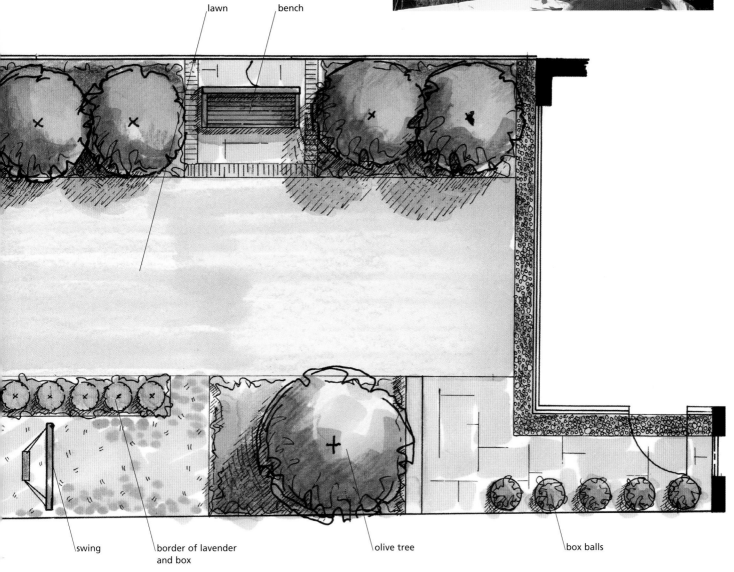

lawn

bench

swing

border of lavender and box

olive tree

box balls

Fish Out of Water

VLADIMIR SITTA / ROBERT FABER – TERRAGRAM PTY LTD

DIMENSIONS 20 x 17m (60 x 55ft)

SOIL imported

ASPECT south-east facing (in southern hemisphere)

KEY FEATURES swimming pool and fish skeleton in vitrine

This space was originally a private zoo. The old walls and some remnants of shed and storage spaces, doors, and ladders all remained on the site. The owners' brief was to incorporate a swimming pool but they otherwise were very open-minded about what should be done with the space.

The resulting contemporary design has a long swimming pool set into the corner of the old walls. The pool is partially elevated above the ground, and on its long side an infinity edge allows a waterfall to flow into a moat bordered with plants to provide the required safety barrier in a creative and exciting way. Thus the pool becomes an integral part of the design and not just a traditional hole filled with water. Access to the pool is from a small, decked platform at the end, and the safety barrier at this point is constructed from a plinth with a large fish skeleton encased in a vitrine set on top. The designer's original idea was to use an aquarium as a pool fence, but logistics and pragmatism ruled that out. On the wall side of the pool, an old door found on the site is set, slightly ajar, against the wall with a single spout of water arcing into the pool; male visitors are often keen to be photographed behind the door!

Old ladders found on the site are used as decorative details against a pergola, and clean, geometric lines of grass and paths keep the design simple. Lighting is used to great dramatic effect in the space and planting is predominantly evergreen.

above *The sharp contrast between the sleek pool and the rustic, antiquated wall reflected in the rippling surface provides the main excitement within this atmospheric garden.*

left *The safety barrier at one end of the pool is constructed from a plinth with a large fish skeleton encased in vitrine on top.*

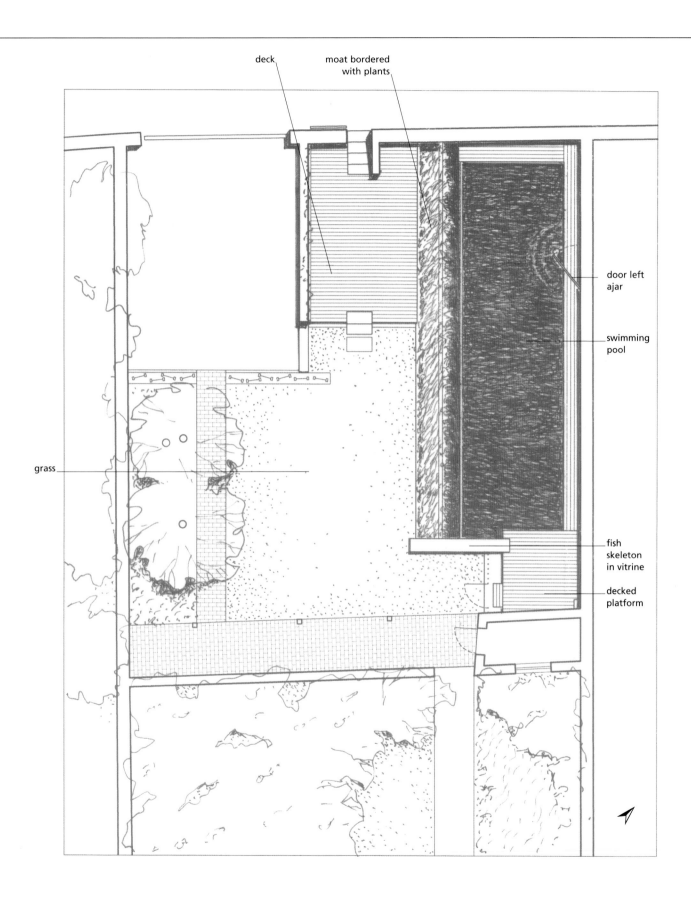

deck

moat bordered
with plants

door left
ajar

swimming
pool

grass

fish
skeleton
in vitrine

decked
platform

Bright, Modern, and Curvy

JULIE TOLL

DIMENSIONS 8.5 x 5m (26 x 16ft)

SOIL poor, light loam

ASPECT south-west facing

KEY FEATURES shallow water feature with
a pressure-activated jet of water

The designer was asked to create a garden for the family. Having refurbished their kitchen, the owners wanted to be able to dine alfresco. It was important that the garden stirred curiosity in visitors as they arrived at the front of the house and glimpsed the space beyond through a small window. Ease of maintenance was also important, as was interest to the children as they grew up.

A low-level terrace, excavated from the existing garden height, provides a sunny sitting area and the designer has incorporated steps to the higher level and seating for the dining table, with the retaining wall holding the rest of the garden back. At the higher level sinuous, low box (*Buxus*) hedges and a path of large stepping stones lead up the garden to flat areas of gravel.

Planting of a *Cotinus coggygria* and phormiums give height and accent to the garden. At the centre, a shallow water feature, formal in shape, contains another rock stepping stone, which activates a jet of water when stepped on to add an element of fun to the garden. Further stepping stones are found among the taller grasses and perennials planting at the back of the garden.

above *The photograph shows the important elements of this garden, including a sunny low level terrace and a shallow water feature.*

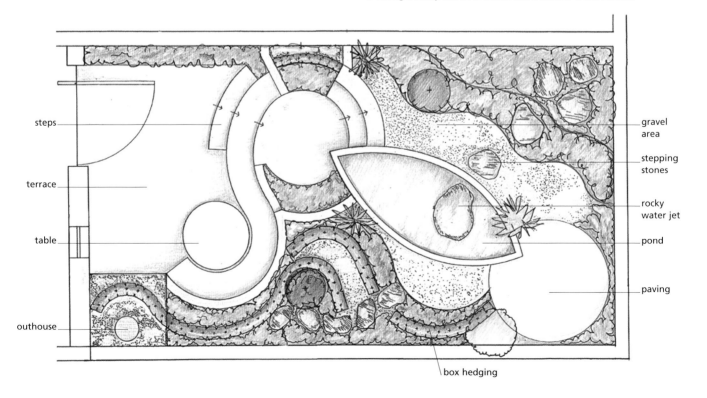

steps

terrace

table

outhouse

gravel area

stepping stones

rocky water jet

pond

paving

box hedging

Diagonal Garden to Deceive the Eye

DAVID R. SISLEY – GARDEN DESIGNS & LANDSCAPES

DIMENSIONS 260 sq m (2,800sq ft)

SOIL clay loam

ASPECT north-west facing

KEY FEATURES trellis to screen children's play area

Screening of neighbouring properties together with provision of a children's play area were crucial requirements in this garden. The owners also wanted colourful planting, which they planned, in part, to do themselves.

The majority of the paving is of old-fashioned, flagstone-style slabs laid diagonally to increase the sense of space. The strong, diagonal lines extend all around the house and are picked up on the south-west boundary with trellis screens. Behind the screens, a large area is set aside for children's play equipment and this section is surfaced in bark for safety. In front of the trellis, a wooden arbour emerges from the trellising, giving a sheltered spot for a bench. Strong planting with trees (*Gleditsia triacanthos* 'Sunburst', *Acer davidii,* and *Amelanchier lamarckii*) and shrubs, as well as lower-level herbaceous plants, surrounds the lawn, which extends into a circle giving a feeling of enclosure. The paving is punctuated by a small area of brickwork laid in a herringbone pattern, which softens the edges of the large area of paving and leads into the lawn's brick edging.

In the paved side return area of the garden, a small self-contained water feature adds interest to the view from the kitchen and entices the visitor out into the garden.

right *Among the trees suggested for this garden design is the deciduous honey locust (*Gleditsia triacanthos 'Sunburst'*).*

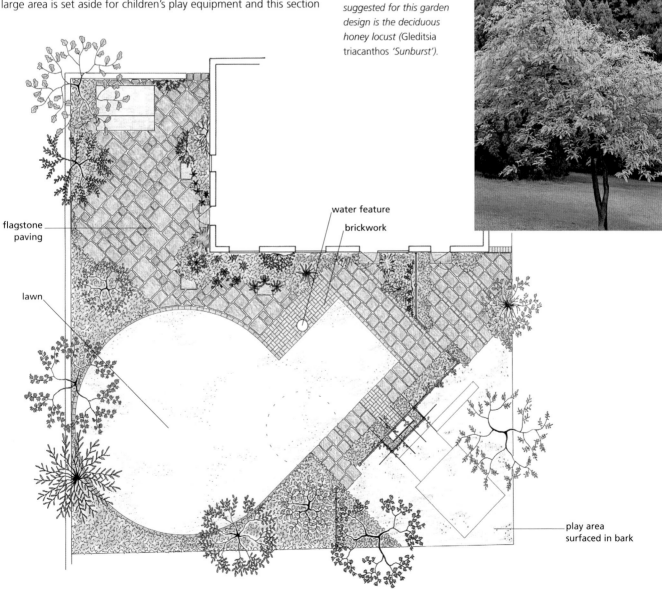

flagstone paving

lawn

water feature

brickwork

play area surfaced in bark

Contrasting Pebbles

DOUGLAS COLTART – VIRIDARIUM DESIGN STUDIO

DIMENSIONS 19.5 x 5.5m (59 x 18ft)

SOIL loam

ASPECT north-east facing

KEY FEATURES use of stones throughout the garden

This small garden is sandwiched between the house and the garage, which is dominant over the space. The owner wanted a comfortable, informal space in which to relax.

The contrast between the brick paving laid in herringbone pattern and the tiered decked areas is marked. The brick defines the pathway from the house to the garage, with the decked areas offset to the sunnier side of the garden. Planting is mainly in a square block outside the kitchen window but with long, narrow beds surrounding the larger decked area. Tall *Juniperus communis* 'Hibernica' are planted to screen the garage wall at the end of the garden and the stone side walls are also clothed in climbers to give a lush and soft feel.

Pebbles are used in various ways: principally, they are suspended, semi-submerged over a rectangular water feature with fine stainless-steel rods through their centres to hold them in place. Elsewhere, pebbles are set into the edge of the deck, and stacks of varying heights are incorporated into the herbaceous beds.

The planting is predominantly of shrubs and perennials, with topiaried box (*Buxus*) in containers. Lavender (*Lavandula angustifolia* 'Hidcote') and *Hebe albicans* are used along with grasses *Molinia caerula* 'Variegata' and *Pennisetum alopecuroides,* and astrantias, geraniums, heleniums, and sedums for shape and colour.

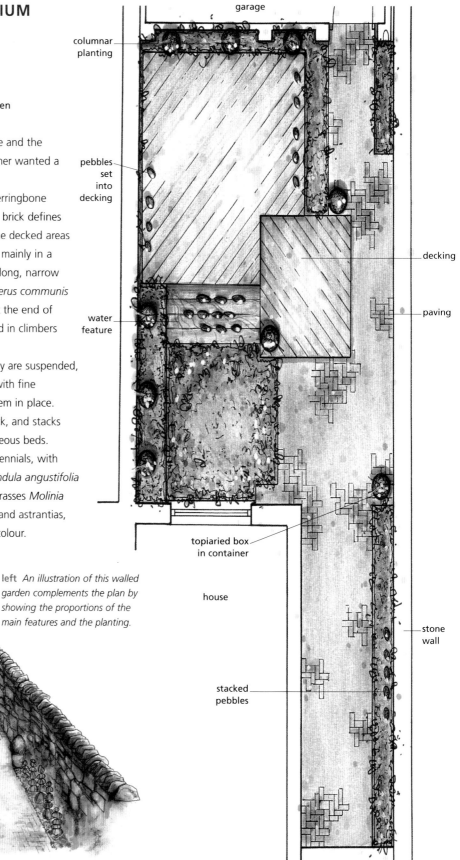

left *An illustration of this walled garden complements the plan by showing the proportions of the main features and the planting.*

Illusion of Space

ANNIE GUILFOYLE – CREATIVE LANDSCAPES

DIMENSIONS 9.5 x 6.4m (31 x 21ft)

SOIL sandy loam containing lots of builders' rubble

ASPECT south facing

KEY FEATURES water wall in heated stainless steel

Recent renovation of the owners' kitchen, which led directly onto the garden through huge glass doors, meant that a design was sought that linked the house and garden. A very striking and contemporary kitchen suggested a similar style for the garden, but with planting to soften the lines of the hard materials. An existing and much-loved *Betula utilis* var. *jacquemontii* had to remain.

Paving is of 900 x 500mm (35½ x 19¾in) limestone slabs laid in stretcher bond to match the flooring of the kitchen. A simple terrace outside the kitchen with a bench and table and chairs is softened by planting of *Melianthus major, Olearia macrodonta,* and *Pittosporum tobira,* among others, as well as perennials *Geranium phaeum* var. *lividum* 'Joan Baker', thalictrum, and phlox. A pinch point in the planting gives a glimpse of the water feature and the impression of more garden to be seen at a distance from the kitchen. Near the far end of the garden a 2m- (6ft-) high, rendered wall is a backdrop for a bespoke metal water feature made from heated stainless steel. The heating creates a wonderful petrol-blue effect and also slightly distorts the metal so that when water tumbles down, it traces the distortion, adding another dimension.

above *This perspective shows the importance of the contemporary metal water feature near the end of the garden.*

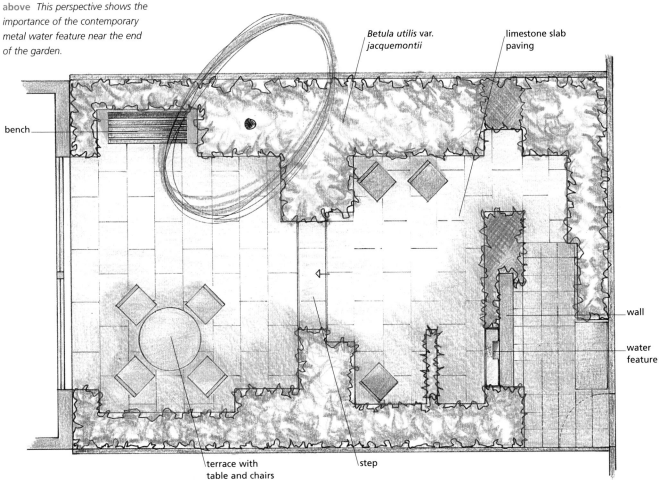

bench

Betula utilis var. *jacquemontii*

limestone slab paving

wall

water feature

terrace with table and chairs

step

Year-Round Interest

TIM THOELECKE – AMERICAN ACADEMY OF LANDSCAPE DESIGN LLC

DIMENSIONS 1,200sq m (13,000sq ft)

SOIL clay

ASPECT south facing

KEY FEATURES terraces

Looking for a garden for all seasons for entertaining, reading, and napping, the owners of this garden also wanted the space to be attractive from inside the house for the winter months: they were looking for a garden to lure them outside.

The design provides a voyage of discovery with a coherent framework to guide the trip through the garden. All around the house different areas for sitting have their own characters and are linked by views from one to another. Repetition of materials and of favourite plants has a unifying effect and bluestone paving, hydrangeas, roses, and box are all repeated throughout the garden. Gently curving outlines of the planting beds combined with lush planting disguise the angles of the house and create an air of informality. Perennials are planted in broad sweeps, with large numbers of a single plant grouped together to give a strong emphasis to the chosen colour and shape.

A small, naturalistic pond fed by a stream is placed near the house, bringing the sound and reflections of water. The natural look is enhanced by blurring the edges of the water with boulders at the margin. Outside each of the doors from the house to the garden, a different sitting space is contrived. A large, triangular pergola with a swing seat suspended from it is positioned to obscure a neighbour's house, and at the back of the house two terraces provide a view out over the garden for a different mood or time of day.

above *The curving beds and planting groups lead the eye across the garden and toward the house.*

right *An atmospheric corner of the garden is based on the simple combination of textured paving and luxuriant foliage planting.*

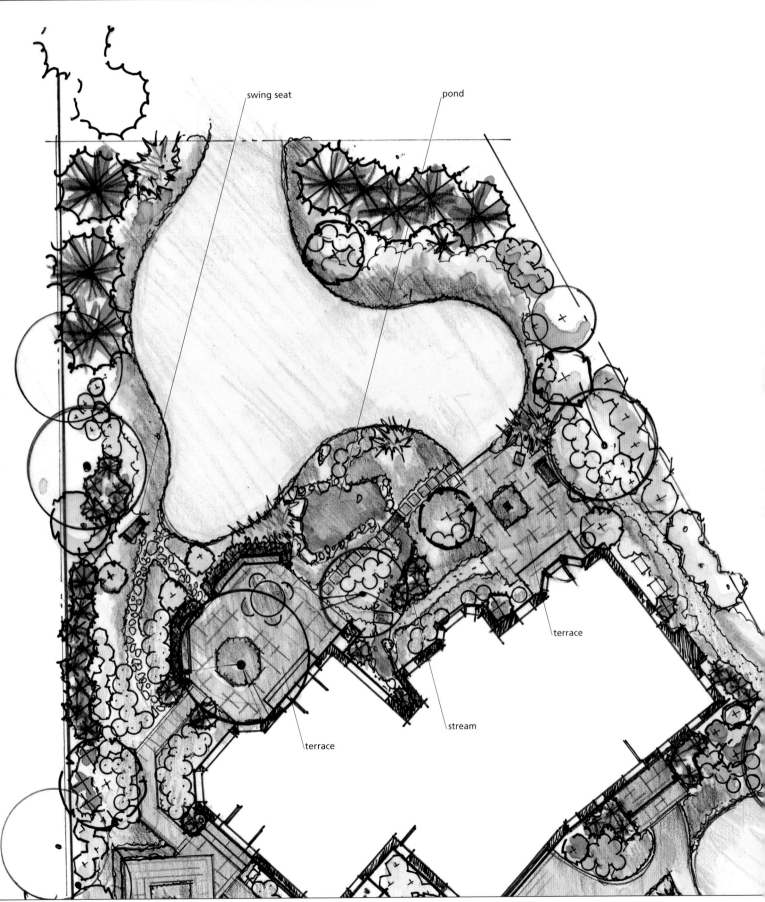

swing seat

pond

terrace

stream

terrace

Fun and Tactile Family Space

PAUL DRACOTT

DIMENSIONS 15 x 10m (50 x 33ft)

SOIL deep silty loam

ASPECT east facing

KEY FEATURES vertical walls and divided spaces

The owners of this property wanted a modern family garden with an emphasis on fun and sound. From the house, a deck was essential to link with a timber floor inside and to raise the garden to the same level. Water, lighting, a children's area, and a dining area were also needed.

Because no lawn was required, it was possible to divide the garden into two proportionate spaces using white, rendered wall sections and free-standing glass panels. A large deck, forming the main thoroughfare for the garden, leads to a rectangular fish pond covered with galvanized mesh. A steel spout emanating from the wall drops water into the pool, allowing the children to touch the falling water and watch the fish beneath their feet.

In the second area of the garden, another decked space has room for a dining table and chairs, and leads to a children's space with rubber flooring and a raised, white, rendered sandpit with a decking cover.

The large glass panels with steel frames that divide the garden are lit from behind with dual-coloured L.E.D. units to create "Chinese lantern"-type projections of children or plants or whatever is behind them. Coloured uplighters and uplighting on the plants give the garden a glow at night.

Planting is of multi-stemmed trees, palms, and shrubs, giving a textured feel. Tall grasses and *Verbena bonariensis* give height and *Chamaerops humilis* add texture. Repetition of *Rudbeckia fulgida* var. *deamii* creates harmony throughout the site.

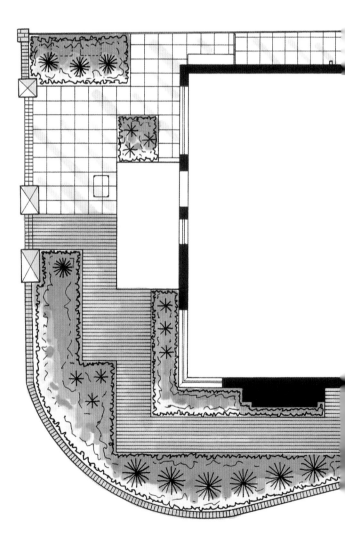

above *Part of a design for a modern family garden, the second decked area provides space for a dining table and chairs.*

left Used to divide the garden areas, these large glass panels are lit from behind with dual coloured LED light units.

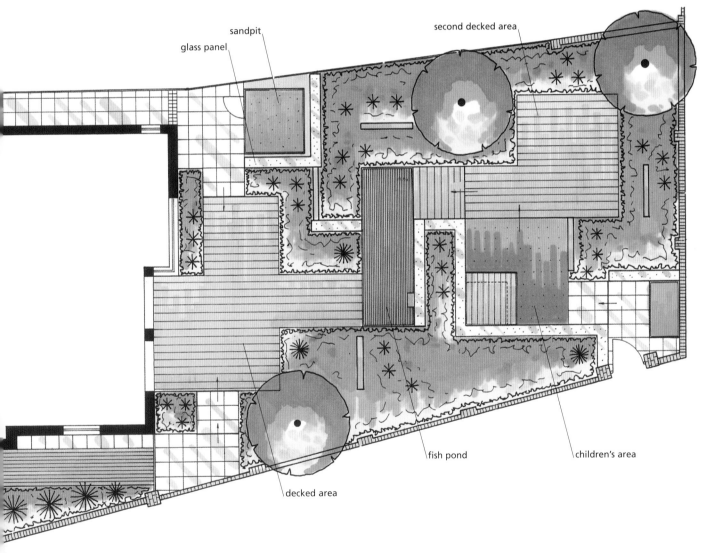

glass panel

sandpit

second decked area

fish pond

children's area

decked area

Soft, Informal, Textured Planting

ANDREW WILSON ASSOCIATES

DIMENSIONS front 9 x 6.5m (30 x 21ft); rear 10 x 6.5m (33 x 21ft)
SOIL neutral silt / loam
ASPECT front north-east facing; rear south-west facing
KEY FEATURE slate detailing and glass verticals

Designing these front and rear gardens was part of a larger refurbishment of the house that included the construction of a small conservatory decorated with floor-mounted uplighters, a feature that was carried into the gardens. The client wanted interesting planting but no lawn and asked for a relatively low-maintenance garden overall.

The rear garden receives sunshine throughout the day but is shaded by a substantial and ancient fig tree that carries a tree-preservation order and gives the garden a sense of character.

In order to relate the garden to the architecture of the Regency villa, slate is introduced into the more randomized limestone paving to create a focus and a sense of some formality. This feature is used in the front and back gardens, giving a sense of continuity between the spaces. At the south end of the rear garden, a tall water feature of slate and polished metal spills a narrow jet of water onto a paved

dish at ground level. Arranged around the garden are a number of mirage glass panels to give vertical emphasis and visual interest.

Planting is randomly positioned in small associations and is primarily of ornamental grasses, herbaceous perennials, and shrubs. The effect is of plants self-seeding into relaxed but textured planting. The soil is covered by gravel to match the paving; this in turn matches the colour of the interior terrazzo floor.

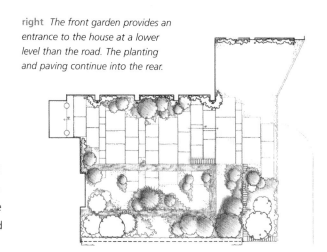

right The front garden provides an entrance to the house at a lower level than the road. The planting and paving continue into the rear.

Front garden

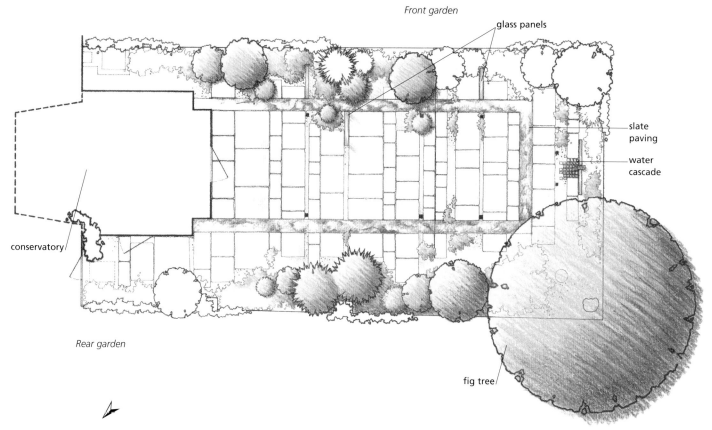

Rear garden

Rose Garden

NIGEL FULLER

DIMENSIONS 8 x 8m (25 by 25ft)

SOIL neutral

ASPECT south facing

KEY FEATURES green oak pergola

This garden was already terraced and the main steps from the house at a lower level had previously been constructed, so it remained only to design a level sitting area at the top of the garden. The garage was at the far end, so a pathway was needed to connect the steps up into the garden and the garage. Local stone had already been used for the hard landscaping in the garden and it was proposed that any additional paving use the same material. The owners were keen to tackle the planting on their own, with suggestions from the designer to include as many roses as possible. An old apple tree was to remain in the garden.

At the higher level of the garden, a round lawn with surrounding planting beds gives space for textural and colourful planting and brings shape to the space. A paved area with a green oak pergola offers a shady spot to sit and relax. Stepping stones through the planting give access to the lawn.

above *The owners of this garden wanted the designer to include as many roses as possible. The colourful planting scheme also included irises and euphorbia.*

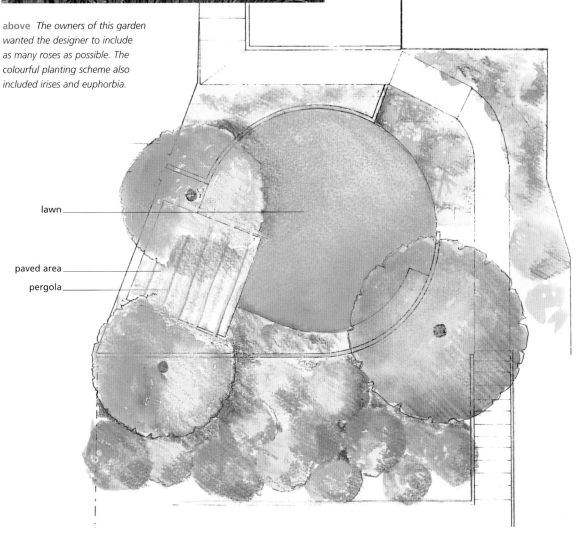

lawn

paved area

pergola

Floating Deck and Divided Space

FISHER TOMLIN

DIMENSIONS 28 x 9m (85 x 30ft)

SOIL rich loam

ASPECT south facing and very hot

KEY FEATURES Ipe decking and upright

panels to divide the space

The owners wanted an adult garden offering division of the space and interest. A striking new glass extension to the house needed to be complemented by the design.

Compacted gravel paths edged with stone lead the visitor slowly through the garden space. From the house, a decked step as wide as the building leads down onto an Ipe decked dining area. This is lit around the edges at night by a simple rope light, which creates the impression that the deck and everything on it is floating.

To the side of the deck is a small area planted with culinary herbs. This leads to the rest of the garden along the compacted

left *A section of the L-shaped pool – a key feature for dividing the garden into different areas of interest.*

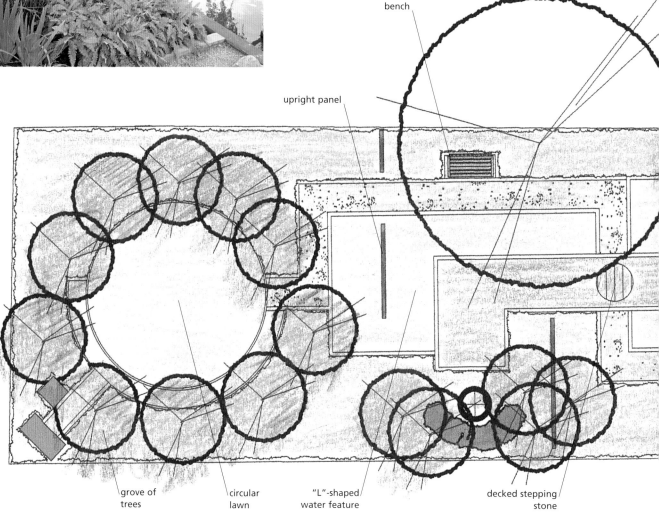

bench

upright panel

grove of
trees

circular
lawn

"L"-shaped
water feature

decked stepping
stone

gravel path, past a small lawn, and across an L-shaped water feature that entices the eye down the garden. A circular decked stepping stone leads across the channel to the path on the other side, which continues down the garden, past a bench, and on to the final, circular lawn, which is surrounded by a grove of trees.

Throughout the garden, upright panels constructed in lpe timber 1.2m (4ft) high divide the space and create views over and through the garden, leading the eye to different features. From a bench halfway down the garden there is a vista across the shorter part of the shallow pool to a focal point on the opposite boundary.

right *The main feature in the final area of the garden is a circular lawn surrounded by a grove of trees.*

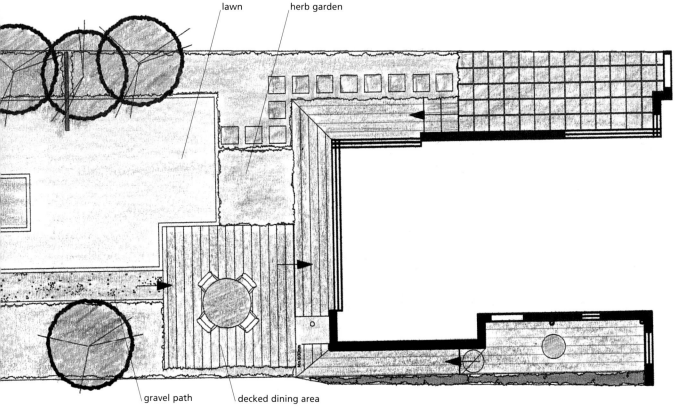

lawn

herb garden

gravel path

decked dining area

Prairie in Miniature

MARY PAYNE

DIMENSIONS 7 x 9m (23 x 30ft)

SOIL clay loam

ASPECT south-east facing

KEY FEATURES slate monoliths and an arbour

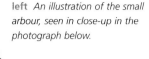

left An illustration of the small arbour, seen in close-up in the photograph below.

The designer wanted to prove that the large-scale "steppe" planting style with which she is associated would work on a very small scale. This front garden is mulched completely in gravel and uses sleeper-effect stepping stones as a pathway to the front door. The path is slightly sunken to give a contoured effect to the space.

The garden is defined by low picket fences painted a soft silvery grey, meaning that a neighbour's quite plain garden can be "borrowed" to offset the complex picture of this space. A small arbour provides a place for morning coffee and three slate monoliths of varying heights act as focal points among the planting.

Vegetation is selected as much for its winter looks as for summer colour, and planting is very random, with species changing places as they self-seed and older ones are removed. The planting includes vibrant hot colours with kniphofias (*Kniphofia* 'Nancy's Red' and 'Brimstone') selected for their compact habit. Grasses such as *Stipa tenuissima* and *Carex comans* add movement, and height comes from *Verbascum olympicum,* which send up great candelabra-style flower heads that last for months.

above The style of planting is a small-scale version of the random "steppe" planting, where different species change places over the years as they self-seed.

right A key focal point in this garden is the small arbour shown right and in the illustration above. Here, the owner can sit and read or enjoy the planting.

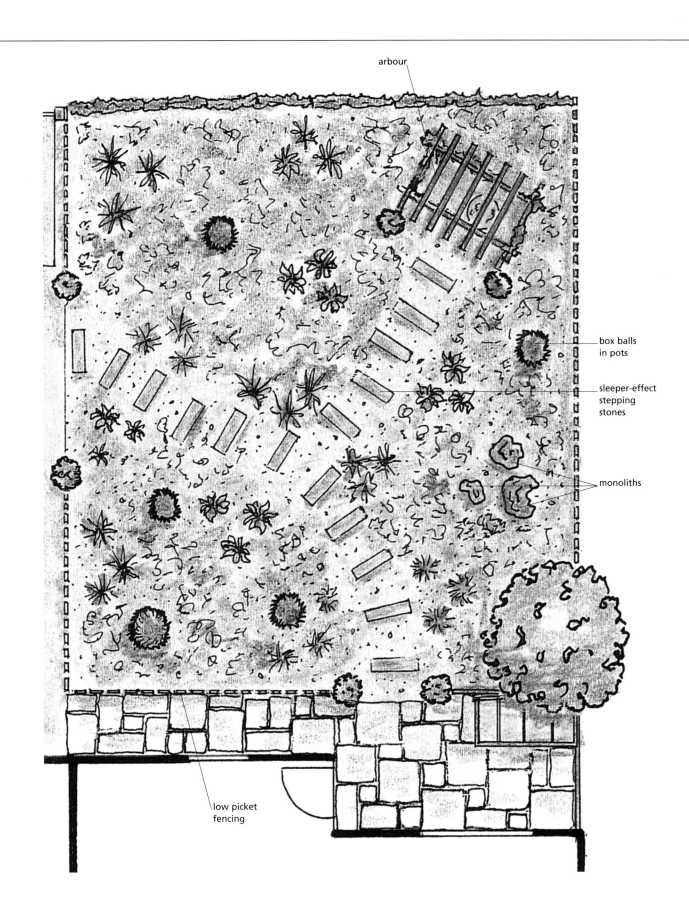

arbour

box balls
in pots

sleeper-effect
stepping
stones

monoliths

low picket
fencing

Taming a Windy Garden

NIGEL L. PHILIPS LANDSCAPE AND GARDEN DESIGN

DIMENSIONS 15 x 9.5m (50 x 31ft)

SOIL loam over chalk

ASPECT south facing but exposed to the wind

KEY FEATURES garden rooms and trellis

The owners did not want practical considerations to impact on their enjoyment of this windy site, but space to park a car was essential. Level changes had to be incorporated into the design and the upper level of the garden needed to relate to the interior of the house.

By dividing the space with pergolas and trellising, both the visual and sheltering requirements of the brief are fulfilled. Movement between areas is guided by openings in the screens and this gives an element of intrigue or mystery when moving around the garden. From the brick-paved driveway two different paths lead into the garden. Rustic trellis is used to screen the parking area from the lower garden, and this lower garden is accessed via a

pergola. It has a large lawn surrounded by dense planting, and a bench for sitting in the evening sun. 'Hidcote' lavender is used for edging and *Clematis* 'The President' grows over the pergola.

From the lower level, trellis screens the wide steps up to the higher dining terrace. From the car parking site, wide, angled stone steps also lead up to this area. An air of formality results from a circle of low box hedging regularly punctuated by pots surrounding the dining table. Two *Cupressus sempervirens* stand sentinel at the corners of this space.

above Dense planting, seating, and a table can be found at one side of the large lawn that dominates the lower garden.

brick driveway

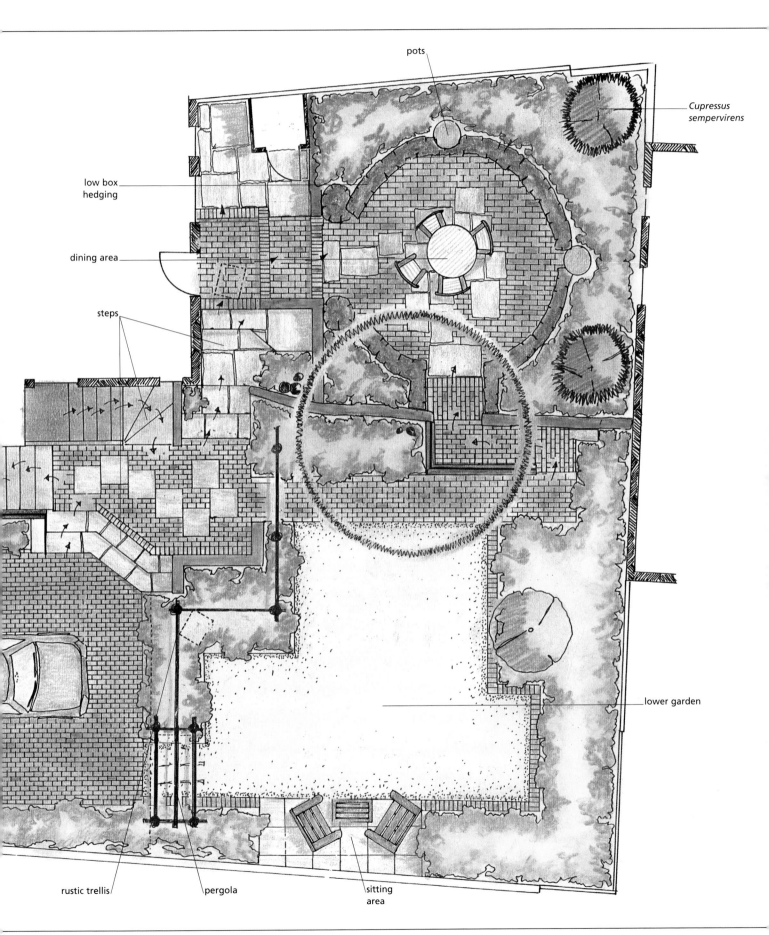

pots

*Cupressus
sempervirens*

low box
hedging

dining area

steps

rustic trellis

pergola

sitting
area

lower garden

Healing Garden

DAVID STEVENS

DIMENSIONS 25 x 30m (80 x 100ft)

SOIL acid and stony

ASPECT east facing

KEY FEATURES Japanese influence, low maintenance

The brief for this garden was to provide tranquillity without nostalgia. The theme was to have Japanese overtones and the area was primarily for quiet contemplation and reflection. Low maintenance was important.

The garden draws upon the modern design influences prevalent in Japan. Sawn-stone paving, in different widths and lengths, leads out from the main doors, taking both feet and eyes into the space. This main sight line is focused by the timber screen to an *Acer*, planted in a glazed bowl standing out in relief against the farthest ochre-painted wall. Low, clipped box hedges echo the line of the paving, providing vertical elements.

A timber bench prevents access to the end of the garden and the path skirts the former, passing the dry garden and then leading behind the timber screen to link with a cross axis into the next garden room to the south.

A diagonal element is introduced by the slate bench and water bowl, the latter spilling water into the dry garden. The line of the bench is echoed by gold-painted boulders, which are repeated in other parts of the garden.

Planting is for year-round interest with a high proportion of evergreens and groundcovers.

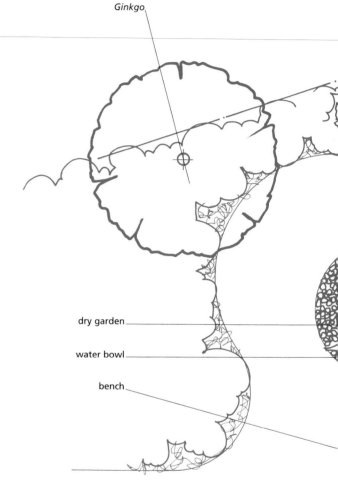

Ginkgo

dry garden

water bowl

bench

left In this garden low-clipped box (Buxus) hedges – similar to those shown in this photograph – echo the line of the sawn stone paving.

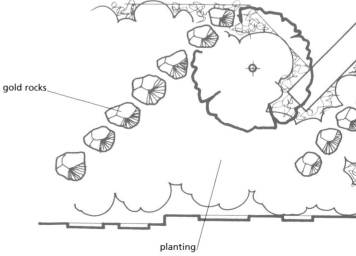

gold rocks

planting

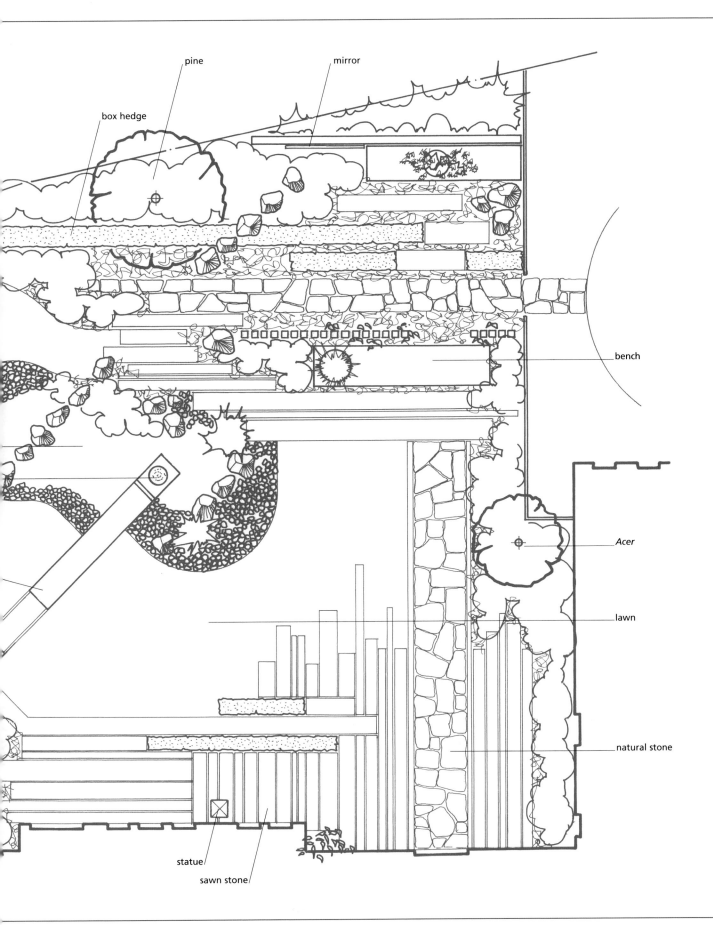

pine

mirror

box hedge

bench

Acer

lawn

natural stone

statue

sawn stone

Elemental Garden

PHILIP NIXON DESIGN

DIMENSIONS 17 x 6m (55 x 20ft)

SOIL neutral to slightly acid

ASPECT south-west facing

KEY FEATURES "conversation" / fire pit

Unusually, this space was to remain open to and part of its surroundings, rather than seeking enclosure and privacy from the redesign. A low-maintenance, contemporary garden was sought using natural elemental materials. A "conversation pit" with an open fire or barbecue was to be included for entertaining.

Outside the house a simple terrace is designed for entertaining and alfresco dining. Very high mesh walls are incorporated to create dappled shade both morning and evening while directing the view outward. Traditional rubble-construction blocks with a clean-cut, modern finish of increasing size feature down the garden, with panels of climbers on the boundaries to echo each mass of wall. In the centre, a "sofa" of the same rubble construction provides an enclosed sitting place at the fire pit. A simple path of long,

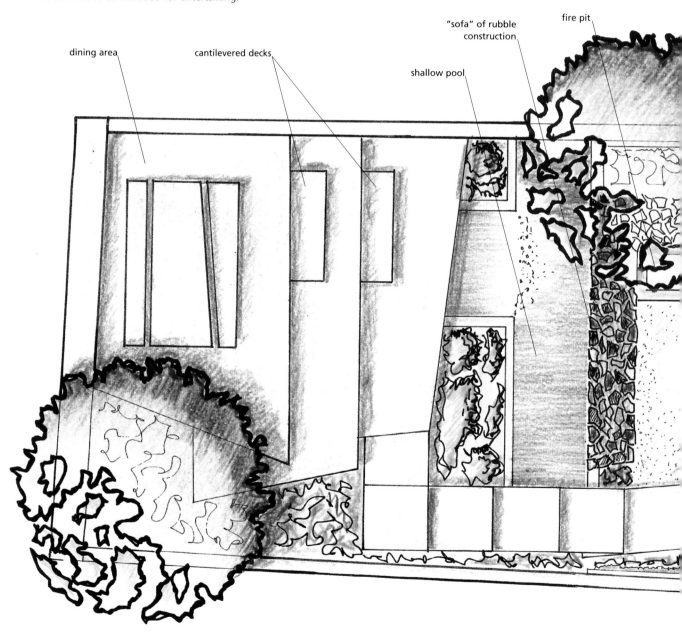

dining area

cantilevered decks

"sofa" of rubble construction

fire pit

shallow pool

overlapping rectangles is formed along the south-east boundary, culminating in a flight of shallow steps leading to a series of cantilevered decks with a dining area by the back wall. From below the decks a shoot spills water into a shallow pool at the base.

Planting is very simple, with an emphasis on yellow. Two *Robinia pseudoacacia* are included and in the centre of the garden is common gorse (*Ulex europaeus*). Other planting is largely of shade-tolerant foliage varieties such as hostas and rodgersias.

right *A perspective provides a more realistic view of the garden than the plan, showing the complex sequence of steps and levels.*

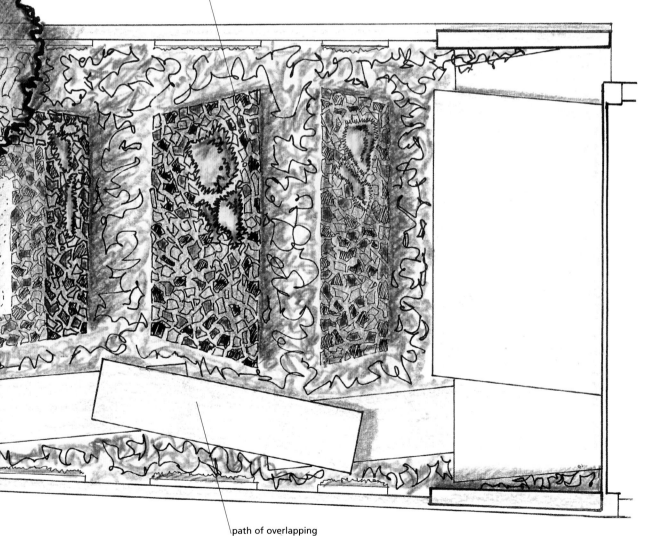

rubble construction blocks

path of overlapping rectangles

Modern Classic

CARO OLDROYD – CLIFTON NURSERIES

DIMENSIONS 9 x 7.7m (30 x 24ft)

SOIL neutral over clay

ASPECT south-west facing

KEY FEATURES: pergola and green oak sleepers

An overall traditional look was requested for this space, with increased possibilities for seating and a "destination" focal point deeper into the garden. The result needed to have an elegant and classical look but require only low maintenance.

Due to the almost square shape of the garden, a strong geometric layout is intended to create an illusion of increased width and depth of the space. York stone is laid in "random rectangular" pattern and is combined with timber detailing in new, green oak sleepers, which are used to retain small, raised beds that continue the line of the new steps, as well as delineating areas of the main garden and softening the formal look. The timber ties in with the timber pergola, arbour seat, and shed. A central planting bed in the garden, along with the sleeper details, helps to break up what would be a large expanse of paving. In the south-western corner, a covered arbour provides a quiet spot to sit. On the north-western wall, a small pergola offers another such location, this time in sunshine during the day.

The main dining area near the house has a new pergola, over which is planted wisteria and *Trachelospermum jaminoides* to create shelter, scent, and privacy from overlooking neighbours.

below *Illustrations of two of the key areas of the garden – a small pergola on the NW wall (below), and the larger pergola, arbour seat, and shed (bottom).*

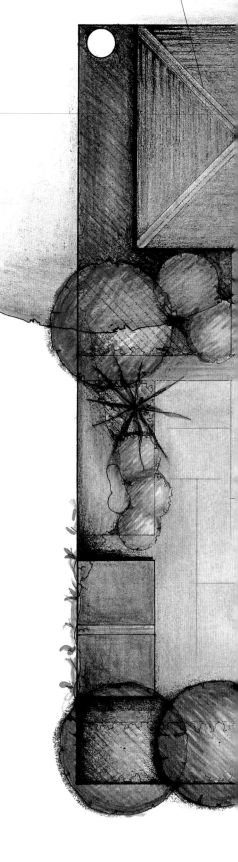

shed

arbour seat

York stone set in
rectangular pattern

sleepers

central planting bed

main dining
area

timber pergola

Seclusion for Modern Sculpture

CHARLOTTE KIERKEGAARD DESIGN

DIMENSIONS 27 x 5m (90 x 16ft)

SOIL loam

ASPECT south facing

KEY FEATURES sculptures and a rill

The owner wanted a garden to show off his collection of modern
sculpture and for enjoyment at night. A hidden retreat at the back
of the garden was requested, with seating sheltered by tall planting.

From the back door of the house, a small terrace is laid with
glasscrete set in aluminium bays. The glass is blue and green, which
sets the colour theme for the garden. A water rill falls from the far
end, along the eastern boundary, and is clad in mosaic. The rising
level is accommodated by wide steps of camomile (*Chamaemelum
nobile*) that cut across the whole garden in steps matching those in
the rill. At the western side of the garden, a glasscrete path leads
up to a small, secluded retreat area in the south-eastern corner,
passing under a *Crataegus laevigata* 'Paul's Scarlet'. A large, square
planting bed is home to a selection of the owner's sculptural pieces
as well as planting of cordylines, fescues, and bergenias.

In the evening, lighting is used along the length of the rill for
the sculptures and to accentuate the steps and the retreat area.

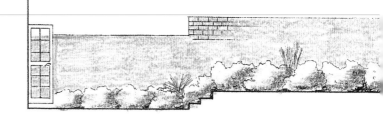

below *The elevation shows the main
level changes within the garden.*

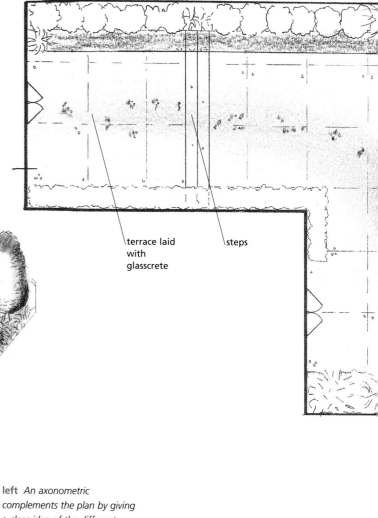

terrace laid
with
glasscrete

steps

left *An axonometric
complements the plan by giving
a clear idea of the different
proportions of the planting.*

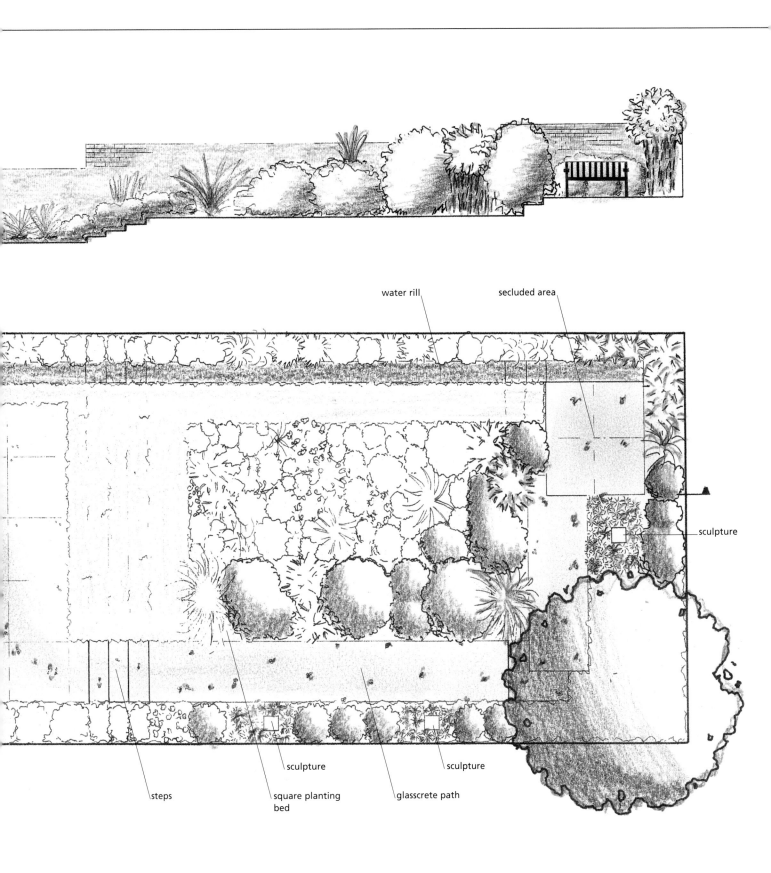

water rill

secluded area

sculpture

steps

sculpture

square planting
bed

glasscrete path

sculpture

Diagonal Decking

JAN KING LANDSCAPE & GARDEN DESIGN

DIMENSIONS 10.5 x 4.5m (34 x 14ft)
SOIL clay subsoil, neutral
ASPECT west facing
KEY FEATURES steel cube water feature

A mixture of traditional and modern design elements was required for this garden. Plenty of room for sitting outside the house, under the existing awning, and moving water were requested.

Setting the design at an angle of 45 degrees allows for a large deck and a large, shallow step down into the garden. The edges of the deck are softened by planting in pots, including scented climbers to lend their perfume to visitors sitting enjoying the garden. An illuminated, steel-cube water feature brings the sight and sound of bubbling liquid into the garden, adding to the relaxing ambiance. The diagonal theme is continued by two lawns, each framed by granite sett edging. These lead to a terrace of setts at the far end of the garden, where a bench would be sited to catch the morning sun. The end boundary is topped with small-gauge mesh for increased privacy in the garden without casting deep shadows.

Planting has strong structure, with grasses (*Carex comans* 'Bronze Perfection') and bamboos (*Fargesia murielae* 'Simba') giving height. Lush and varied climbers clothe the fences, including several different clematis (*Clematis* 'Niobe', 'Elsa Späth', and 'Lady Londesborough'), and 'Iceberg' roses bring colour and scent. A range of other perennials, including *Hemerocallis* 'Night Beacon', *Hosta* 'Royal Standard', and *Geranium sanguineum* 'Elizabeth', brings colour in summer. They are planted to grow together to give a soft traditional feel to the garden boundary.

above *The steel water cube forms a slick focal point close to the main seating area, providing noise and a lively distraction.*

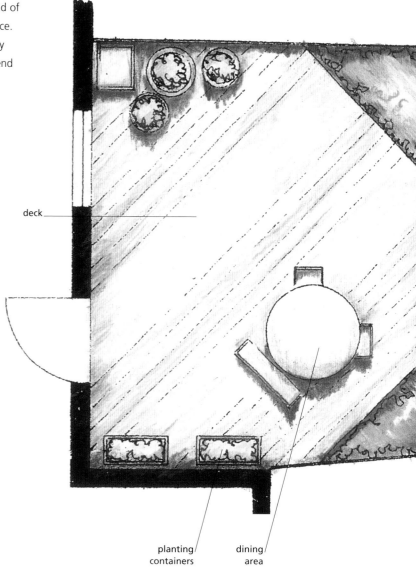

deck

planting containers

dining area

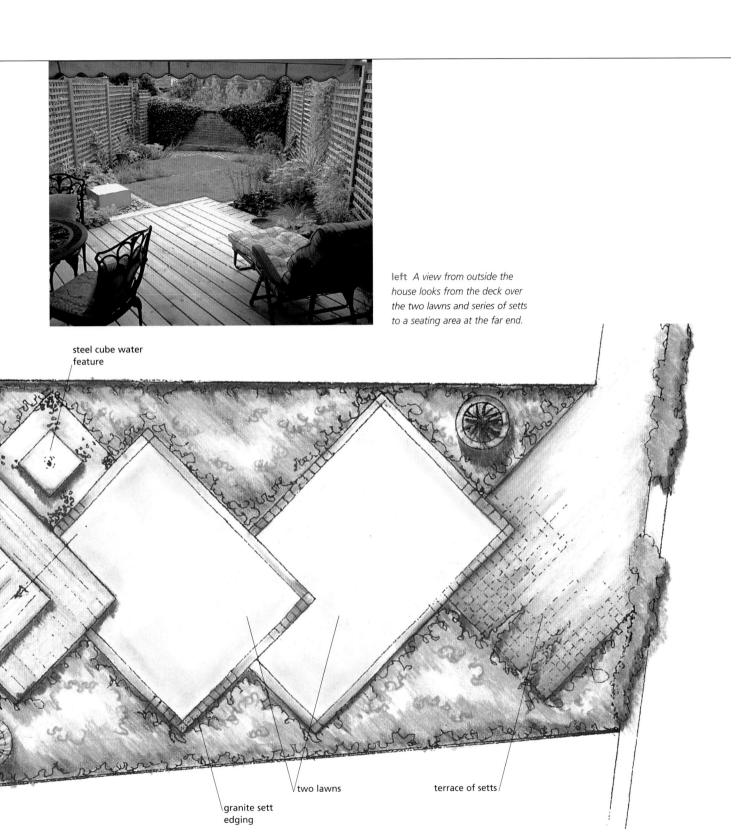

left *A view from outside the house looks from the deck over the two lawns and series of setts to a seating area at the far end.*

steel cube water feature

granite sett edging

two lawns

terrace of setts

Cruciform Design

HELEN BILLETOP GARDEN DESIGN

DIMENSIONS 14 x 11m (47 x 36ft)

SOIL clay

ASPECT north-west facing

KEY FEATURES summerhouse and pergola

This site posed some challenges to the designer because the northern corner is about 1m (1yd) lower than the terrace. The owner was looking to resolve the sloping site and wanted a full garden to encourage use, possibly with some formal elements. Views of neighbouring properties needed to be screened for privacy, and the clay soil posed some difficulties; remedial drainage pipes were to be included in the ground works.

From the house, a diagonal terrace sets up the design to use the longest axes, creating the maximum illusion of space. Wide steps lead down to a rectangular, sunken lawn with surrounding beds retained by brick walls to match the house. At each point of the design, a feature brings interest to the garden: to the west is a summerhouse, in the north corner a built-in oak bench is surrounded by raised beds, and to the east a pergola helps to provide privacy from neighbours. A water feature next to the pergola is positioned as a focal point for the view from the conservatory. Lighting is used in the garden to enhance a feature urn and the bubbling water feature. The seating areas are gently lit for evening use. Planting brings additional interest, using textured and variegated foliage for structure.

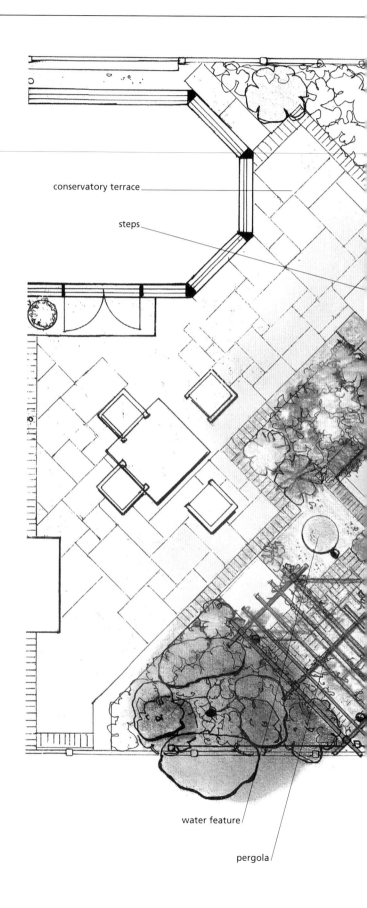

conservatory terrace

steps

water feature

pergola

above *Steps lead down to a rectangular sunken lawn with surrounding planted beds retained by brick walls.*

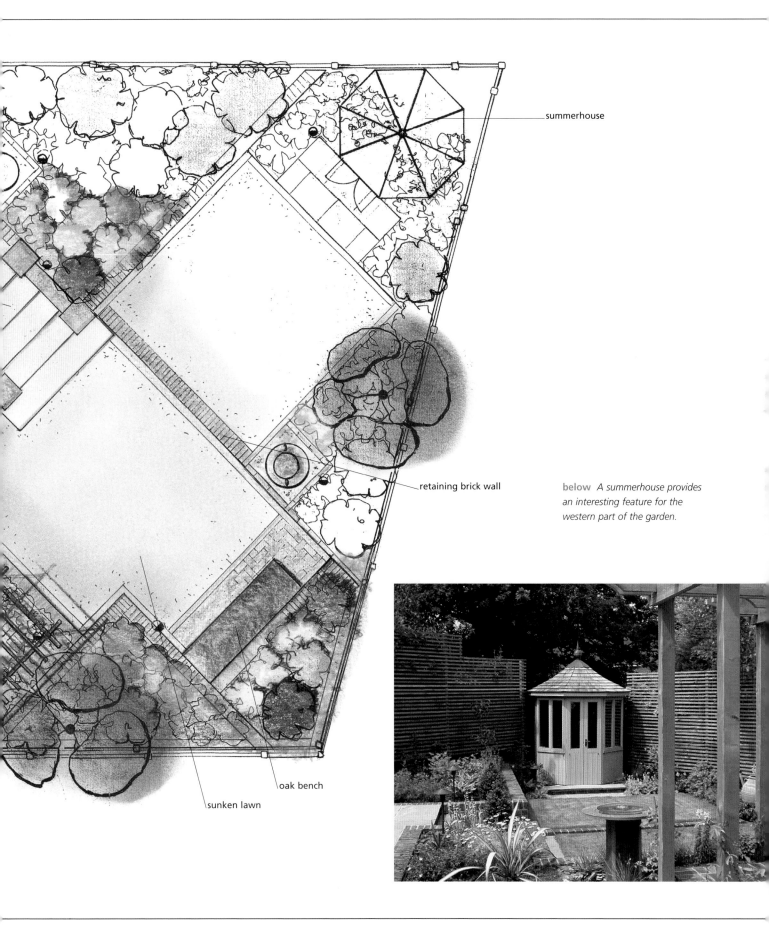

summerhouse

retaining brick wall

below *A summerhouse provides an interesting feature for the western part of the garden.*

oak bench

sunken lawn

Garden for Remembering

NAILA GREEN GARDEN DESIGN

DIMENSIONS 26 x 17m (82 x 55ft)

SOIL neutral

ASPECT west facing

KEY FEATURES Japanese style

The designer was asked to create a commemorative garden for a young teenager who had recently died. The garden was to be sited within the gardens of the girl's school and designed to capture aspects of her interests and personality, as well as providing her friends with a contemplative space in which to remember her.

left *The Japanese maples (Acer japonicum) used within this garden, as here, are prized for their autumn colouration.*

The girl had had a strong interest in Japanese style and this was to provide the theme for the garden.

On entering through a Moon Gate, the Japanese influence is immediately apparent in the planting of Japanese maples, bamboos, and ferns for a contemplative atmosphere, and the hard materials used. A sinuous curve of boulders links all areas of the garden, starting in a Japanese stone garden of gravel, stones, and pebbles, crossing a circular pool simply edged in mown grass, and continuing along a small meandering stream. The boulders are sourced from near the teenager's home and are used to celebrate each year of her life, starting out as low, flattish stones suitable for sitting on and getting larger as they continue through the garden. Each boulder is engraved with words that were personal to the girl, including lines from her favourite poems, lyrics from favourite songs, and favourite words. Soothing bubbles of water emerge from the tops of some of the boulders and fall back into the stream. Occasionally and unpredictably these bubbles spout a sudden and exciting jet of water to surprise and remind the visitor of the fun and challenging side of the teenager's nature.

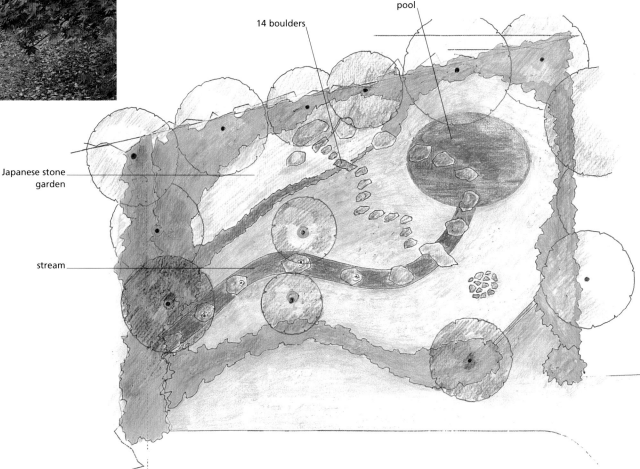

pool

14 boulders

Japanese stone garden

stream

Space for the Evening Sun

MICHAEL DAY

DIMENSIONS 5 x 12m (16 x 40ft)

SOIL downland chalk

ASPECT north-west facing

KEY FEATURES boulders in the planting and the water feature

Originally this garden was entirely gravelled and used for car parking. The owners wanted an attractive space for sitting in the evening sunshine with the car-parking area set off to one side and screened as much as possible. They also requested a water feature.

To complement the house, the paving is in brick and blue grey slate. The decked seating area close to the house is constructed around the base of an existing *Betula pendula* and makes a feature of its bark. A boulder water feature spills water into a stainless-steel rill and then into a small, timber-edged pond, giving a soothing sound and screening any traffic noise. Boulders are positioned throughout the garden, leading the eye through the space, and a sculpture is positioned at the focal point from the front door to the end of the path.

To screen cars on the drive, *Miscanthus sinensis* 'Malepartus' is planted, which then provides a backdrop for four red roses in pots between the grasses and the rill. For winter scent, an evergreen *Sarcococca hookeriana* var. *digyna* 'Purple Stem' is placed near the front door. Other planting of asters, hemerocallis, and *Stipa gigantea* continue the rural feel of the garden.

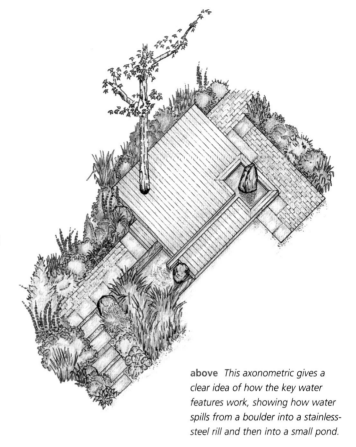

above *This axonometric gives a clear idea of how the key water features work, showing how water spills from a boulder into a stainless-steel rill and then into a small pond.*

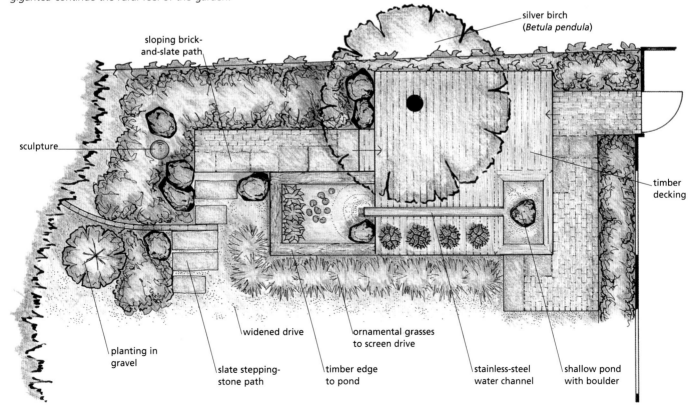

sloping brick-and-slate path

silver birch (*Betula pendula*)

sculpture

timber decking

planting in gravel

widened drive

ornamental grasses to screen drive

slate stepping-stone path

timber edge to pond

stainless-steel water channel

shallow pond with boulder

Garden with Views

RACHEL MYERS GARDEN DESIGN

DIMENSIONS 12 x 8.5m (40 x 26ft)

SOIL alkaline

ASPECT north-east facing

KEY FEATURES triangular water feature, decked steps

The architecture of the property demanded a bold, contemporary design with space for entertaining and views back to the house from the far end of the garden.

A low planter created for herbs is built against the existing retaining wall to the lower terrace and a storage space is included by the steps for cooking paraphernalia near to an angled space perfect for positioning a mobile barbecue. This means that the chef can be near to the diners sitting at the table in the return of the house. From the lower terrace level, a flight of steps leads up to the higher level and a series of large decked angular steps continues the journey to the back of the garden. At this level a large deck straddles the main garden and a lower parking area beyond. The built-up vantage point gives a view from the garden over the driveway below and forms useful storage for bicycles and tools beneath the deck. A raised stainless-steel pool on two levels is backed by a triangular rusticated stone wall through which water is pumped into the pools below.

Lighting is an important element in this garden. Halogen lamps are strung over the dining area, giving a feeling of containment, and the steps up into the garden have step lights triggered by sensors that illuminate and extinguish as progress is made through the garden.

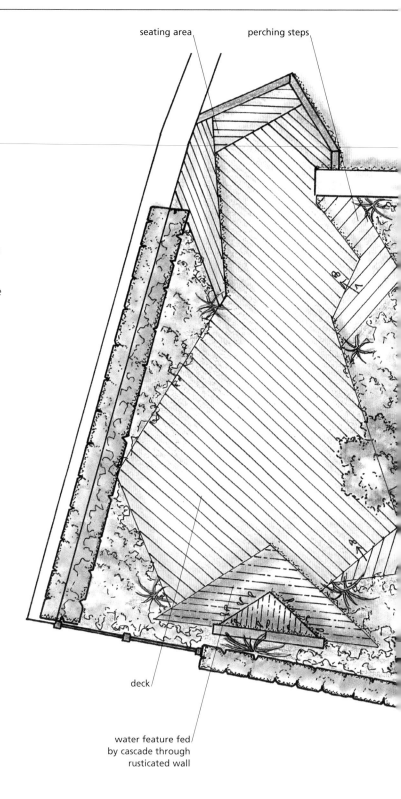

seating area perching steps

deck

water feature fed by cascade through rusticated wall

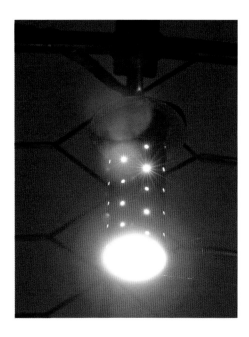

left *Halogen lights – similar to that shown here – were strung up over the dining area.*

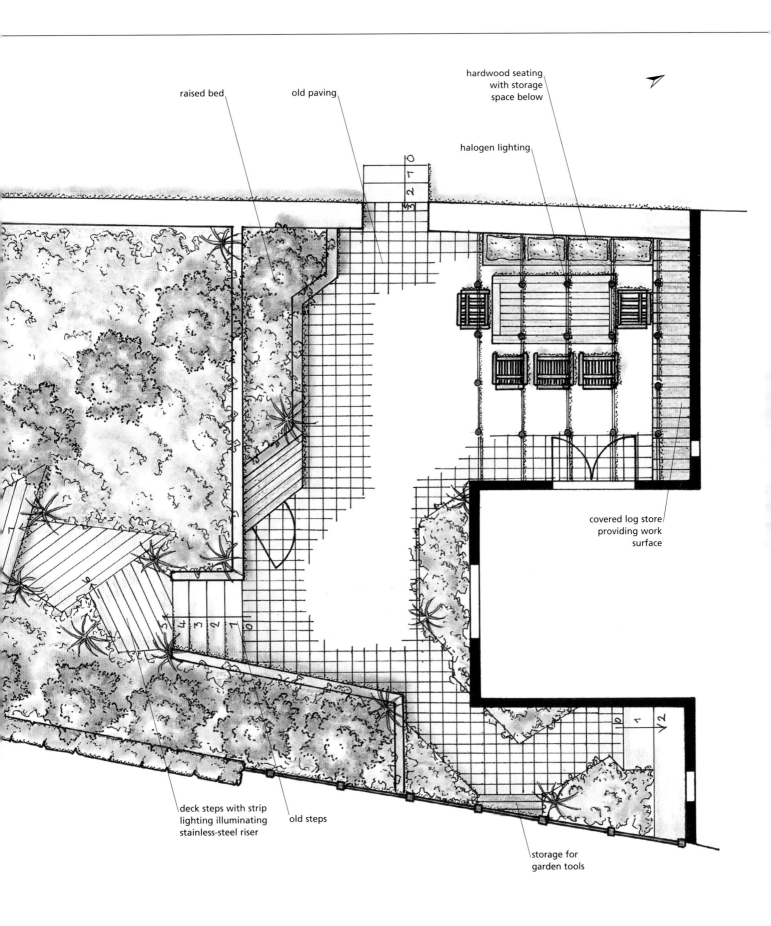

raised bed

old paving

hardwood seating
with storage
space below

halogen lighting

covered log store
providing work
surface

deck steps with strip
lighting illuminating
stainless-steel riser

old steps

storage for
garden tools

Shade and Mystery

SALLY COURT – COURTYARD GARDEN DESIGN

DIMENSIONS 22 x 6.5m (70 x 21ft) maximum

SOIL slightly acid clay

ASPECT north-west facing

KEY FEATURES granite setts

The enthusiastic owner of this garden wanted a variety of different styles in the space. In particular, he wanted it to resemble a garden that he had seen in Paris with plenty of shade and mystery. Room to entertain was important, as was screening for noise at the back of the garden. Leading out of the house at basement level, the garden was rather dark and sloped up towards the rear wall.

Beside the house, a large terrace of random, rectangular, reclaimed York stone paving is interspersed with granite setts. These setts continue as a meandering pathway up through the garden. A large, circular terrace of setts provides a sitting space in the centre of the garden and the pathway then continues again in random

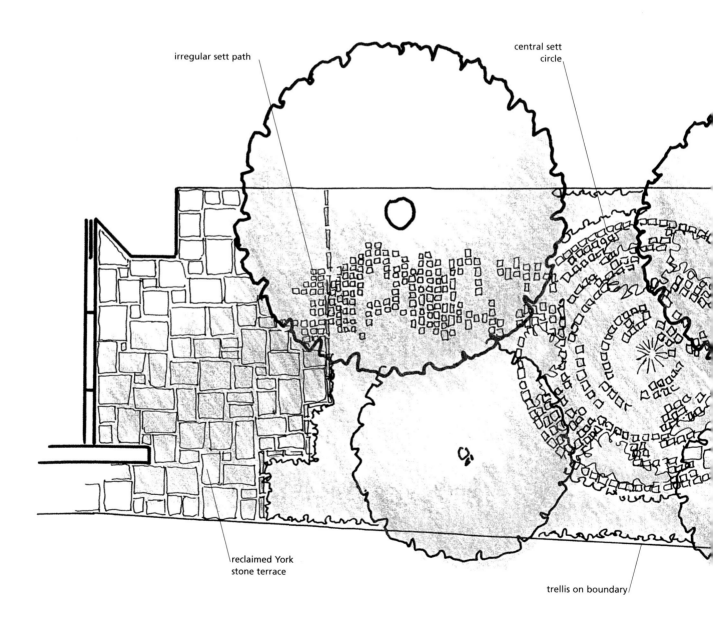

irregular sett path

central sett circle

reclaimed York stone terrace

trellis on boundary

York stone to the rear of the garden, where another large stone-and-sett terrace forms an ideal sitting spot to catch the late evening sun in privacy. The use of just two paving materials unifies the space and creates movement through their changing roles at different points.

Planting is predominantly in a Mediterranean style suited to the microclimate created by the high surrounding walls. Several large specimens, including a *Magnolia grandiflora,* a large vine, and a *Prunus subhirtella,* are included, having been craned over the house and into the garden. Shade-loving acers and camellias are planted for structure, and wisterias clad the walls on either side.

above *One of the larger specimens of planting was a Higan or rosebud cherry (*Prunus subhirtella*). The specimen shown here is growing in a different garden.*

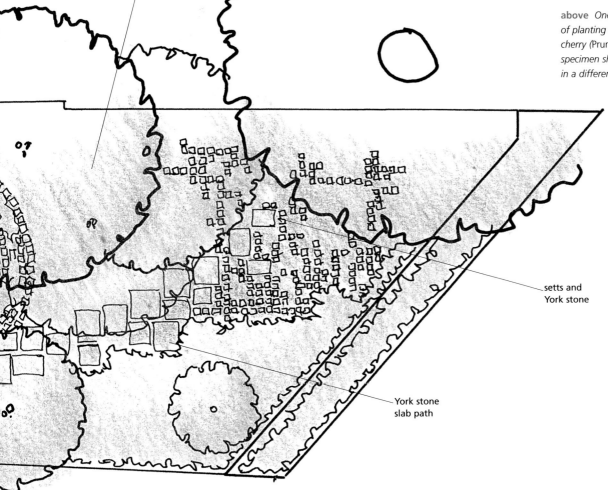

planting to create "secret" areas

setts and York stone

York stone slab path

Plantsman's Garden

KEITH PULLAN GARDEN DESIGN

DIMENSIONS 15 x 12m (50 x 40ft)

SOIL alkaline

ASPECT south facing but on a north-facing incline

KEY FEATURES different planting areas for a wide variety
of plant types

This was a very steep garden with a slope rising away from the
house and almost no view out from the house from the ground
floor. The owner wanted spaces for sitting, a pond, and a purpose-
built orchid house, as well as a big area for planting a large variety
of different plant types.

From the house several interconnected levels are used to create
seating and planting areas and water features within a confined
space. A rectangular grid forms the basis of the design, providing
consistent shapes in both plan and elevation. Against a backdrop
of a dense conifer hedge at the back of the garden raised beds
of very dense planting are at a higher level than the rest of the
garden. Within this shelter, a small, intimate sitting area is
constructed with an overflowing basin water feature as a focal
point. Leading back to the house, rockwork is built into a slope
as a habitat for rock and scree planting. Stepping stones lead
back to the house as an informal path.

In the centre of the garden a formal pond, planted with
waterlilies, is fed by a water spill and this borders a larger terrace
for dining near the house. A pergola screens the garage at the
side of the garden and provides an opportunity for the owner
to grow a variety of climbers.

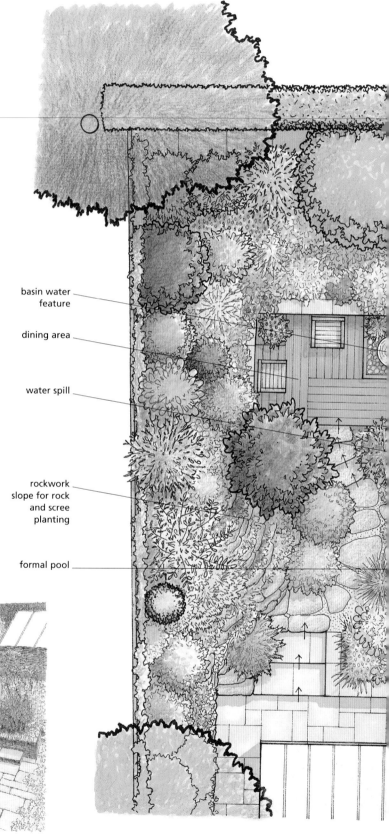

basin water feature

dining area

water spill

rockwork slope for rock and scree planting

formal pool

above *This
sketch shows how the
different levels and planting
types work together, with a
water feature as a focal point.*

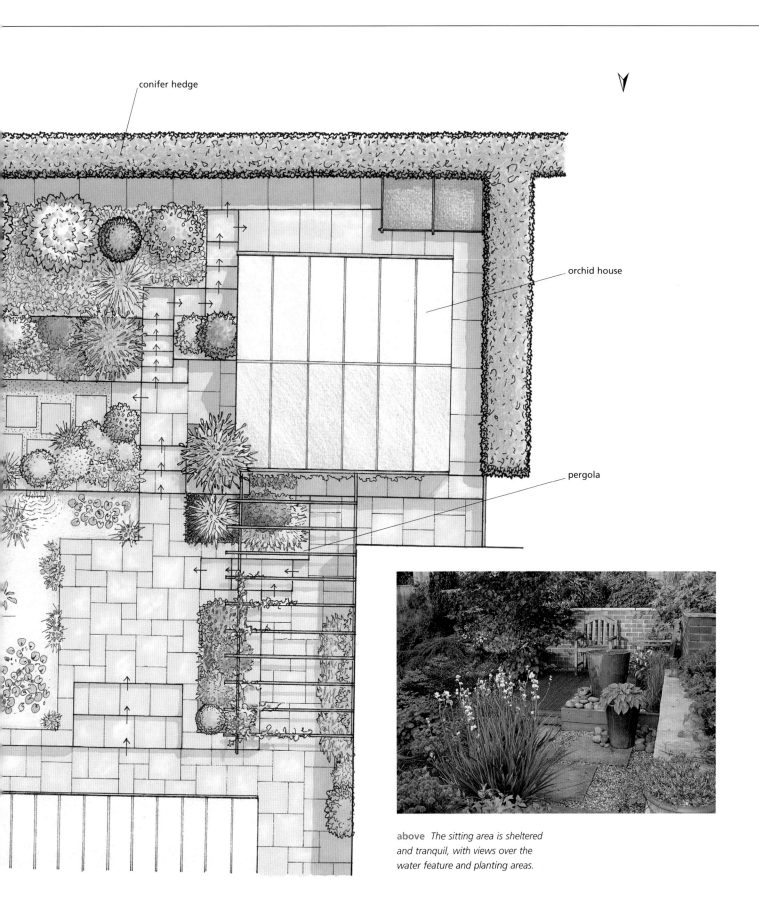

conifer hedge

orchid house

pergola

above *The sitting area is sheltered and tranquil, with views over the water feature and planting areas.*

Three Options for a Long, Narrow Garden

LIZ DAVIES GARDEN DESIGN

DIMENSIONS 13.5 x 5m (44 x 16ft)

SOIL neutral

ASPECT south-west facing

KEY FEATURES exotic planting and a sitting area

This garden was attached to a small, terraced house that was elevated above the garden. Old, stone steps led down into the garden, which was surrounded by a low, stone wall. The space sloped gently away from the house and the owners wanted a strong design because the garden is viewed mainly from above. The brief for planting was mainly for exotic, jungle-style planting such as bamboos, bananas, phormiums, cannas, *Acanthus mollis*, *Crambe cordifolia*, and fatsias.

IDEA 1

This turned out to be the preferred option. A very formal design gives wide terraces with the level change divided into three. Each area is grassed and there is an armillary sphere in the centre circle, edged in red brick to match the house. A pair of topiary trees forms an entrance to the end of the garden. The owners' planting ideas don't sit very easily with this design.

IDEA 2

This shows an offset design with paving in crisp grey-green 600 x 600mm (24 x 24in) slabs to replace all the grass. A sitting area is placed at the end of the garden, and a square water feature on the middle section increases interest in the journey through the garden.

IDEA 3

An informal and cheap option: the garden retains its natural slope leading gently down to a circular, paved sitting area reached through a rustic arch.

Idea 1

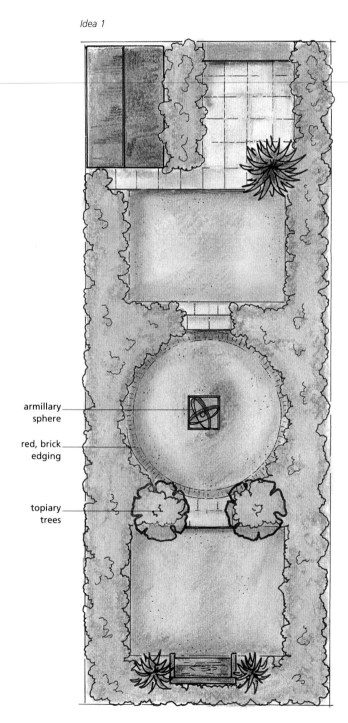

armillary sphere

red, brick edging

topiary trees

left *Few plants give a greater sense of the exotic than cannas. In this garden they were to be planted with other "jungle" planting such as bamboos and bananas.*

Idea 2

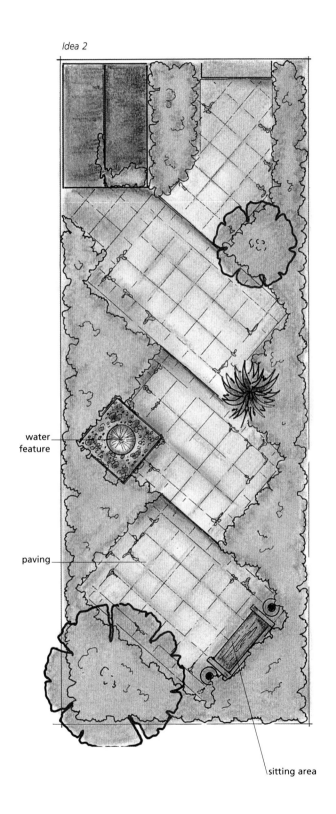

water
feature

paving

sitting area

Idea 3

rustic arch

sitting area

Sunbathing and Dining Garden

SALLY COURT – COURTYARD GARDEN DESIGN

DIMENSIONS 9 x 5m (30 x 16ft)

SOIL no soil, just gravel over concrete

ASPECT north-east facing

KEY FEATURES raised decking plinths

An intimate courtyard was requested by the owners of this property. Because the space backed onto a communal courtyard, this was a challenge. The main constraint to the design, however, was that the area was formed from one large, concrete slab constructed over an underground car park with two large air grilles set into it. Any design would need to incorporate these vents.

Two raised decks set at 45 degrees to the building were constructed, with the dining deck set one step up from the base and a further step up to the sunbathing deck. Around the outside of the decks, raised beds were constructed to contain new soil for some planting within the garden. They were rendered to match the existing walls and provide a warm, sheltered environment for Mediterranean-style planting. Against the rear wall of the garden, a bespoke feature spills water from a glass-and-copper waterfall into a triangular pool.

Two *Acacia dealbata* trees provide much-needed screening from neighbours, their feathery evergreen structure contrasting with the hard angles of the raised beds. Planting is primarily evergreen, including cistus and *Convolvulus cneorum,* with climbers clothing the walls to increase the sense of privacy and seclusion.

left *The predominantly evergreen planting in this scheme included the shrubs* Convolvulus cneorum *(shown left), and the rock rose* Cistus x loretii.

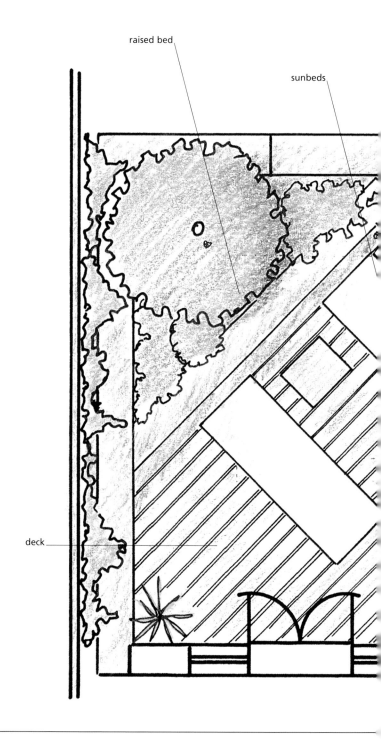

raised bed

sunbeds

deck

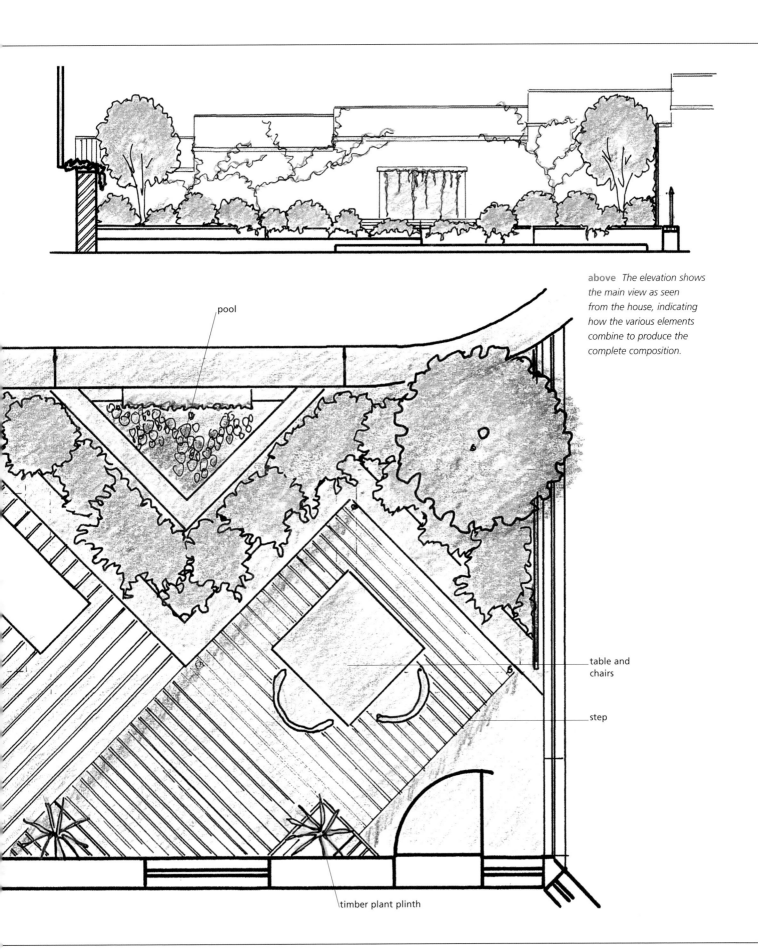

pool

above *The elevation shows the main view as seen from the house, indicating how the various elements combine to produce the complete composition.*

table and chairs

step

timber plant plinth

Wildlife Haven in the City

HELEN BILLETOP GARDEN DESIGN

DIMENSIONS 12 x 7.25m (40 x 23ft)

SOIL neutral loam

ASPECT north-west facing

KEY FEATURES wildlife pond

When the owners of this garden had a conservatory added to their house, a fish pond was removed in the process, so their brief to the designer was to build a replacement. Existing trees in this garden and that of a neighbour provided considerable shade at the back of the garden and it was hoped that this area could be given a more appealing look.

A change of level from the house down to the end of the garden presented an opportunity to have a pond on two levels, with a waterfall from the upper to the lower pool. To the south-west of the pool, a rockery of Lakeland green slate forms the edge to a raised planting bed at the boundary. To the other side of the pool, a deck overhangs the water providing sanctuary from the fish from the ever present herons.

From the terrace near the house, a boardwalk runs between two small areas of lawn, dropping down two timber steps to the deck and the summerhouse. The lower level at the far end of the garden conceals a work area with composting facilities and is paved in permeable timber setts to allow rainwater to continue to water the existing trees. At the focal point from the boardwalk down the garden, three specially made timber planters hold *Hydrangea quercifolia,* which will thrive in the shade; a tree fern (*Dicksonia antarctica*) is also planted here.

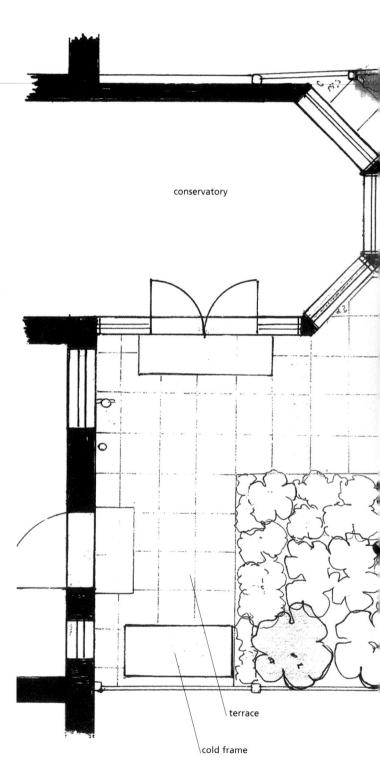

conservatory

terrace

cold frame

above *The key feature of this garden was a wildlife pond built on two levels, with a waterfall taking water from the upper to the lower pool.*

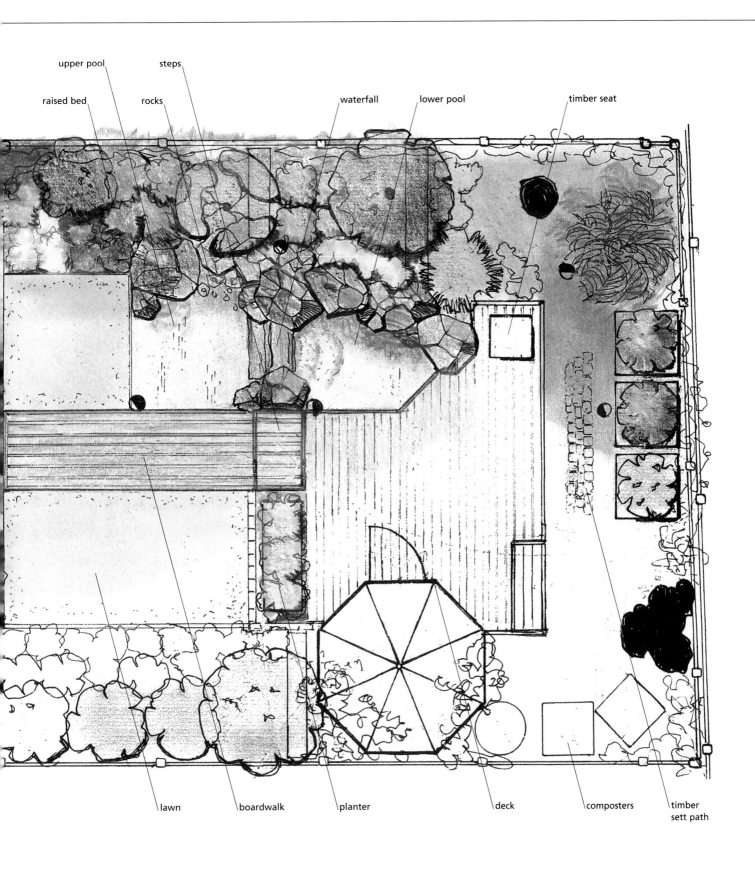

upper pool

steps

raised bed

rocks

waterfall

lower pool

timber seat

lawn

boardwalk

planter

deck

composters

timber
sett path

Garden for a Healthy Lifestyle

ANDY STURGEON GARDEN DESIGN

DIMENSIONS 23 x 10m (71 x 33ft)

SOIL not known

ASPECT south facing

KEY FEATURES pavilion and lap pool

For the Chelsea Flower Show 2006, this designer created a garden to promote a healthy lifestyle. A lap pool forms the dominant feature, with a smaller plunge pool beside the pavilion. Integrated into the planting are a large number of herbs and fruit bushes. The trees surrounding the pavilion are carefully sited to cast shade at key times of the day so that visitors can always be shaded. A water wall cascades from the pavilion into a lower pool, with the water then falling to surround a small, outdoor seating area.

A lawn the same size and shape as the small pool is on the other side of the lap pool, offset to the other end of the pool to balance the design.

The shape of the pavilion is inspired by the shape of the seat at the front of the garden, and the angle at which the pool sits allows the maximum length of lap pool possible in the garden, with the surrounding planting for interest and privacy. Paving in the garden is in stone which is honed and sand blasted to give a non-slip surface.

Key trees in the design are *Quercus phellos,* semi-evergreens that can be clipped to allow light through. Through the planting beds, low tables of clipped yew provide structure and contrast. General planting is a mix of evergreens and herbaceous perennials.

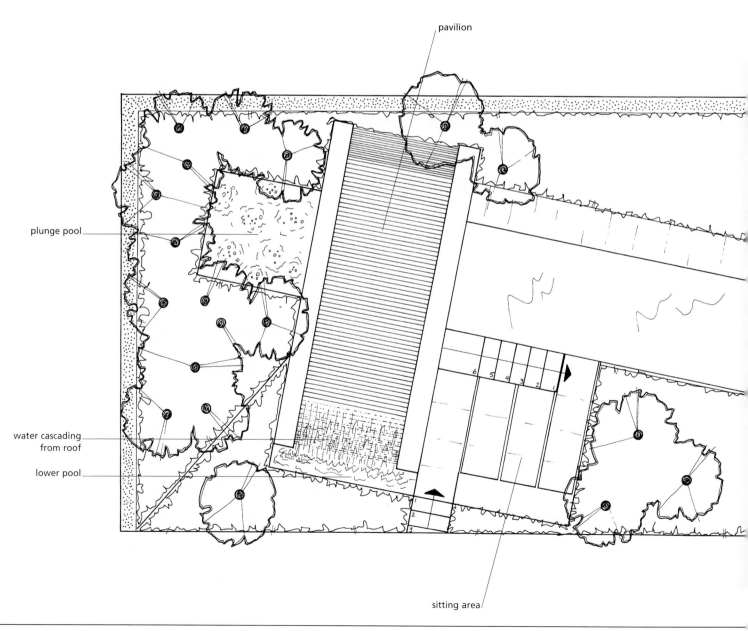

pavilion

plunge pool

water cascading from roof

lower pool

sitting area

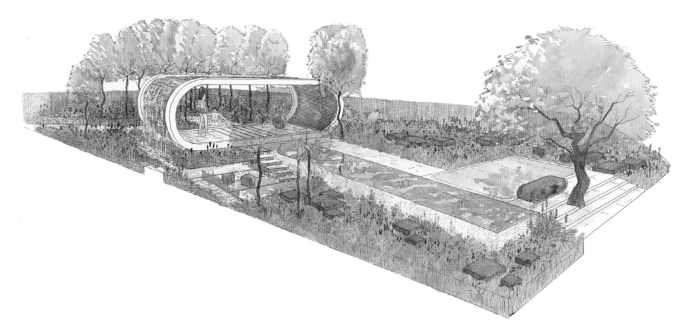

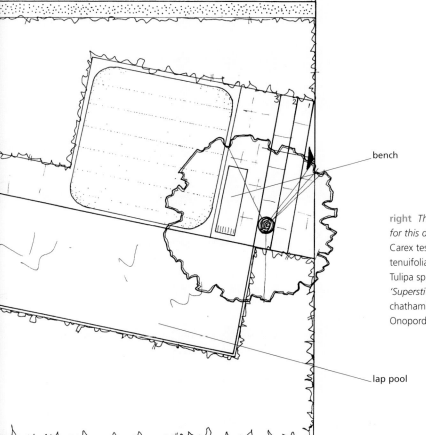

bench

lap pool

above *This illustration shows how the shape of the pavilion was inspired by the small seat at the front of the garden.*

right *The planting for this design includes* Carex testacea, Stipa tenuifolia, Salvia sylvestris, Tulipa sprengeri, *Iris 'Superstition',* Astelia chathamica, *and* Onopordum acanthium.

Plant Showcase

ANDREW WILSON ASSOCIATES

DIMENSIONS 28 x 17m (92 x 55ft)

SOIL slightly acid

ASPECT north facing

KEY FEATURES York stone on edge paths

This garden was originally designed as an on-paper showcase for rich plant associations in a design setting for a site at the RHS garden at Wisley, Surrey, in England. The garden was never built.

The house was assumed to stand along the boundary closest to the main circular terrace, which was pulled farther into the garden to allow for shadow cast by the imagined property. There is a level change of approximately 1.2m (4ft) across the site, which means that the lawn sits lower than the terrace level.

A wide range of planting types is showcased in the garden, but the whole composition is controlled by large sentinels of yew hedging that run through the entire space. The main view across the gardens at Wisley inspired the angled layout of the York stone paving, laid on its edge to create a textured pattern in contrast to the brick paving. A plinth created along this axis provides a position for prized specimens in a decorative pot. The steps drop down between the terrace and the plinth onto a more formal, regularly shaped lawn. The main concept is to demonstrate how design can provide a coherent structure to a disparate plant collection.

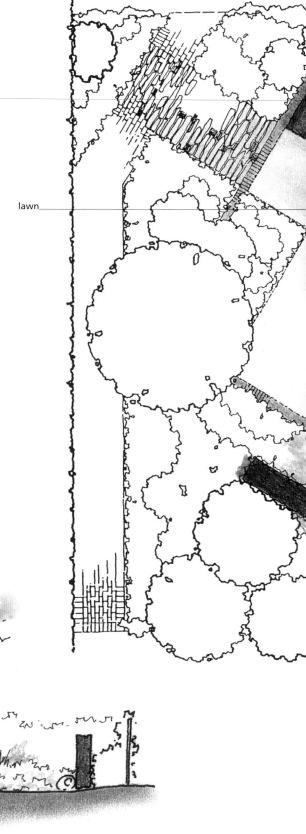

lawn

below The sectional elevation shows the main level change and the importance of the sentinel-like yew blocks in defining the main spaces and providing scale.

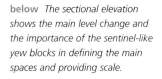

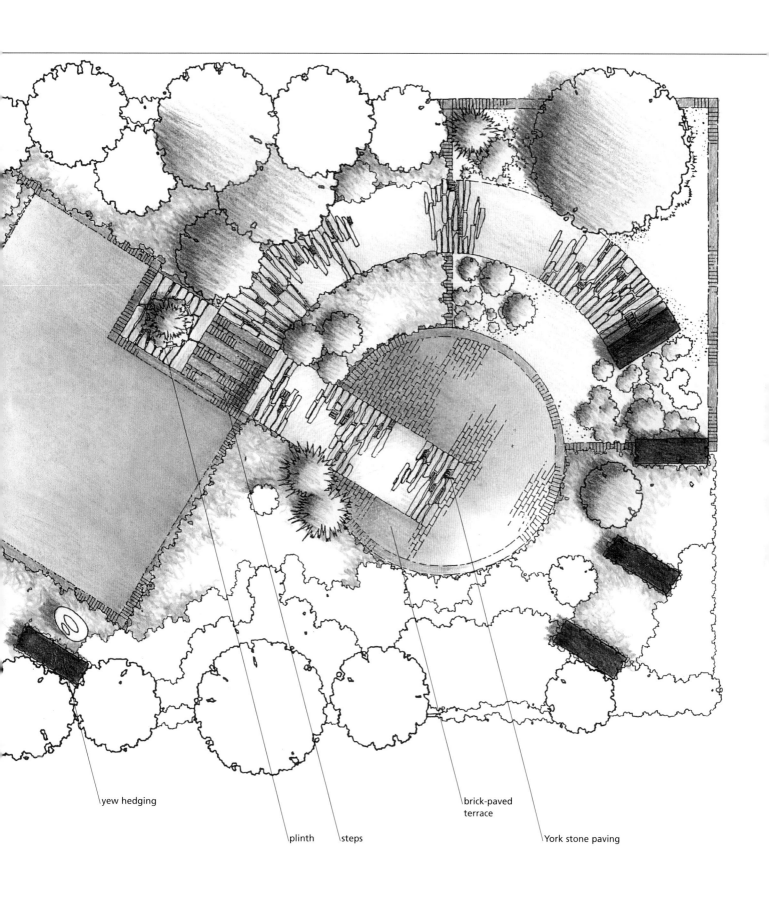

yew hedging

plinth

steps

brick-paved
terrace

York stone paving

Comfortable Retreat

DEBBIE ROBERTS – ACRES WILD

DIMENSIONS 12 x 6m (40 x 20ft) with 6 x 2.8m (20 x 8ft)
side passage

SOIL clay

ASPECT north-west facing

KEY FEATURES hedges to divide the space

Creating a private and comfortable garden was the brief for this commission. To complement the terraced Victorian house, planting was to be lush and naturalistic. A small dining table needed to be accommodated, and a focus at the end of the garden was sought from the house.

A large deck conceals existing concrete paving, rationalizes levels, and unifies the area. Dining space on the deck is thus in the sunniest and most private part of the garden. Leading down the garden, concrete paving slabs are set in gravel, forming a "path" that ends at a seat beneath a metal arbour. Clipped hedges of gradually increasing height semi-divide the space, hide a compost bin, and provide textural contrast to frothy and sculptural planting.

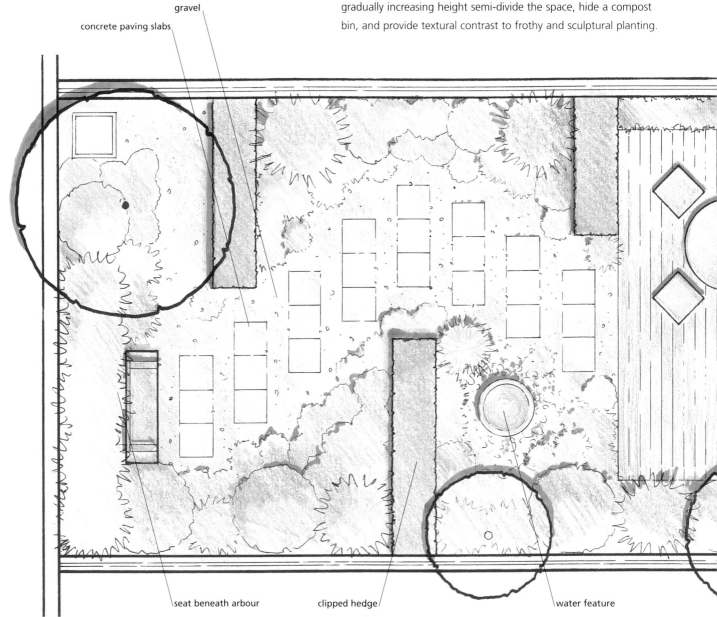

gravel

concrete paving slabs

seat beneath arbour

clipped hedge

water feature

A small water feature animates the space and provides another focal point, partway along the garden's length.

The planting has a soft and sensuous feel and includes plants that spill, flop, and intertwine, contrasting with more clipped and architectural specimens. A *Prunus serrula* and bamboos provide screening at the end of the garden, and phormiums are used as focal plants. Colourful perennials such as kniphofia, hemerocallis, crocosmia, and verbena are set off by low-growing ferns and grasses and groundcover plants that spill over the path and merge with the gravel.

right *Through this perspective it is easier to see how the clipped hedges have semi-divided the space, giving the garden's occupants a degree of privacy.*

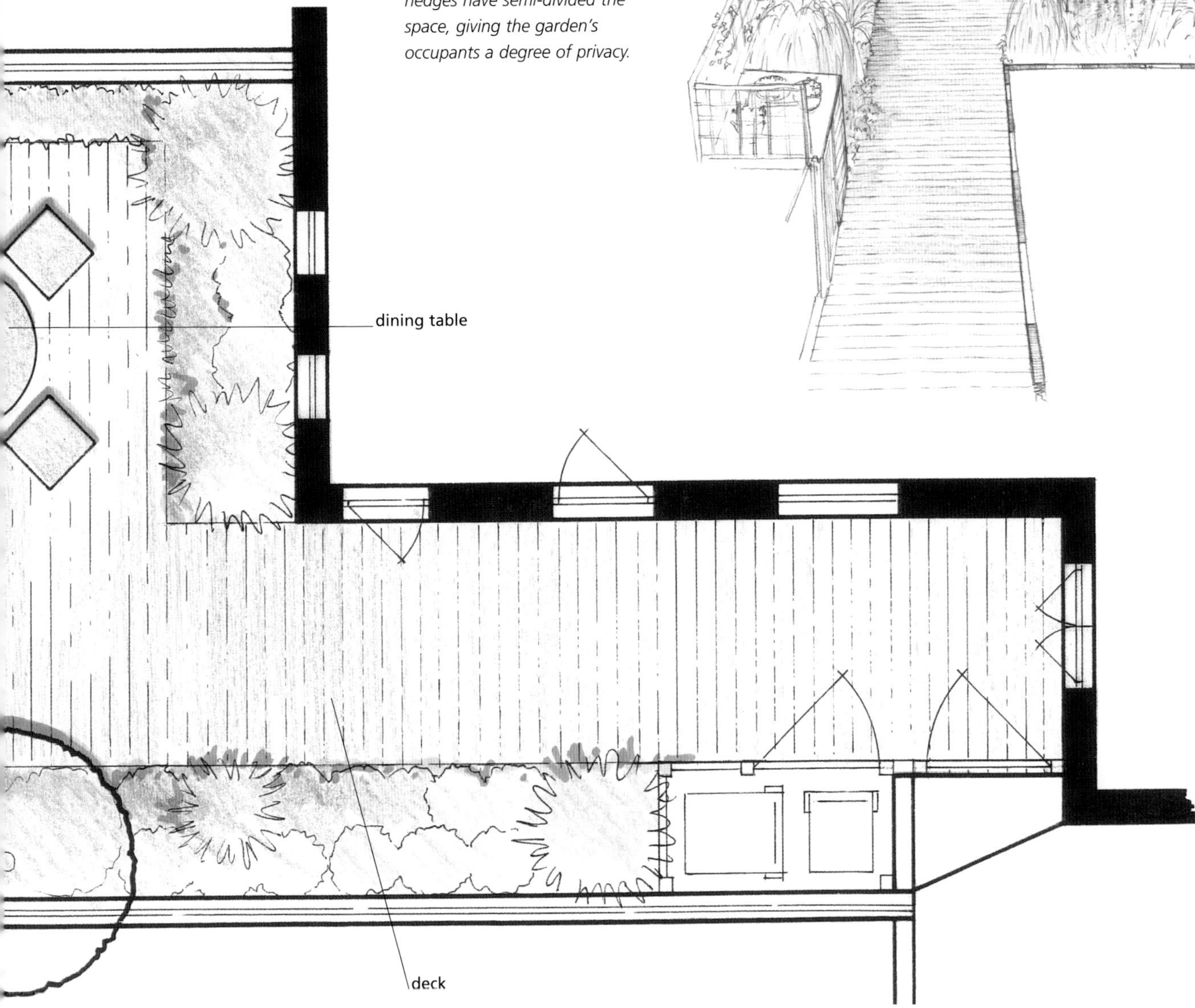

dining table

deck

Three Gardens in One

SARAH LAYTON

DIMENSIONS 25 x 12.5m (80 x 41ft)

SOIL clay

ASPECT north facing

KEY FEATURES soft, pink walls

above *The central feature of this garden is a lawn whose formality is softened by the cottagy plants in the surrounding borders.*

Entry to this garden is from the basement level of the house. The existing basement terrace area was very stark and modern, with clean-cut white paving and copings, and the challenge was to create a traditional "cottage" feel in the rest of the garden to link with the modern basement as well as to incorporate a significant level change up to the far end of the garden. A large tree casts a shadow at the end of the garden for much of the day.

To soften the lower terrace, the walls are rendered in soft pink and a planting bed is introduced beside the steps up to the rest of the garden. The white coping and pink render for the retaining walls is used throughout the garden to unify the space. A formal lawn sits at the centre of the garden, surrounded by crisply edged beds that are then planted with soft, cottage plants to spill over the edges, softening the whole look. A bench at this level gives a place to stop and enjoy the view, and sculptures are nestled in among the planting for added interest.

Steps lead up again to the back of the garden, where a woodland area is planted under the canopy of the tree. A dry-stone wall and bench are focal points, and planting of anemones, euphorbias, and ferns adds to the soft woodland feel.

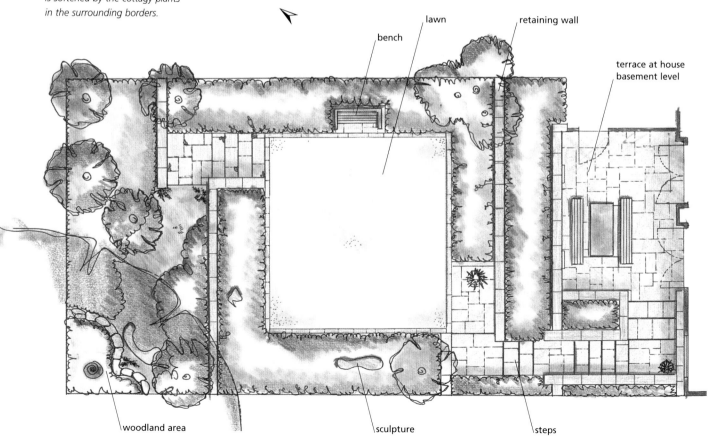

Sweeping Front Driveway

NAILA GREEN GARDEN DESIGN

DIMENSIONS 30 x 14m (100 x 47ft)

SOIL loam with patches of clay

ASPECT north-east facing

KEY FEATURES granite sett driveway

The approach to this large house had an ugly driveway that needed to be moved and refined to stay in keeping with the house. The owners wanted a resolution to the steep level change at the front of the house and to create an approach that would be welcoming and visually pleasing at all times of the year.

First, the driveway was transformed to a large, sweeping curve in front of the existing double garage, with paving of granite setts and narrow lines of pebbles to break up the large expanse. The curving lines of the driveway continue throughout the design and are formalized in some areas as circular planting beds. Curved retaining walls built of rendered blockwork make the garden more plant friendly, and a coping of blue slate on edge brings interest and unity to the design. Gravel paths then link the driveway and the front and side of the house, using slate as a detail.

A number of *Betula pendula* are planted along the garden's boundary to soften the visual impact of the large house and to provide vertical accents to the garden. In addition, *Prunus*

subhirtella 'Autumnalis' are planted to bring interest in winter and to act as hosts to summer-flowering clematis. The planting is mostly of evergreen flowering shrubs to furnish the garden and reduce maintenance. Near the front door, scented shrubs are planted and sculptural yew spheres act as focal points, echoing the slate and granite sett circles.

above *The dramatic sweeping curve of this driveway is emphasized by the granite sett paving.*

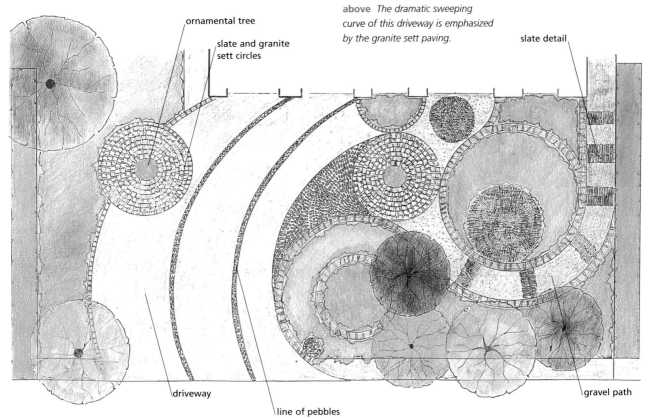

Garden for Retirement

LIZ DAVIES GARDEN DESIGN

DIMENSIONS 11 x 9m (36 x 30ft) and 9 x 4.5m (30 x 12ft)

SOIL acid to neutral

ASPECT west facing

KEY FEATURES high walls, fish pond, acers

With garages on either side of the garden near the house, this area needed to be made more enticing and colourful, and it also needed to encourage further exploration of the larger garden. The owners were retired and planning to travel extensively, so wanted a very low-maintenance space with interesting planting and a pool for their fish. The garden was surrounded by high Welsh pennant stone walls of great character and two large sycamore trees overhung the space.

A new dining area is created in the smaller garden just outside the house, with planting beds for climbers to screen the garages on either side. Planting includes clematis, lonicera, jasmines, and x *Fatshedera lizei* for evergreen cover. An arch marks the entrance to the larger garden area, again planted with climbers for a soft and interesting appearance. Once into the back garden space, the reclaimed grey, flagstone paving turns on the diagonal, giving the impression of greater space. A small, geometric pond edged with granite setts and crossed by a timber bridge is planted with water lilies. On the far side of the pond, a path of flagstones leads to a small Chinese lantern, just visible from the main garden.

Planting includes *Gleditsia triacanthos*, *Acer pseudoplatanus* 'Brilliantissimum', *Acer palmatum* 'dissectum', and eleagnus for colour, texture, and interest throughout the year.

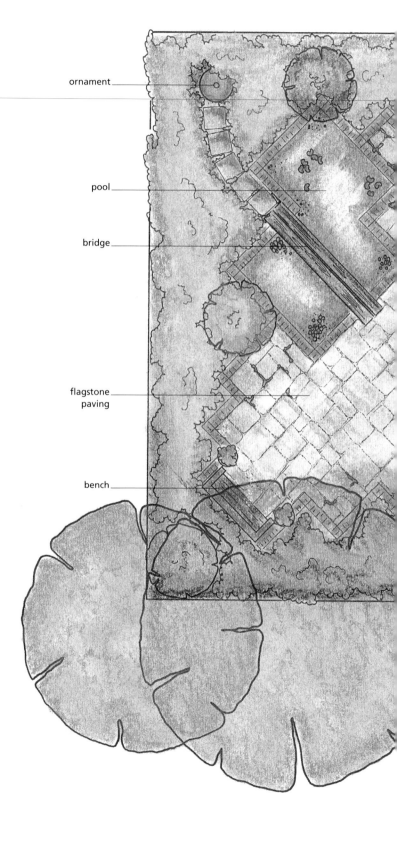

ornament

pool

bridge

flagstone paving

bench

left *The sycamore (Acer pseudoplatanus 'Brilliantissimum') is a fast-growing deciduous tree that can reach 6m (20ft). Another acer suggested for this scheme was the Japanese maple (A. palmatum 'Dissectum'.*

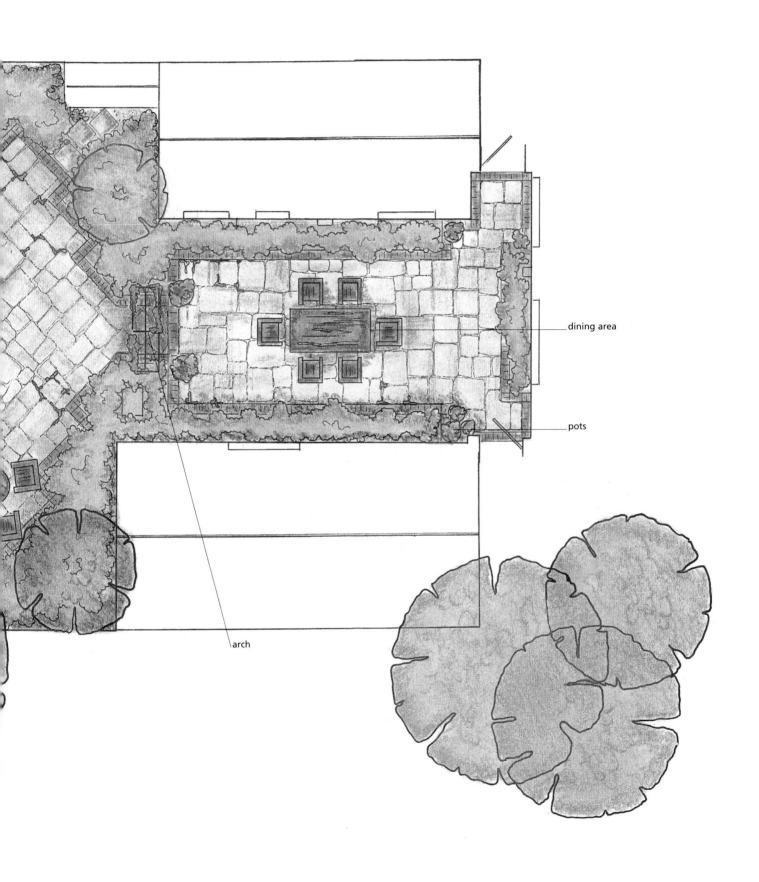

dining area

pots

arch

Garden for Enthusiastic Gardeners

SARAH LAYTON

DIMENSIONS 15 x 6m (50 x 20ft)

SOIL clay

ASPECT north facing

KEY FEATURES lots of seating spaces

Two passionate gardeners wanted a space in which they could pursue their hobby, sit to enjoy the fruits of their labour, and entertain visitors. A large work area was required, with a potting shed and space for a large water butt.

Slightly offsetting the design from the main axis of the garden adds greater interest and movement to the space, as well as causing the garden to appear much longer than it actually is.

From the back of the house, a large step leads out onto a terrace of small, square slabs. Nearby, deep alcove beds paved in golden polished pebbles, surrounded by shrubs and perennials, provide a space for the owners to showcase the results of their annual planting in beautiful terra cotta pots. Tulips, cannas, and lilies are planted here each year.

A narrow path leads through deep, textured planting to another garden space with a bench and a large table and chairs for entertaining. At the back of the garden, an area is fenced off with trellis to create a work space. A shed, a potting area, and a water butt are housed here, and a bespoke potting bench is made to be wheeled into the garden when in use.

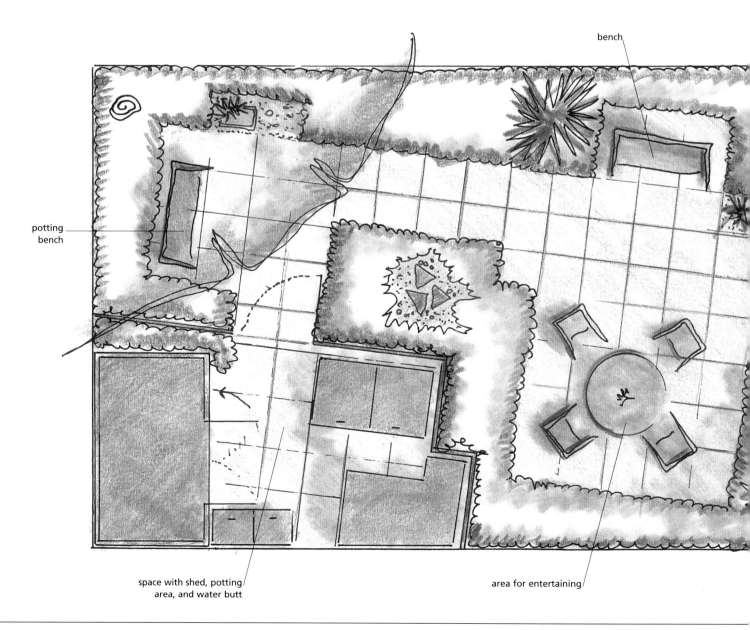

bench

potting
bench

space with shed, potting
area, and water butt

area for entertaining

left An important aspect of this scheme was plenty of seating so that the garden's owners could relax and entertain.

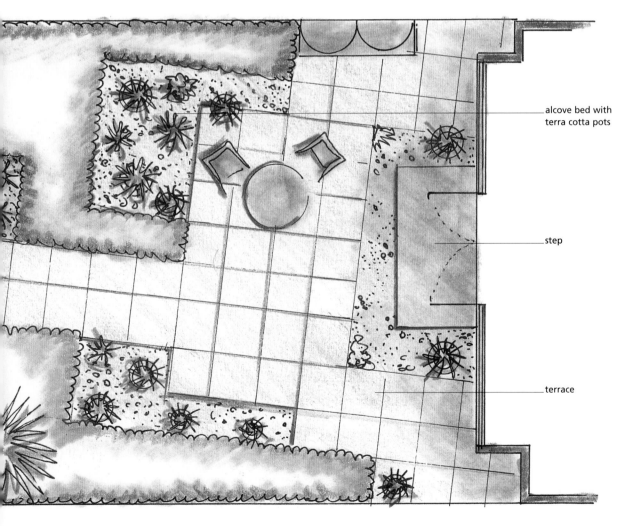

alcove bed with terra cotta pots

step

terrace

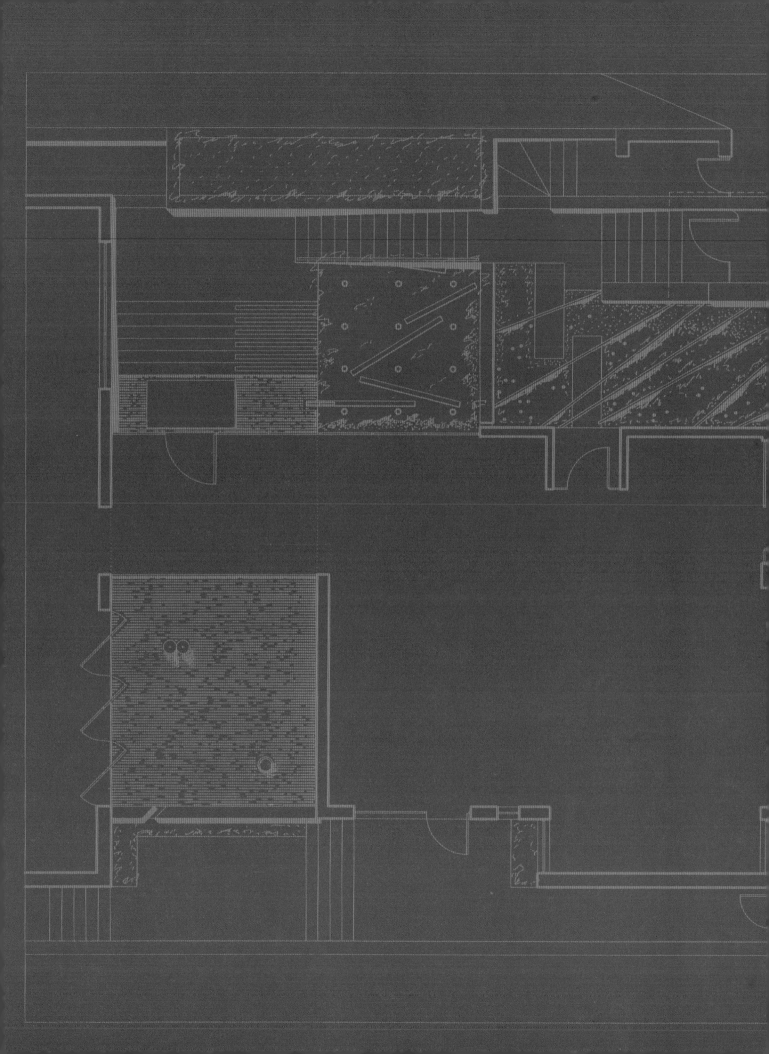

ROOFGARDENS

The design of roof gardens is dictated more by the structure of the roof and its capacity to hold weight than by the application of stylistic concepts. Other issues such as ownership, safety, and the location of services such as air conditioner units, vents, and skylights must also be carefully dealt with. Purpose-built roof gardens will be much less problematic; converting an existing roof space into a garden will provide more headaches and can prove extremely costly. Exposure is a major problem that must be dealt with once the structural issues are resolved. Roofs are harsh environments, open to extreme temperature fluctuations, much less sheltered than ground-level gardens, and there is no ground to excavate for planting. Screens in fabric, glass, or timber protect against wind; trellis or perforated screens reduce wind speed rather than blocking it. All fixings need to be strong and durable to prevent wind damage or loss. Select planting to cope with extreme conditions, and consider larger raised beds if weight restrictions allow rather than smaller containers, because the latter will dry out quickly. Drainage must be carefully designed to shed water quickly and effectively, and care must be taken not to damage any waterproofing materials used to seal the roof surface. Also think about the practicalities of importing or exporting materials and planting.

City Formality

GEORGE CARTER GARDEN DESIGN

DIMENSIONS 18.5 x 11m (58 x 36ft)

SOIL imported

ASPECT west facing

KEY FEATURES lead planters and formal paving

These small spaces were very close to a busy thoroughfare only 12m (40ft) from the back of the house, and street noise was intrusive. Two different outdoor spaces, one 2m (6ft) above street level and one 2.4m (7ft) below street level, needed to relate to each other and to bring as much light as possible into the lower level. The spaces were as much for viewing from inside the building as they were for going into, so the colour schemes had to complement the muted neutrals of the interiors.

At the boundary, a 2m- (6ft-) high hedge of *Prunus lusitanica* was installed to reduce road noise and to mask double-decker buses at the bus stop immediately outside. On the main terraces, specially designed formal lead fountains and lead water cisterns are incorporated for height and interest. Tall planting at the lower level, of *Cupressus sempervirens,* is designed to be "read" through both the lower and the upper floors. The design follows strictly formal, symmetrical lines, and this is enhanced by the pattern of the paving as well as the layout of planters and planting. At the lower level, a series of back-lit, acrylic columns helps to add light to the area.

above *Taken from above, this photograph clearly shows the way the garden is divided into three different spaces.*

right *This view of the main terrace shows how the pattern of the paving and the layout of the planting follow strictly formal lines.*

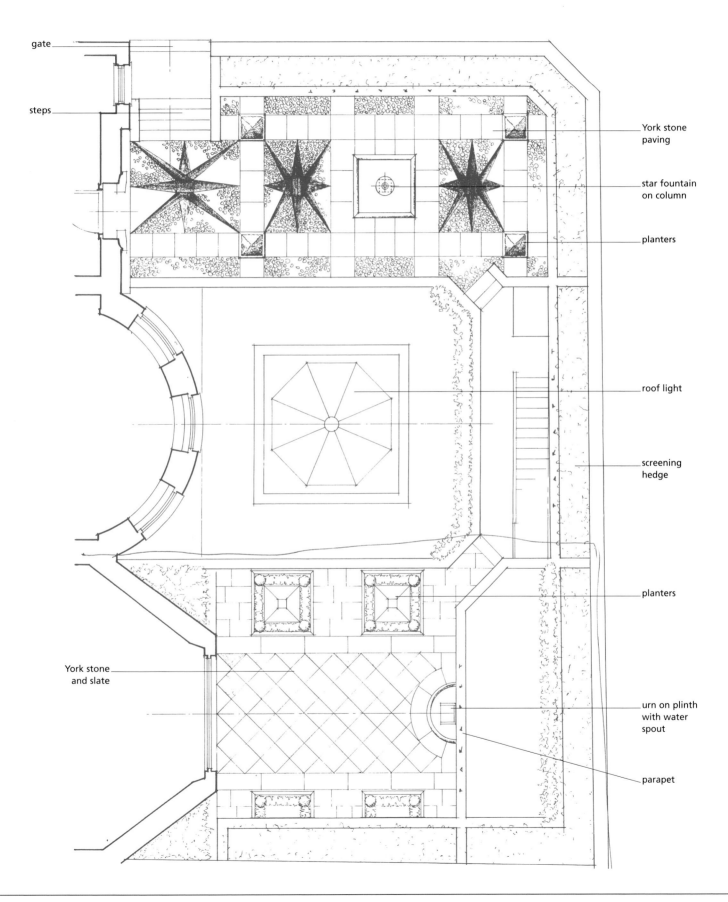

gate

steps

York stone
paving

star fountain
on column

planters

roof light

screening
hedge

planters

York stone
and slate

urn on plinth
with water
spout

parapet

Glass-Roofed Garden

DANIEL McCARTHY – WOODHAMS LANDSCAPES

DIMENSIONS 15 x 5m (50 x 16ft)

SOIL clay loam

ASPECT east facing

KEY FEATURES acrylic light pergola

With this city roof, the owners wanted a formal but relaxing atmosphere that would unify and simplify the boundaries. Two glass roof structures were already in place and needed to be incorporated into a garden setting. High-quality materials were to be used in a sympathetic way.

An acrylic light pergola is used above the main glass roof, emphasizing the height of the two-storey room below. The lighting columns also visually contain the space around the glass roof section, enhancing the anticipation of looking down to the room below. Internally lit, these fittings give a stunning display at night. It was suggested that clear acrylic dining furniture be placed, when required, on the glass roof for an extreme dining experience. At the end of the garden, an illuminated neon ring is set on a frosted, acrylic panel as a focal point to the design.

Louvred panels are used to simplify visually the boundaries and to emphasize the outdoor-room effect being aimed at.

Paving is predominantly of square, black slates bisected with sustainable Iroko decking to define the sitting area. Planting is in bespoke planters and is mainly for texture to enhance the relaxed atmosphere.

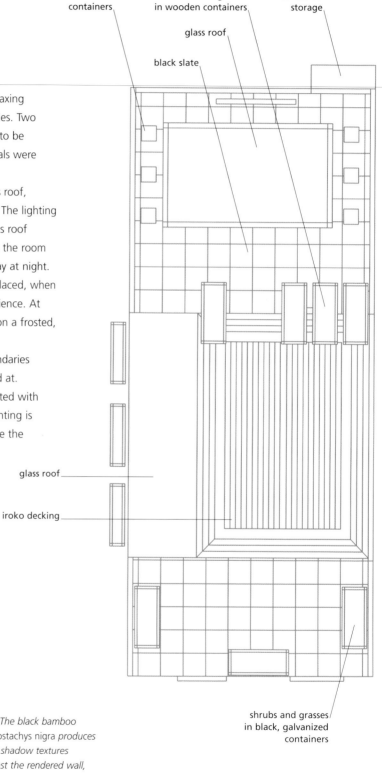

box balls in wooden containers

shrubs and grasses in wooden containers

concealed storage

glass roof

black slate

glass roof

iroko decking

shrubs and grasses in black, galvanized containers

left The black bamboo Phyllostachys nigra *produces lively shadow textures against the rendered wall, contrasted with the sheen of the steel containers.*

"L"-Shaped Garden

DOUGLAS COLTART –
VIRIDARIUM DESIGN STUDIO

DIMENSIONS 17 x 12m (55 x 40ft)

SOIL imported loam

ASPECT unknown

KEY FEATURES directional decking to enhance space

The owners of this awkwardly shaped roof terrace required a design that would unify the space and make the garden usable for entertaining. They especially wanted to incorporate use of the narrower of the two sides. In the resulting design, decking is used outside the back door, laid along the line of vision to increase the apparent length of the area. There is a small, paved space for a barbecue to stand, and a water feature is placed against a timber screen wall backdrop, directly in line with the doors. This creates a calm and enclosed space for sitting and entertaining. In hot weather, a canopy can be extended over this portion of the garden to provide screening from the sun.

An area of decking squares leads to a further decked area, which can accommodate a dining table and chairs, and this in turn leads to another decked area where it is proposed that either a sculpture or a screen be erected to end the vista. To reduce maintenance, these areas of decking are surrounded by gravel and pebbles through which bamboo (*Phyllostachys nigra*), grasses (*Carex buchananii*), and alpines (*Sempervivum ciliosum*, *Thymus serpyllum* ambig, and *Trifolium repens* 'Purpurascens') grow. Planters of *Miscanthus sinensis* 'Zebrinus' are placed at intervals so that when fully grown they will divide the space, creating garden "rooms", and providing movement.

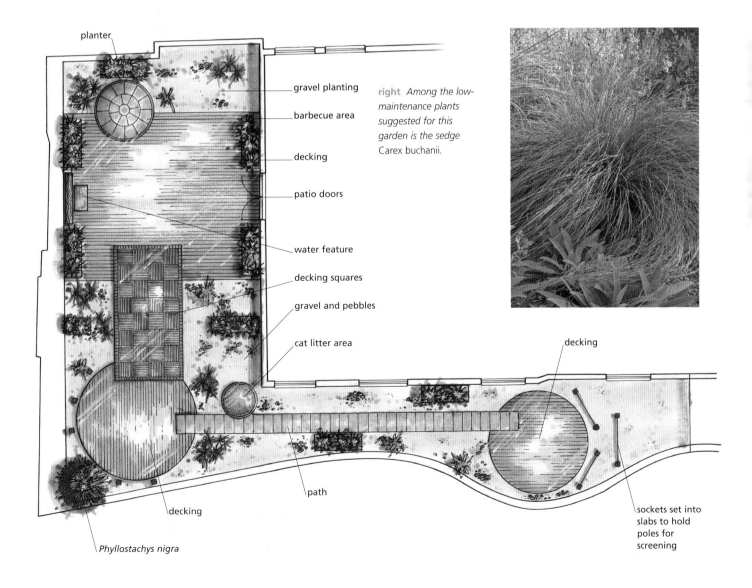

planter

gravel planting

barbecue area

decking

patio doors

water feature

decking squares

gravel and pebbles

cat litter area

path

decking

Phyllostachys nigra

decking

sockets set into slabs to hold poles for screening

right *Among the low-maintenance plants suggested for this garden is the sedge Carex buchanii.*

Theatrical Roof

PHILIP NASH DESIGN LTD

DIMENSIONS 9 x 3m (30 x 10ft)
SOIL imported
ASPECT south-west facing
KEY FEATURES seating and an atrium

There was very limited access to this roof terrace on the sixth floor: all material needed to be carried up by elevator and then through a newly decorated apartment. This is clearly a very confined space, but the owners' brief was to create a "garden" and not just a terrace with planters, in order to enjoy views out over the city. Part of the terrace has a glass floor, which is the ceiling of the atrium on the level below.

Innovative use of a steel frame to support the paving allowed other elements, such as the table and seating, to be supported on the same structure. Paving is of Turkish limestone, butt jointed and laid on rubber strips protecting the steel supports. Blue LED strip lighting is laid around the perimeter of the paving for an ambient and unusual lighting effect.

Steel planters of different heights are planted with, among others, *Agapanthus africanus*, *Yucca recurvifolia* 'Variegata', *Carex oslimensis* 'Evergold', and phormiums.

The original design included a square stone table, bordered on two sides by glass benches, but due to budgetary constraints these elements were replaced by timber versions.

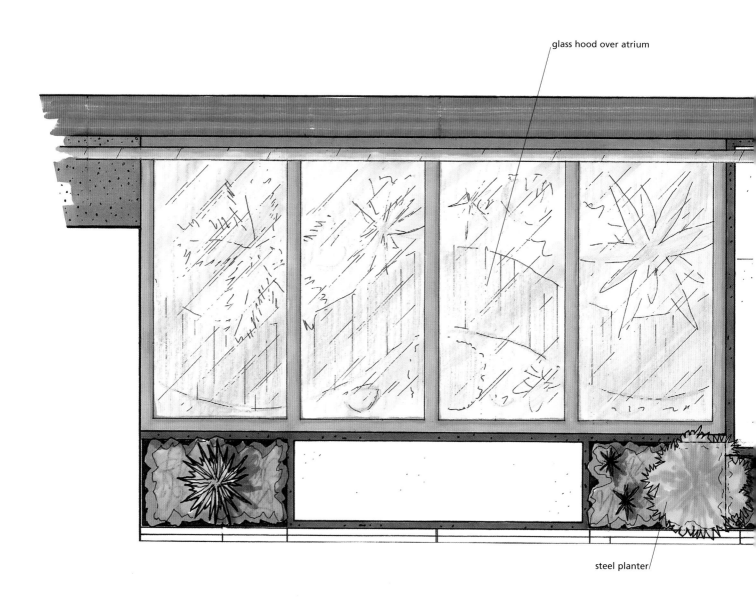

glass hood over atrium

steel planter

left Considering the narrowness of the site, this shows how space can be optimized without compromising style.

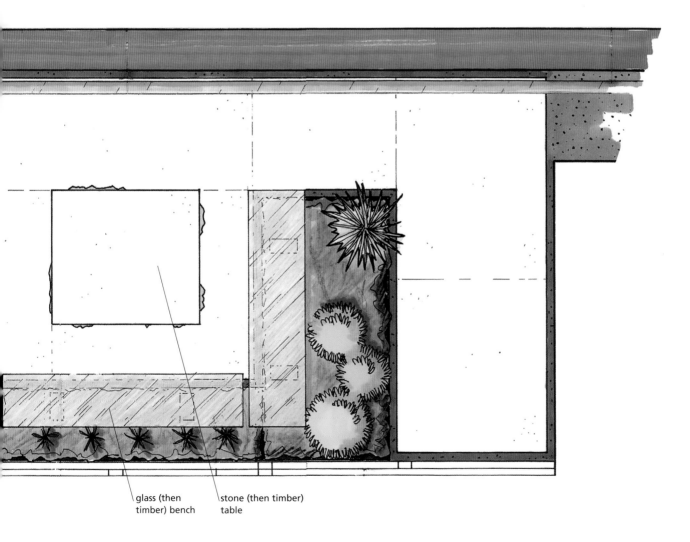

glass (then timber) bench

stone (then timber) table

Entertaining on the Roof

ROBERT MYERS – ELIZABETH BANKS ASSOCIATES

DIMENSIONS 13.5 x 10m (44 x 33ft)

SOIL imported "John Innes No 2" planting medium

ASPECT west facing

KEY FEATURES sinuous, curved decking

An existing roof terrace was to be updated and upgraded to provide a space for client entertainment and staff use as well as for events organized by the owners. Loading on the roof, wind levels, and exposure were the major design constraints.

To maximize the space available for use of the garden, the majority of the space is given to paving and decking. The area is defined by curved decking steps with stainless-steel risers for a crisp look. The paving is of silver-grey, granite slabs. New glass balustrades with timber handrails give a clean, modern look to the boundary and views out to the surrounding buildings. The majority of the planting is contained in two generous, curved planters that are filled with a mixture of sun-loving shrubs including lavender, roses, rosemary, and rock roses *Pittosporum tobira* and *Convolvulus cneorum*. For year-round structure and foliage, two specimen pine trees (*Pinus sylvestris* and *Pinus nigra*) are included, with an *Acer griseum* and an *Amelanchier lamarckii* for autumn colour and decorative bark. Around the deck, free-standing pots are planted with *Yucca filamentosa* and grasses. In front of each large planter is a curved, timber seat to echo the lines of the planters.

above Paving and decking dominate this roof space, producing a shallow amphitheatre or viewing deck for the cityscape beyond.

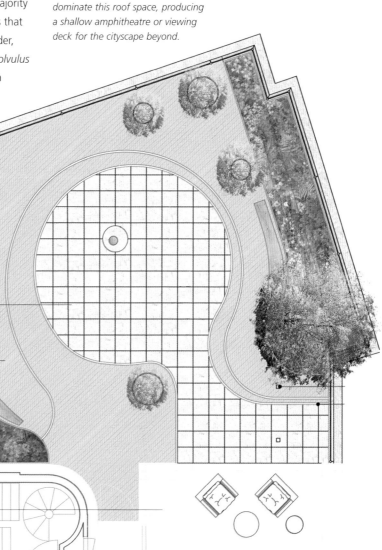

freestanding pot

granite paving slabs

curved, decking steps

timber seat

planter

boardroom

Calming Space

AMIR SCHLEZINGER – MYLANDSCAPES

DIMENSIONS 32sq m (345sq ft)

SOIL not relevant

ASPECT north-east facing

KEY FEATURES "Echo" water sculpture

The views from this fifth-floor city terrace were a mixed architectural jumble, and the owner was seeking a beautiful, calm, and relaxing space that would be visible from the living room and the kitchen, and could be used for entertaining. Access to the site was extremely difficult and a crane was necessary to lift all materials up to the working area.

New paving of specially quarried 900 x 450mm (36 x 18in) grey, Chinese sandstone was used, laid lengthways to make the space appear deeper. A long, rectangular planter is planted with a yew (*Taxus baccata*) and box (*Buxus microphylla* 'Faulkner') hedge trimmed into a curved and sculptural shape to echo but simplify the surrounding buildings. A stainless-steel water feature, "Echo", is placed at the end of the hedge planter, lending a focal point and interest to the space. In the south-eastern corner of the terrace, a raised bed was made of plywood with an Iroko coping; it contains a sculpture and dense planting of multi-stem birch, ferns including *Blechnum novae-zelandiae* and *Blechnum discolor*, and grasses (*Festuca glauca* and *Ophiopogon plansicarpus* 'Nigrescens'), as well as *Edgeworthia chrysantha* planted near the door for winter scent.

above *The main focal point of this roof garden is the stainless steel water feature placed at the end of a hedge planter.*

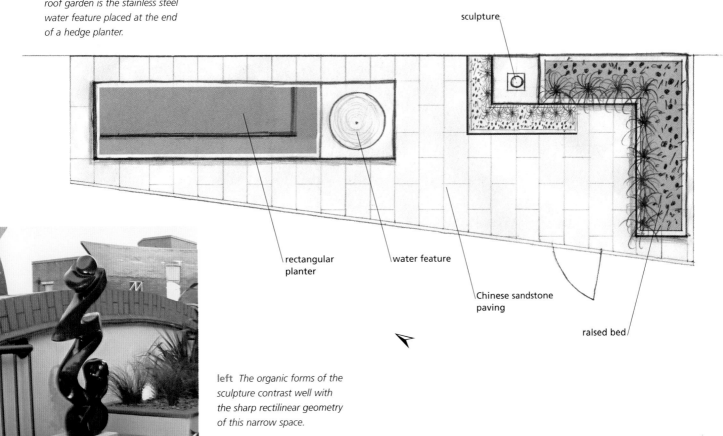

sculpture

rectangular planter

water feature

Chinese sandstone paving

raised bed

left *The organic forms of the sculpture contrast well with the sharp rectilinear geometry of this narrow space.*

Awkward Roof Space

AMIR SCHLEZINGER – MYLANDSCAPES

DIMENSIONS 44sq m (474sq ft)

SOIL imported compost

ASPECT south-east facing

KEY FEATURES moveable planters

This long and awkward roof space needed to be transformed for owners who wanted to seat eight for dining, and needed additional seating for a group and space for a large gas barbecue. The road needed to be screened for both sight and sound.

The original buff concrete slabs were relaid, reoriented to a 45-degree angle to increase the feeling of space and replaced every so often with bands of specially quarried lilac gritstone to create rhythm and space division. To maximize use of the area, moveable planters, made of plywood with an Iroko coping and swivel castors for easy movement, are placed at an angle to the paving. In keeping with the design of the chosen dining set, a bespoke bench was built in Iroko and stainless steel to echo the shape of the planters.

At one end of the main terrace is a sculpture, which is echoed at the other end by a lightweight concrete planter containing a silver birch. The birch screens a very small area that is set aside as a private sitting area for a bedroom with a balcony door.

Bamboos, contorted hazel, astelia, heuchera, and variegated *Carex* form the majority of the planting, giving structure and interesting leaf colours. Red cobbles are used to mulch the planting beds while adding to the harmonious effect.

above *Wooden planters and a sculpture add character to this dining space overlooking an urban landscape.*

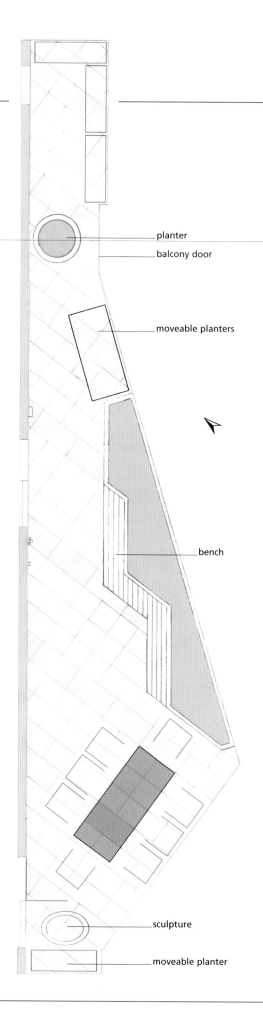

planter

balcony door

moveable planters

bench

sculpture

moveable planter

Classical Roof Garden

BARNES WALKER LIMITED

DIMENSIONS 24 x 21m (78 x 63ft)
SOIL specially mixed rich sandy loam for free drainage
ASPECT south facing
KEY FEATURES clipped topiary and box hedging

A low-maintenance, traditional entertaining space was requested for the roof of this listed building. A structural engineer calculated the maximum loadings that the framework could support, which was particularly useful when determining the positions of the larger trees and shrubs. It was also necessary to obtain what is known in the UK as Listed Building Consent before the work could be done.

The garden's entrance is marked by a grid of granite setts, which turns the visitor's eye to a stone pathway. This in turn leads into the garden through planted borders of lavender. Up ahead, a large topiary tree planted in a square bed edged with setts forms a focal point, pulling the eye into the heart of the garden.

As the path gives onto the wider area, low box hedging takes over the framing and forms the edges of herbaceous borders on either side. The planting is colour themed, using a combination of blue, white, and lime-green vegetation to unify the space and give it a traditional feel.

A paved area for a dining table and chairs is offset to the east side of the garden, where a bench is set into the planting, and there are two topiary specimens as sentinels on the boundary. There is a matching bench on the opposite side of the lawn, set slightly less formally on an elliptical area of paving. The balustrade running around the outer edge of the roof area is planted with wisteria to soften its appearance.

above *The traditional formal design is clear in this photograph of the centre of the garden.*

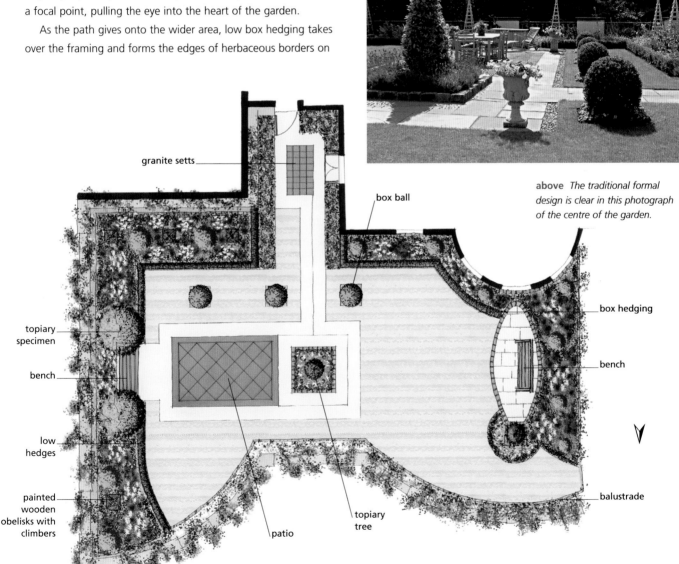

granite setts

box ball

topiary specimen

bench

box hedging

bench

low hedges

painted wooden obelisks with climbers

patio

topiary tree

balustrade

Gallery Terrace

AMIR SCHLEZINGER – MYLANDSCAPES

DIMENSIONS upper terrace 31sq m (334sq ft); lower terrace
47sq m (506sq ft)

SOIL not relevant

ASPECT South and west facing

KEY FEATURES bespoke planters

The owner had an extensive art collection within the apartment and was looking for a strong, contemporary, and beautiful space on the terraces to complement the interior. Views over the City of London were important from both levels and needed framing for maximum impact. The existing decking was to stay. Access was very difficult and meant employing cranes.

To link the inside and outside spaces, bespoke planters were created, suitable for both situations. These have planting spaces at the top and the lower section is hollow, giving a sculptural shape and allowing the eye to travel through and see beyond. These planters allow light into the space and create interest with their curvaceous shape and varied colours. On the upper terrace, a line of these planters leads the eye to a view of St Paul's Cathedral in the distance. The hollow space also allows a view through the glass handrail and out over the city, increasing the sense of space on the narrow terrace. All the rooms have glass sliding doors and, when these are open, the terrace flows around the whole space, linking the rooms. The existing decking is stained to a sophisticated walnut colour. On the lower, more shaded terrace, a *Ginkgo biloba* frames the view. Night-time lighting enhances the space and is particularly effective with the planters.

A sculpture and plinth provide focal points within the space and planting is predominantly of *Acer palmatum,* grasses, and bamboos giving height and structure.

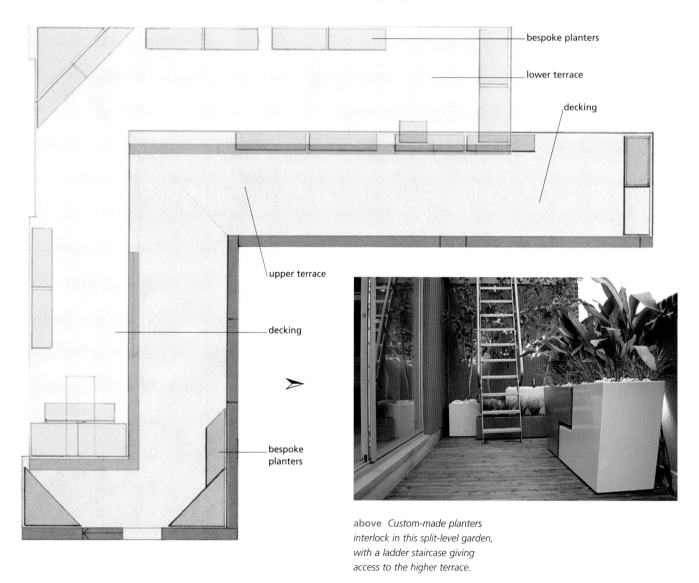

above *Custom-made planters interlock in this split-level garden, with a ladder staircase giving access to the higher terrace.*

Modern Materials and Neon Lights

DAVID STEVENS

DIMENSIONS 10 x 7m max (33 x 23ft)
SOIL lightweight general-purpose compost
ASPECT shaded by surrounding buildings
KEY FEATURES: decking and slatted glass seats

A roof garden situated on a period house in the city, this was an uncompromising space, surrounded by high-rise buildings, central-heating flues, and general bad views. The brief was for a very contemporary garden that would provide room for entertaining with minimal maintenance.

This is the classic "outdoor room", but the materials used are far from classic. The high walls are framed out with translucent dichroic glass into which are inserted mirrors and light strips in blue neon. The garden is floored in precisely detailed decking, to minimize roof loading, which is lit with recessed, low-wattage uplighters. The slatted seat is constructed from plate glass, illuminated from within.

As the garden wraps around the building, an overhead structure of grey, steel beams supports stainless-steel chains, down which water tumbles into the pool below. On the other side of the garden a mirror water wall, 6m (20ft) high, conceals a heating flue set behind it.

Planting is simple and architectural, with bamboo growing through a mulch of blue, glass beads, and yucca planted in tall terra cotta pots. One tree, a specimen *Acer,* frames the view.

above *An elevation shows the height of the mirrored water wall that forms a dramatic focal point within this restricted space.*

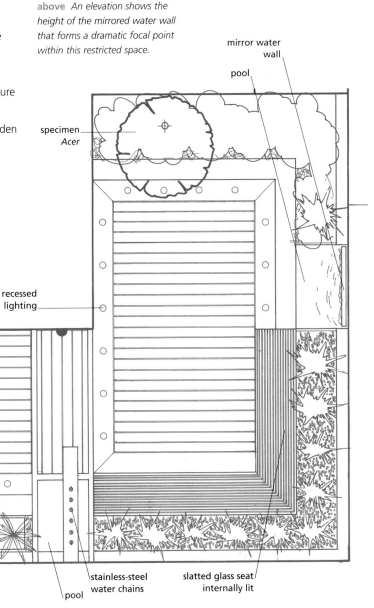

Garden of Reflections

VLADIMIR SITTA / MAREN PARRY – TERRAGRAM PTY LTD

DIMENSIONS 20 x 15m overall (60 x 50ft)
SOIL imported
ASPECT south facing (in southern hemisphere)
KEY FEATURES glass and water

In this strikingly modern house, the sound of water is used to entice the visitor into the interior. Coming from the driveway, one passes a roof garden sitting on top of a new garage. This space is dissected by granite slabs that undulate, becoming gradually higher and able to contain soil to sustain small plants. From this level, a flight of cantilevered and stainless-steel-clad concrete steps leads down to the main entrance of the house. A further set of wide, stone steps continues down to a stepping-stone bridge set into a dark pool of water in front of the doorway. These steps have long, narrow beds set into them, planted for leaf texture. To the side of the steps, a small courtyard is planted with a bamboo grove and it is only as the visitor descends the steps to the house that the source of the sound

of the water is revealed. Horizontal, light reflecting, zigzagging slabs of laminated glass are discharging water into a pool by the front door. At night this effect is enhanced by fibre optic lighting, creating a fairy-tale atmosphere.

Within the house itself, a double-height space forms a sculpture court filled entirely with water, interrupted only by one *Phyllostachys nigra* and a light, copper mesh that seem to emerge from the water. From this point, views out over the city and harbour become apparent, finally appearing over an elevated, "edgeless" swimming pool.

left *The steps leading down to a stepping stone bridge have long narrow planting beds set into them for growing plants with unusual leaf texture such as sedges or grasses.*

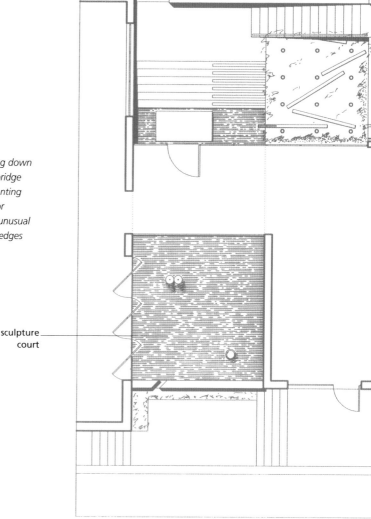

sculpture court

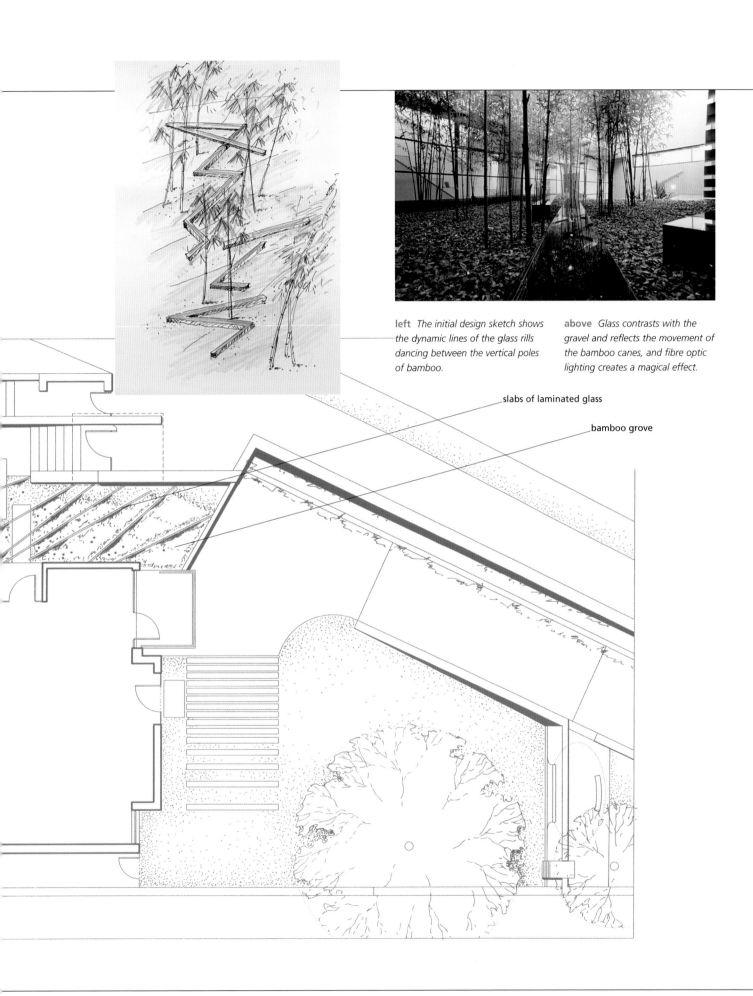

left *The initial design sketch shows the dynamic lines of the glass rills dancing between the vertical poles of bamboo.*

above *Glass contrasts with the gravel and reflects the movement of the bamboo canes, and fibre optic lighting creates a magical effect.*

slabs of laminated glass

bamboo grove

City Landmark

ARABELLA LENNOX-BOYD

DIMENSIONS 0.25ha (0.5 acre)

SOIL neutral

ASPECT north-east facing

KEY FEATURES distinct garden spaces, bold planting, City views

Forming the roof of a landmark city building, this garden needed to show the city skyline to best advantage as well as offering a social and focal space for a restaurant. Constraints included incorporating the building's many hard surfaces and an existing pergola into the design, as well as the problems of extreme climatic conditions and shallow soil depth. Access for the public was another consideration.

The space is divided into three gardens: an apex garden to the north east, an inner garden in the centre, and outer gardens on either side of the restaurant. The apex garden is open to its surrounding and has views over St Paul's Cathedral and the City of London. A simple lawn is bordered by "ploughed rows" of box inspired by the ridge-and-furrow formations of ploughed fields. Large, sandstone balls give the garden a modern edge. At night these are lit from beneath to give the illusion of floating spheres.

The inner garden is enclosed within a high, circular wall with a pergola along the inside perimeter planted with edible grapes (*Vitis* 'Fragola') and *Wisteria floribunda* 'Alba'. The circle is softened by irregular borders within the paved grid. Narrow openings in the wall lead to the outer gardens, which are used for alfresco dining. Serpentine raised beds create dining pockets along previously straight passages. These are planted with beech columns for architecture and height, and underplanted with roses, ceanothus, and ivy to soften the hard edges.

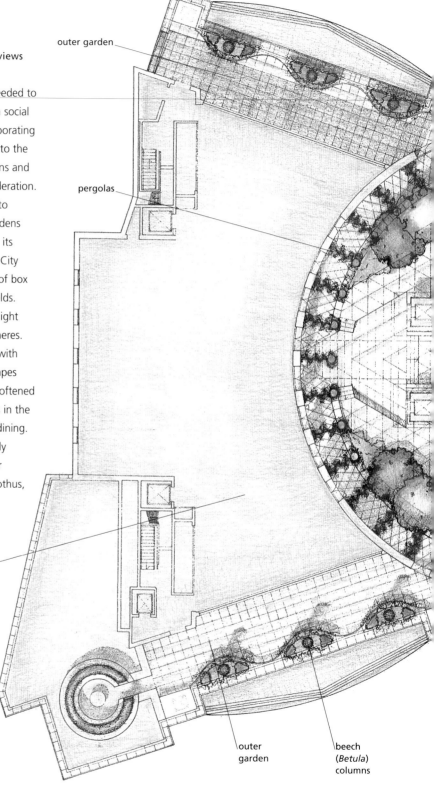

outer garden

pergolas

restaurant

outer garden

beech (*Betula*) columns

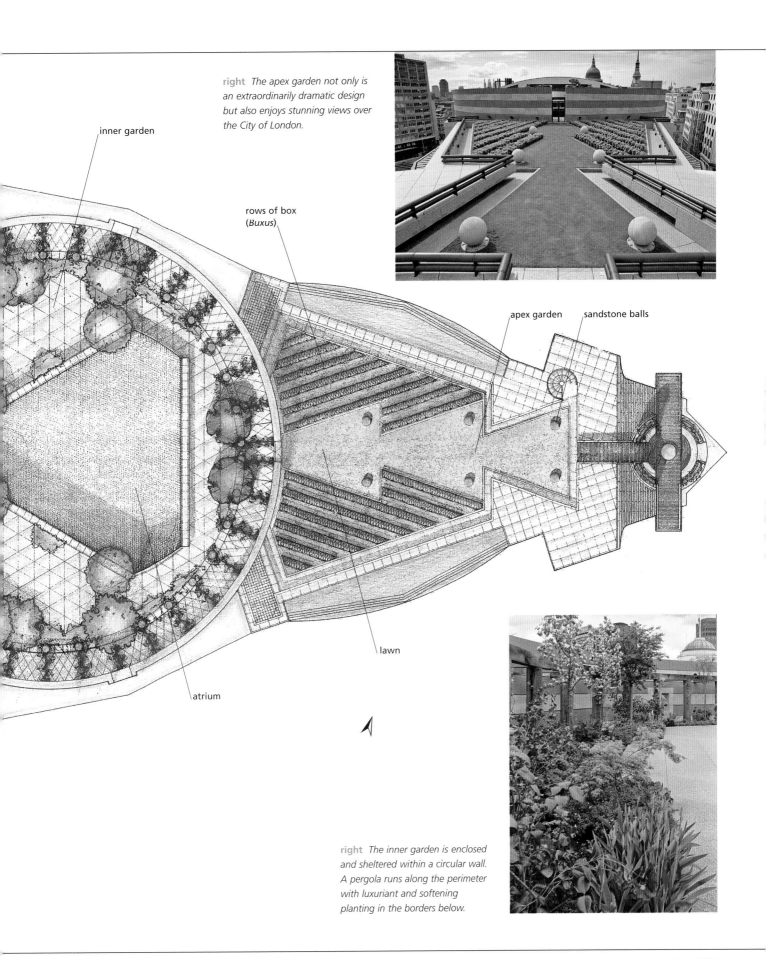

inner garden

right *The apex garden not only is an extraordinarily dramatic design but also enjoys stunning views over the City of London.*

rows of box (*Buxus*)

apex garden   sandstone balls

lawn

atrium

right *The inner garden is enclosed and sheltered within a circular wall. A pergola runs along the perimeter with luxuriant and softening planting in the borders below.*

Interconnecting Circles

DOUGLAS COLTART – VIRIDARIUM DESIGN STUDIO

DIMENSIONS 15 x 7.5m (50 x 24ft)

SOIL imported

ASPECT south facing

KEY FEATURES two circular areas

Designed to complement a modern apartment, this roof garden needed to include space for informal relaxing as well as a more formal dining and entertaining area. The roof had spectacular views over the city but these needed to be enhanced.

By setting out two distinct, circular areas, the two major functions of the garden are catered for. A circular deck is surrounded by raised beds of low-maintenance planting, which provides screening and shelter and also frames views of the city. Paving is used to link the two sitting areas, and a small, paved circle sits on the edge of the entertaining deck as the site for a patio heater.

The other circular space includes several raised areas drawn from the same centre but at different radii for interest. Astroturf is used to contrast with the decking because it provides a comfortable surface without needing any maintenance. A small, cascading water feature provides movement and sparkle, and sculptures and planted containers bring further interest. Two *Sorbus vilmorinii* frame the view over the city from the eastern side of the garden.

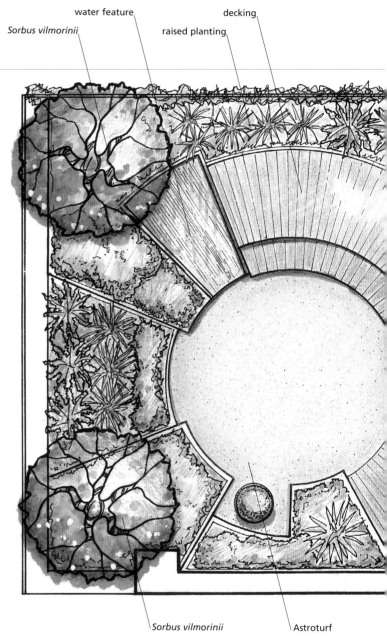

water feature

Sorbus vilmorinii

raised planting

decking

Sorbus vilmorinii

Astroturf

above *In this roof garden two specimens of the spreading shrub or tree* Sorbus vilmorinii *frame the view over the city.*

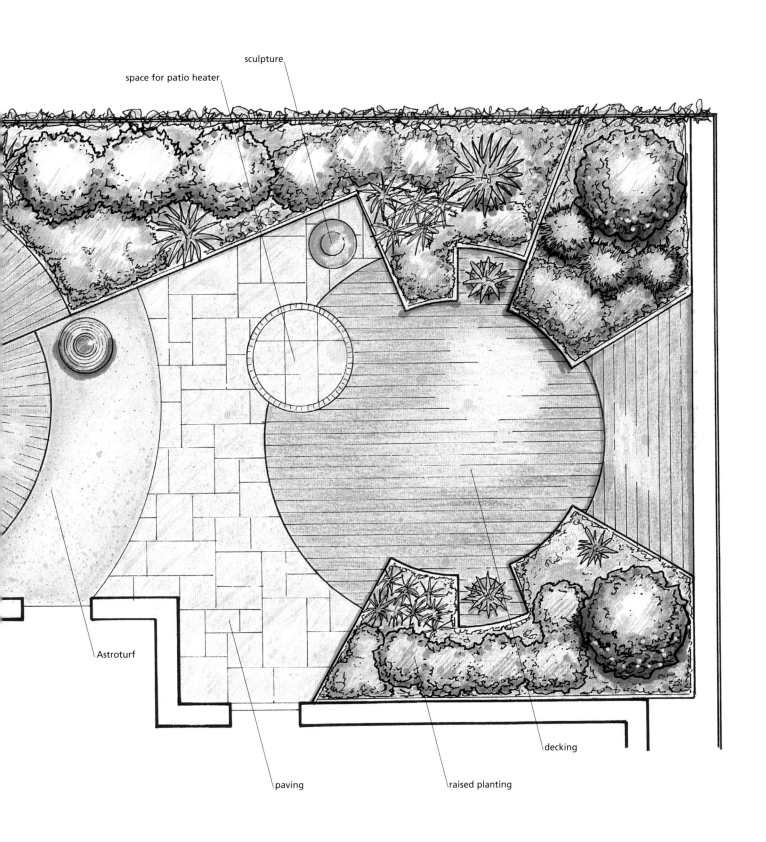

space for patio heater

sculpture

Astroturf

paving

raised planting

decking

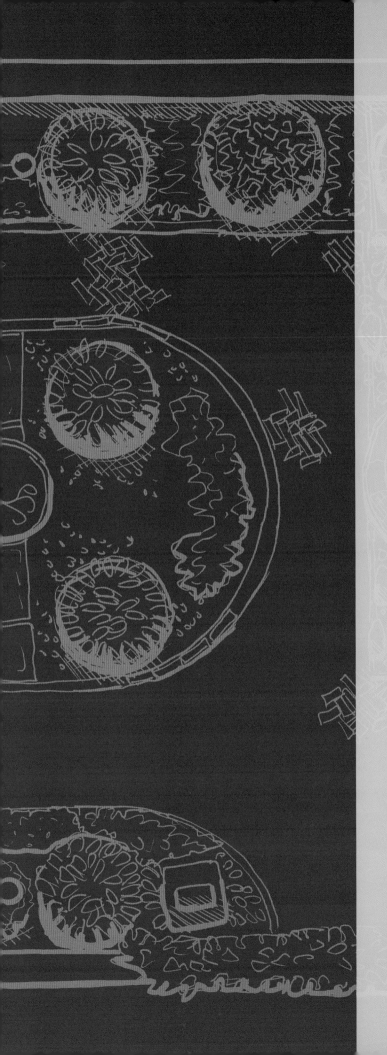

FORMALGARDENS

Symmetry and formality have always been popular as ways of asserting regularity and control on the natural landscape. Axial routes, symmetric patterns, repetition, and mirror-image geometry impose a clear system on a garden. In small spaces, complete formality can be difficult to achieve because few areas will be regular in shape. In addition, the house or apartment may not share in the symmetry intended for the garden, creating a mismatch. The informal approach may suit these situations better. Dense or large-scale planting can disguise and fill the perimeter of awkward plot shapes, within which a regular ground plan can be created. Plants can also be used in this way to camouflage or neutralize the impact of the house.

Within the formal garden, the accuracy of the symmetry is an unrelenting consideration. Central views or pathways must be accurately centred; planting bed dimensions or the positioning of containers and artifacts must relate to the regime and to each other. Attempted formality that is not accurately laid out creates ambiguity and visual discomfort. Keep ornament and sculpture large and generous, despite the restricted space. This will create drama and interest and will potentially attract the eye from indoors, creating an invitation to explore.

Architecture and Structure

XA TOLLEMACHE LANDSCAPE AND GARDEN DESIGN

DIMENSIONS 10 x 6m (33 x 20ft)

SOIL neutral

ASPECT north facing

KEY FEATURES canal and bridge

A high surrounding wall and two large plane trees were major constraints to the design of this garden; in particular, the root systems of the trees could not be disturbed by any works. The brief was for the garden to be "architectural" with structure using evergreens, and that it should look as good when viewed from above as it did at ground level.

The new layout is very formal and symmetrical, with the design slightly offset from the main house to maximize the small space. Low, wide steps lead up into the garden from a lower terrace. Water is introduced as a canal along the central axis. At the focal point of the garden is a concrete obelisk designed by George Carter. Water drips down the frost work on the obelisk, into a raised holding pool, and thence into the canal. Behind the obelisk is a reflective panel of galvanized steel with glass panels. Versailles planters and trellis work, also designed by George Carter, are positioned around the canal for structure and interest. The planters originally contained *Cupressus sempervirens* to emphasize the verticals in the garden but these suffered from the dust created by the plane trees so they have been replaced by wire-work obelisks planted with clipped ivy.

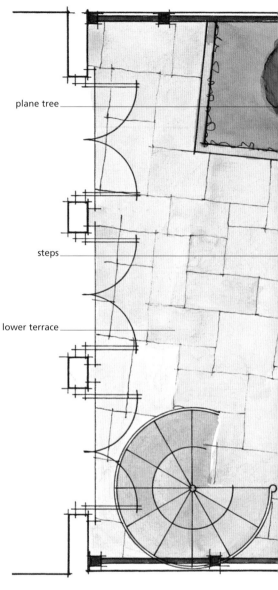

plane tree

steps

lower terrace

left *The focal point of this garden is a concrete obelisk from which water drips down into a raised holding pool and then into a canal.*

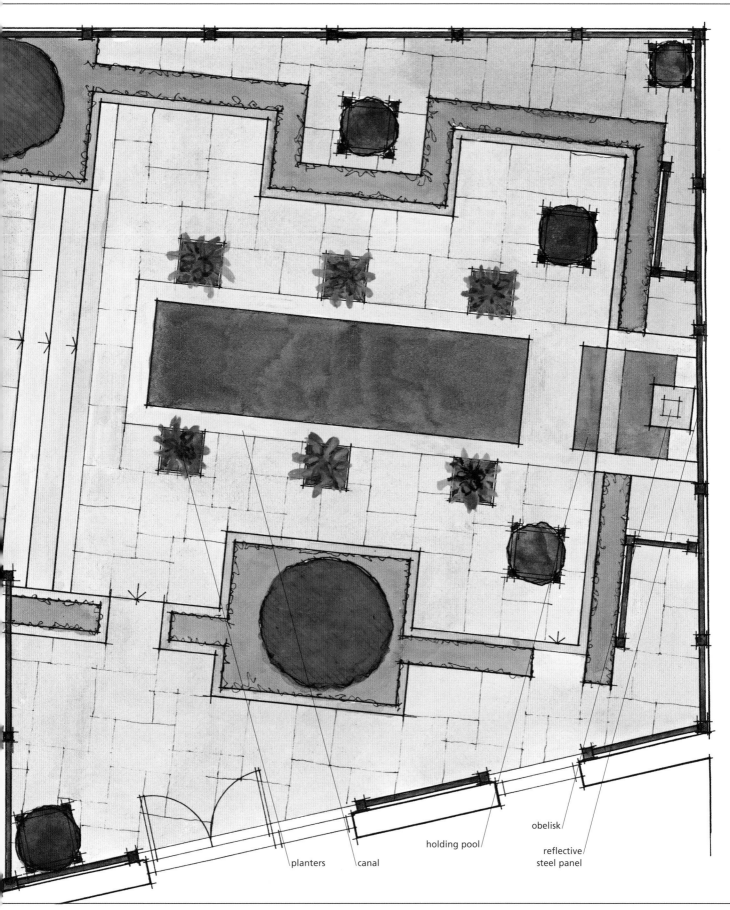

planters   canal   holding pool   obelisk

reflective
steel panel

Minimalist Party Space

PAUL DRACOTT

DIMENSIONS 11 x 8m (36 x 25ft)

SOIL heavy clay loam

ASPECT north facing

KEY FEATURES blue-lit rill leading to a stainless-steel water feature

This garden is owned by a single man who wanted an external party space that would flow seamlessly from the minimal interior space. He wanted a contemporary water feature, built-in seating, and coloured lighting.

The design creates one simple, open space surrounded by planting and bisected with a central, stainless-steel rill covered with galvanized mesh. The rill leads the eye directly to a stainless-steel waterfall. Built-in, rendered seating at the foot of the garden creates a gathering space and provides a destination. A hardwood timber deck leads from the interior hardwood floor out, through folding glass doors and steps down, onto cream sandstone paving laid in a simple chequerboard pattern.

Topiarized privet (*Ligustrum*) standards in black rectangular pots line the rill, narrowing the view and focusing the eye on the central axis. Etched-glass panels provide screening and are washed with coloured light to create light boxes around the garden. Blue LED strips light the rill and blue uplighters pick out the rendered seating and light the rear façade of the house. Massed planting of *Phyllostachys nigra* gives height and structure in the corners.

above *This exciting party space really comes into its own at night when the lighting, including blue LED strips and glass panels, is turned on.*

timber deck

left *Even without the dramatic night-time lighting the garden has plenty of interest, including the topiarized privet (*Ligustrum*) in black containers.*

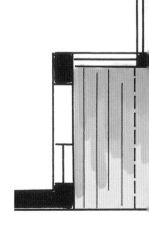

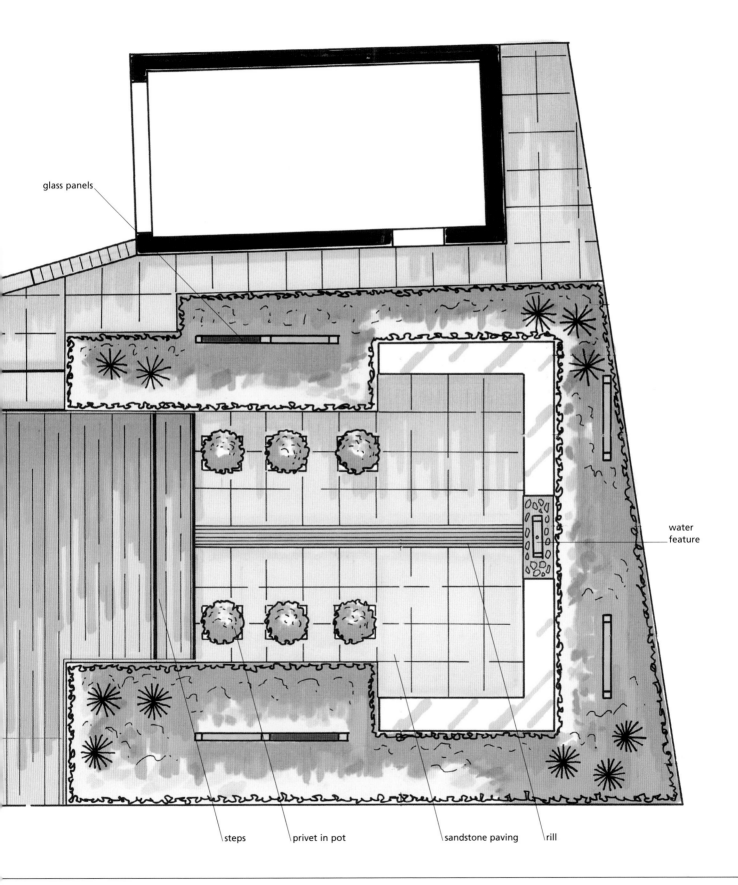

glass panels

water feature

steps

privet in pot

sandstone paving

rill

Courtyard for Entertaining

MARCUS BARNETT DESIGN

DIMENSIONS approx 12 x 16m (40 x 53ft); part of a larger garden

SOIL acid

ASPECT south-west facing

KEY FEATURES box structures and "hot" planting

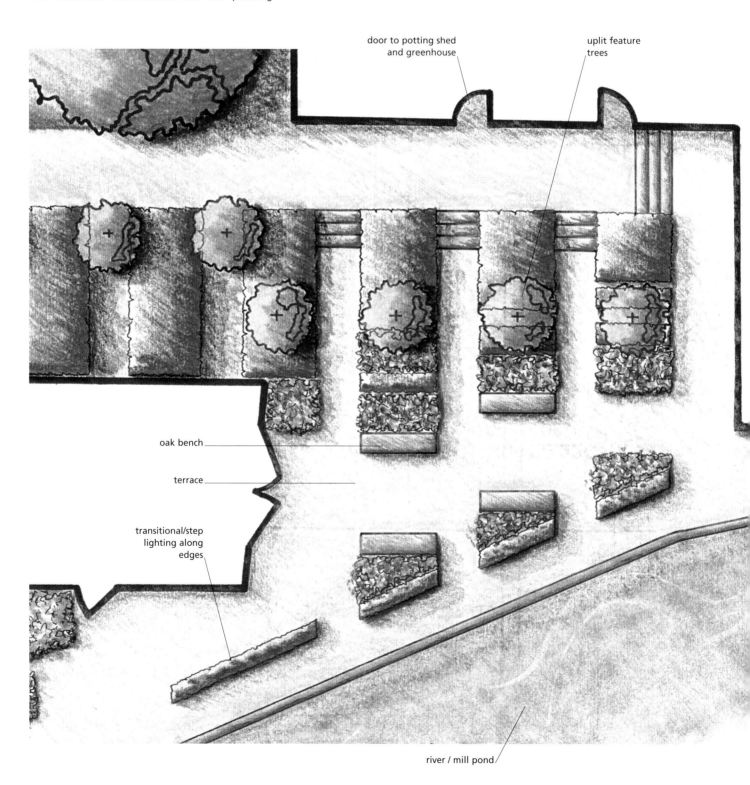

door to potting shed
and greenhouse

uplit feature
trees

oak bench

terrace

transitional/step
lighting along
edges

river / mill pond

Entertainment is the principal function of this area within a much larger garden. A courtyard is formed by the house, an old, flint-walled potting shed, and a forge that has been transformed into an outdoor dining room. From the house there are unimpaired views of a river and these were to remain. The design had to allow for enjoyment, whether it was used by a few people or by a group of up to 30, and it must allow for back-casting during fly-fishing.

To resolve the awkward shape of the space, large rectangles of *Buxus sempervirens* provide structure and geometry. They also provide an evergreen backdrop for the planting and dilute the grey,

flint walls. Large, oak "benches" 500 x 500mm x 2m (20 x 20in x 6ft) provide summer seating and winter structure and echo the history of the buildings.

Trees planted include multi-stemmed *Amelanchier lamarckii* pruned into mop-heads. Other planting of grasses and perennials is designed to look very "hot" against the backdrop of the flint walls. The key colours are scarlet, blood red, fresh lime green, and bronze, including *Penstemon* 'Firebird', *Calamagrostis brachytricha, Papaver orientale* 'Beauty of Livermere', *Atriplex hortensis* var. *rubra,* and *Alchemilla mollis.* Apart from the *Buxus* all planting is deciduous.

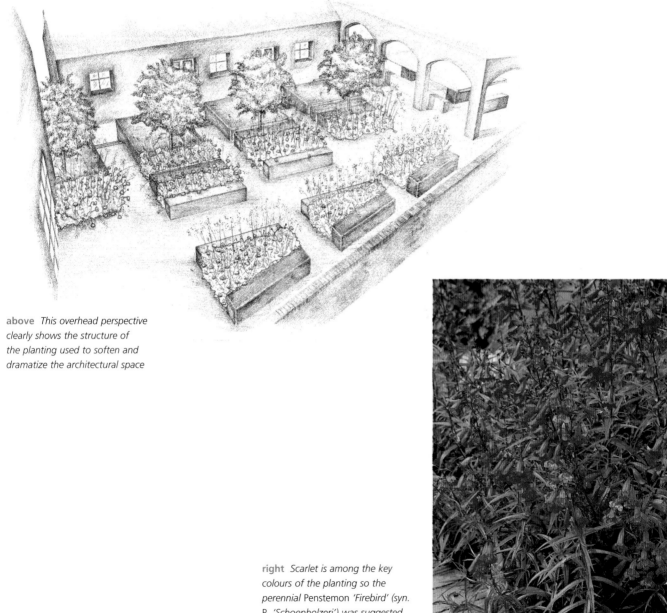

above *This overhead perspective clearly shows the structure of the planting used to soften and dramatize the architectural space*

right *Scarlet is among the key colours of the planting so the perennial* Penstemon *'Firebird' (syn. P. 'Schoenholzeri') was suggested.*

Classical Structure

ANDREW DUFF

DIMENSIONS 180sq m (1,939sq ft)
SOIL clay
ASPECT south facing
KEY FEATURES pergola

In an overlooked city space, this garden needed to become much lighter and brighter but also more private. The internal and external spaces needed to work together and a level change of 650mm (28in) from the lower basement level up into the main garden needed to be addressed.

To unify the indoor and outdoor spaces, limestone paving for both is laid in a grid. A small play area outside the house has wide stone steps leading to a square, sitting area with raised beds capped with a 500mm- (20in-) wide timber seat, bringing a sense of enclosure to the space. At the rear of the garden, a gate leads onto open parkland. A York stone pathway leads from the house to this gate, past the sitting area and under a contemporary pergola consisting of three simple beams that provide a sculptural element to the garden and increase privacy. Planting is predominantly in the form of an urban woodland underplanted with low, evergreen groundcover, seasonal bulbs, and bedding. The owners were eager to add a sense of humour to the space, but their gardening knowledge was limited. In response to this, Versailles planters on castors are planted with vegetables and set on the terrace by the house.

above *In an overlooked city space, an informal, woodland style of planting contrasts well with more formal limestone paving.*

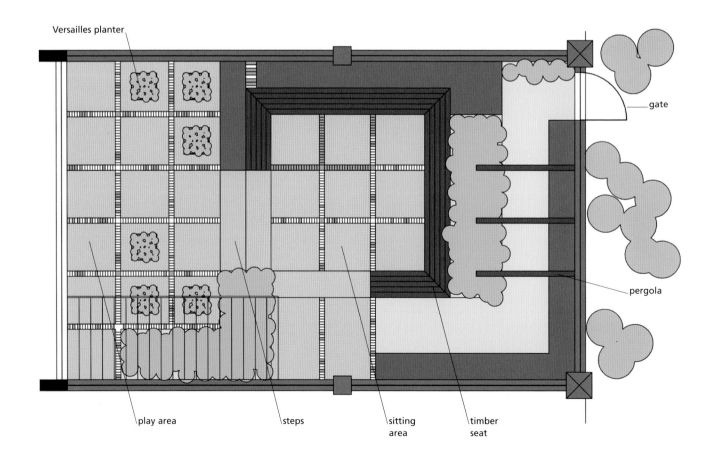

Versailles planter

gate

pergola

play area

steps

sitting area

timber seat

Mediterranean-Style Courtyard

NATALYA SCOTT – MOOREA LANDSCAPES LTD

DIMENSIONS 7 x 5m (23 x 16ft); walkway is 7 x 1.5m (23 x 4½ft)

SOIL neutral

ASPECT east facing

KEY FEATURES topiary in pots and symmetrical planting

This small, formal space was inspired by the owner's desire for a "Mediterranean" garden. From the house, the view of the garden is along a narrow walkway and a key part of the design was to enhance this area to entice the visitor into the garden. The courtyard garden was already paved in dark red bricks laid in a herringbone pattern.

Lining the walkway to the garden is a miniature "avenue" of *Prunus laurocerasus* (cherry laurel) in galvanized steel pots. Either side of the stone paving are ribbons of blue glass aggregate for interest and colour. From the window at the end of the walkway, the view is enhanced by a sculpture at the far end, just into the main garden, leading the eye out.

In the main garden a formal layout of beds and planting is softened by lush planting. *Cupressus sempervirens* in large, square,

copper planters provide an elegant backdrop with olive trees and lavenders, thymes, and *Trachycarpus fortunei* continuing the Mediterranean theme. In the centre of the garden is a sitting area with a water feature and sculpture.

left The narrow passageway into the garden provides an introduction to the main space with sculpture used as a way marker and focal point.

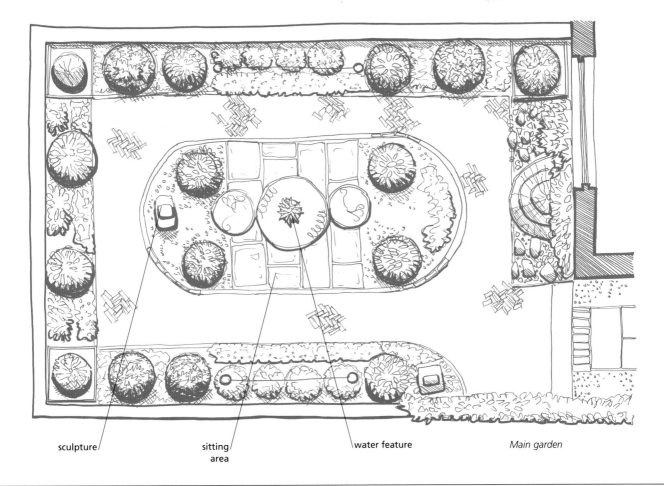

sculpture   sitting area   water feature   *Main garden*

Incorporating the Wider Landscape

ALISON BRETT – HORTUS DESIGN + BUILD LTD

DIMENSIONS 15 x 14m (50 x 47ft) and 11 x 12m (36 x 40ft);
part of a much larger garden

SOIL light, sandy, and acidic

ASPECT south facing

KEY FEATURES far-reaching views

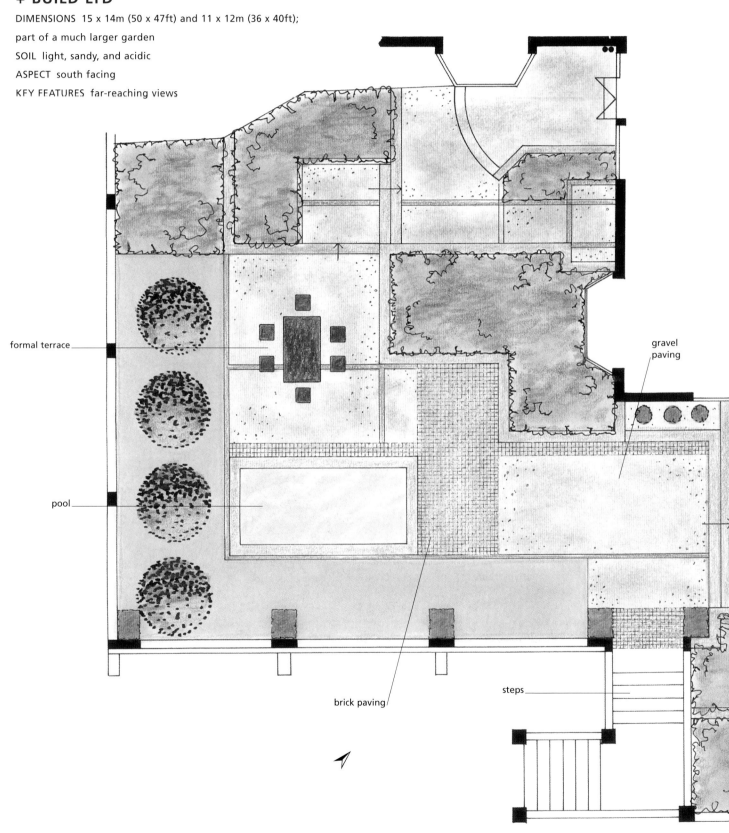

formal terrace

pool

gravel paving

brick paving

steps

above *This view shows how the formal structure of the terrace contrasts with the more informal low maintenance planting.*

On a windy and exposed hill-top site, this terrace forms part of a much larger garden with fantastic, far-reaching views across downland countryside. The area around the house is contained by original brick walls and stone balustrades. The remainder of the garden falls away steeply. New access was needed from the kitchen and screening from neighbours was necessary.

A generous flight of steps down to the terrace was constructed to be in scale with the rest of the house. Changes in level require more stone steps and raised beds with textured render and stone copings. A contemporary feel is brought to the design using a grid of geometric lines linking the different areas. Variously sized rectangles give a dynamic and interesting look, with either stone or gravel infills for movement and texture. Two sitting areas are provided, one a private, intimate space outside the kitchen and the other a more formal spot to the west of the house. The pool shown in the design was omitted at the construction stage.

Planting is low-maintenance with green structure and lots of flowers. Evergreen structure is provided by yew hedging, clipped standard *Elaeagnus* x *ebbingei,* and box balls in blocks. Elsewhere "naturalistic" planting includes grasses, lavenders, and rosemary.

steps

kitchen terrace

above *A view of the terrace from the other side of the house shows how the changes in level require a number of stone steps.*

Box Hedging and Limestone Strips

CHARLOTTE KIERKEGAARD DESIGN

DIMENSIONS 11 x 7m (36 x 23ft)

SOIL loam

ASPECT north facing

KEY FEATURES small box hedges and camomile in the paving

Creating a garden that would look as good in winter as in summer meant this small space required structure. The existing lawn was adversely affected by a mature tree, and the owners wanted to replace the grass with hard landscaping that would look good and need less maintenance. Because the garden is north facing and has the tree, bringing light into the space is very important.

Steps outside the house lead on to a small, decked area with a tiny water feature to the side, giving the movement and sound of water. The garden's structure is provided by low box hedging, forming "frames" within the planting beds on either side. These lines are continued across the garden at ground level in camomile (*Chamaemelum nobile*) to soften the limestone paving. Longer lengths of hedging hide the basement of the house, and form an entry into the secluded sitting area at the far end. A high rendered panel screens the shed in the corner of the garden and provides a backdrop to the limestone bench under the tree. Cedar decking, trellis, and furniture link the wooden elements.

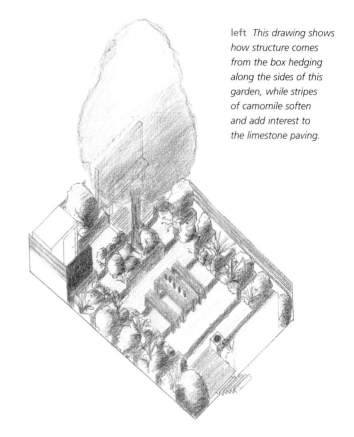

left This drawing shows how structure comes from the box hedging along the sides of this garden, while stripes of camomile soften and add interest to the limestone paving.

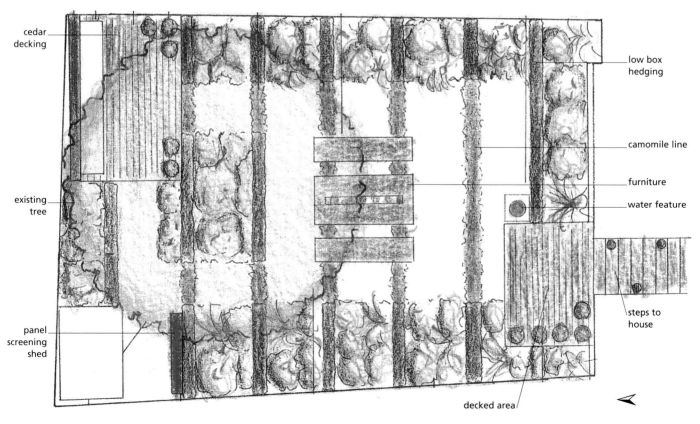

cedar decking

existing tree

panel screening shed

decked area

low box hedging

camomile line

furniture

water feature

steps to house

Mediterranean Pool Garden

NAILA GREEN GARDEN DESIGN

DIMENSIONS 23 x 18m (70 x 57ft)

SOIL woodland loam over clay subsoil

ASPECT south facing

KEY FEATURES formal swimming pool and Cretan pots

The owners' Mediterranean background was the main inspiration for this garden. They wanted a large, rectangular swimming pool to be surrounded by areas for sitting and dining, and the different elements had to be integrated into a cohesive garden.

The pool is set at the centre of the garden, with two parallel rills running linking the other garden spaces. Vistas through the garden are created by high, sandstone-coloured walls set perpendicular to the pool; the rills pass through these on each side of the pool. The different spaces in the garden are linked by Cretan pots set on plinths and planted with *Cupressus sempervirens* to lead the eye through the space and to add a touch of classical Greek influence. At each corner of the garden, a sitting area with its own unique character gives purpose to the whole space.

A terra cotta tile-paved sitting area covered by a large pergola constructed with twisted-tile column supports forms the main dining area in the garden and a bar is built in for the clients' enjoyment. From this space the view along the rill shows a more relaxed sitting space where scented vegetation spills over the paving. A further gravel area is more densely planted with Mediterranean foliage for scent. Following the other rill along from there, a shaded garden at the far end is planted with a mature olive tree, and has terra cotta stepping stones leading back to the pool.

above *This perspective shows how Cretan pots planted with* Cupressus sempervirens *lead the eye from the pergola-covered paving along a rill beside the pool.*

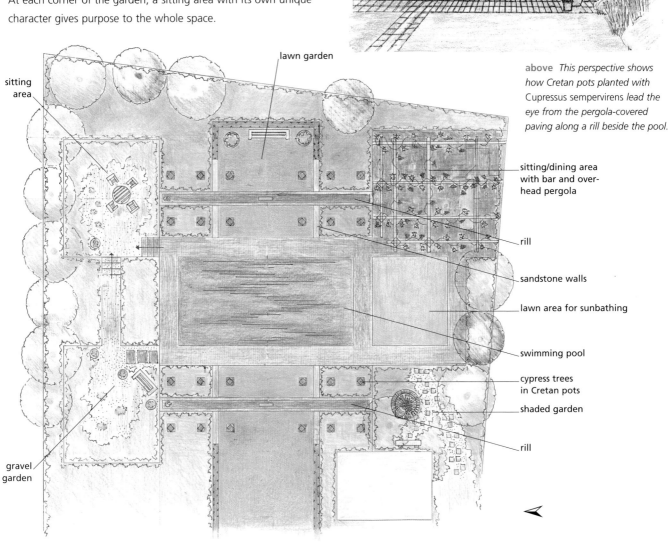

- sitting area
- lawn garden
- gravel garden
- sitting/dining area with bar and overhead pergola
- rill
- sandstone walls
- lawn area for sunbathing
- swimming pool
- cypress trees in Cretan pots
- shaded garden
- rill

New Zealand Influence

ANNIE GUILFOYLE – CREATIVE LANDSCAPES

DIMENSIONS 6 x 5.5m (20 x 19ft)

SOIL no existing soil because of paving

ASPECT south-west facing

KEY FEATURES architectural planting and "L"-shaped canal

The garden owner was a busy professional with a strong design awareness who was looking for a bold, contemporary design using plants predominantly from New Zealand and of architectural presence. The tiny back garden was constantly on view from the sitting room and an upstairs study. The owner's busy lifestyle and frequent travelling meant that the garden needed to be very low maintenance but she likes to entertain so was looking for an exciting garden in which to dine.

Portland stone is used for the paving and Iroko wood for the fencing and gate. The water feature and channel are made from rendered concrete blockwork that has been waterproofed with fibreglass. Leading out from the house, a small terrace is visually cut off from the rest of the garden by planting, and the water channel and is crossed by a stepping stone. Here, two oak cube seats give a welcoming spot for perching to catch the evening sun. The strong, architectural planting includes *Eriobotrya japonica, Pseudopanax laetus, Pteris cretica, Olearia macrodonta, Persicaria amplexicaulis* 'Firetail', *Dicksonia antarctica,* and *Muehlenbeckia complexa.*

left *Because the planting in this garden needed to be low maintenance, grasses were included in the scheme.*

water feature

oak cube seats

stepping stone

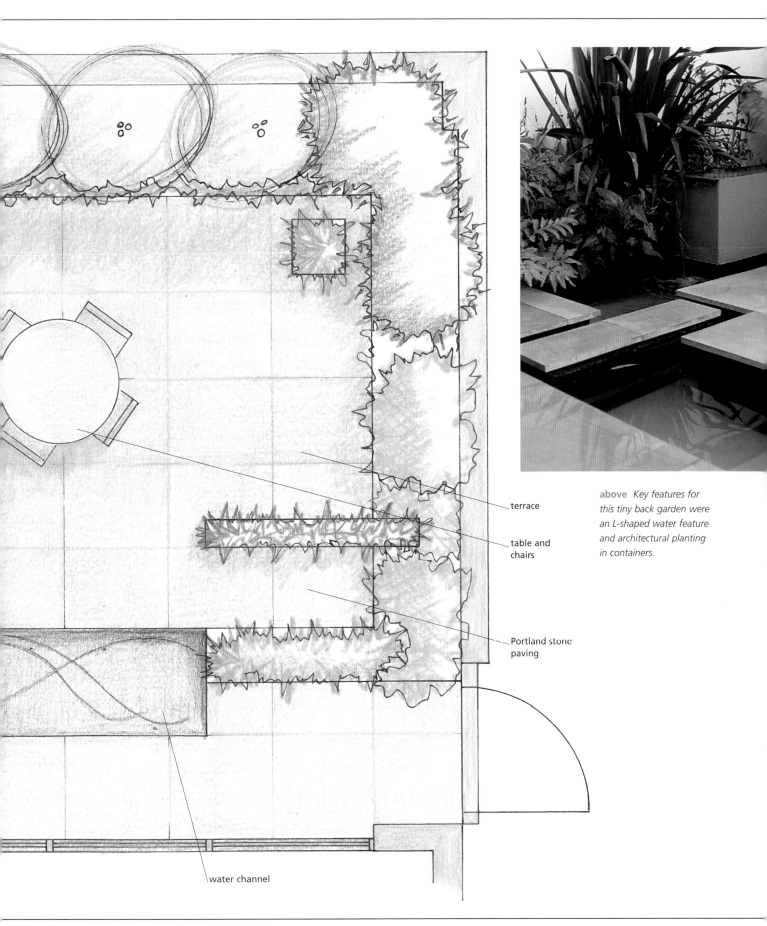

terrace

table and
chairs

Portland stone
paving

water channel

above *Key features for
this tiny back garden were
an L-shaped water feature
and architectural planting
in containers.*

Maze Garden

KEITH PULLAN GARDEN DESIGN

DIMENSIONS 8.5 x 4m (26 x 13ft)

SOIL alkaline

ASPECT south-west facing

KEY FEATURES clipped box hedges

For this front garden of a terraced house, the owner's requests were very specific: a semi-formal garden, but "quirky", possibly with a maze of some kind, and with a direct path from gate to front door. Herbs also needed to be included near the house.

Low, clipped box hedges are often associated with traditional, formal designs; here, they are used to create sculptural form as a central element of the design, with a careful balance of mass and void both within the maze area and between that and the stone path. The varying heights of the box add further interest, with rusted, iron obelisks, as sculptural forms, lending vertical elements.

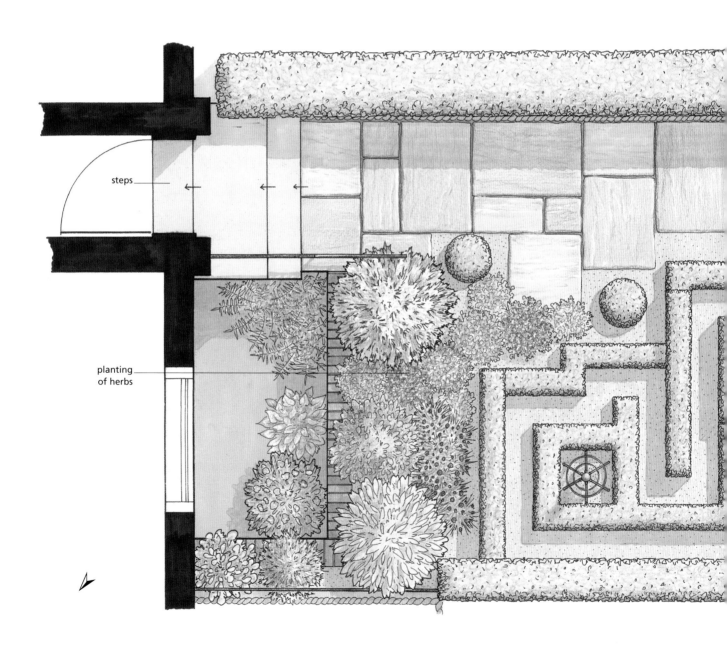

steps

planting of herbs

Clipped box balls also enhance the rhythmic pattern through the garden and contrast in shape and form with the maze, leading the eye up the path to the front door. Gravel surrounds the hedging and the box balls, softening the edges of the pattern and providing mulch around the informal planting near the house.

Herbs with contrasting foliage, form, and texture against the formality of the clipped box soften the front of the house and give splashes of colour to the otherwise predominantly green garden. They also balance the massed planting of ophiopogon at the front of the garden.

above *Among the suggested planting in this predominantly green garden was massed planting of the evergreen perennial* Ophiopogon.

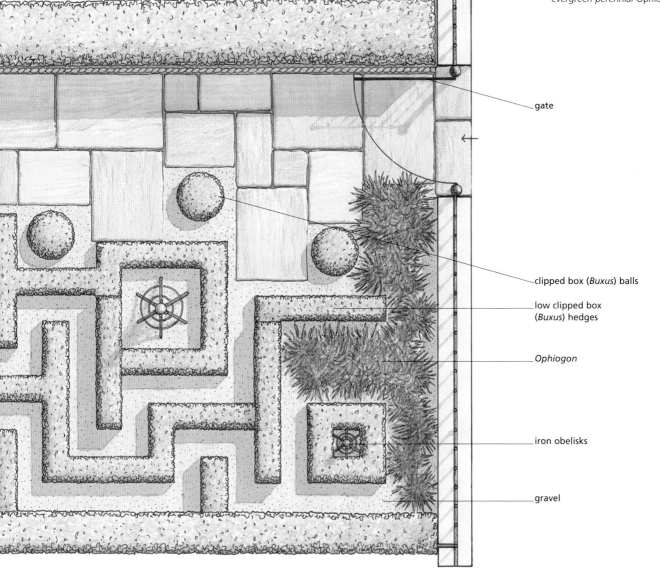

gate

clipped box (*Buxus*) balls

low clipped box (*Buxus*) hedges

Ophiogon

iron obelisks

gravel

Jungle Retreat

JAMES ALDRIDGE GARDENS

DIMENSIONS 7 x 5m (23 x 16ft)

SOIL new loam

ASPECT north-east facing

KEY FEATURE water spout and obelisk

For this formal house with classical motifs, the owners were looking for a retreat from city life, with jungle-like planting. Privacy from neighbours was important and a water feature was required to help mask the noise of the city. A very high wall at the back of the garden needed to be incorporated into the design.

To detract attention from the high wall, a large, square pool was built at the back of the garden, 100mm (3ft) high, with a water spill over which water drops into a wide canal at the garden level. This low pool is colour-washed in a rich blue and is partly covered in an intricate mosaic by Cleo Mussi. The mosaic also appears on a garden table and on the bases of two urns in the garden. A tall obelisk is set in the centre of the pool, providing a formal focal point for the garden.

The space is formally paved in a reclaimed granite sett grid inset with green slate slabs. The boundaries are trellised in a square grid to reflect the paving, and pleached limes (*Tilia platyphyllos* 'Rubra') at a height of 2.5m (7½ft) give a sense of seclusion and privacy. Other planting is chosen for a luxuriant, tropical feel in summer.

above *A highly architectural plant, the succulent* Agave americana, *was part of the planting scheme.*

below *The elevation shows the depth of water and how the levels work to create the cascade. Beyond, the pleached limes and tall trellis provide valuable privacy.*

paving grid of granite setts filled with squares of green slate

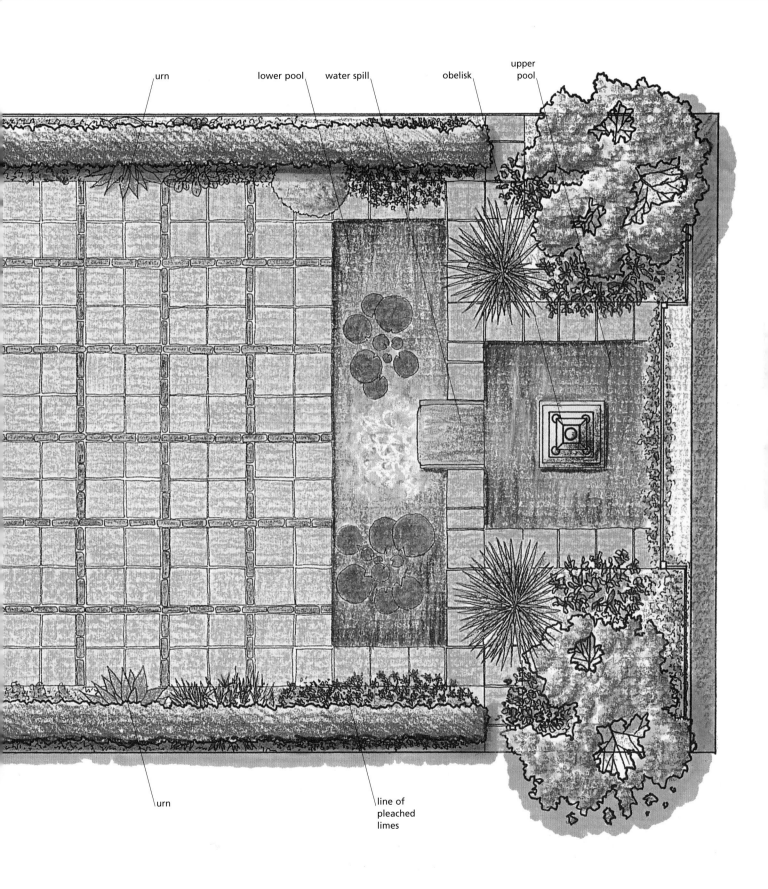

urn   lower pool   water spill   obelisk   upper pool

urn

line of pleached limes

AWKWARDGARDENS

Irregular or angular plot shapes make it difficult or uncomfortable to introduce regular and coherent designs. Most problems arise when we try to maximize usable space by pushing planting and artifacts back to the boundaries. Planting becomes squeezed into tight borders and acts as wallpaper, allowing the awkward angles to assert themselves and dominate. Angles create movement and direction and can focus our view very efficiently, often creating dynamic but restless spaces. This affects our experience of the garden, meaning that intended focal points fail to compete with the wider distraction. By imposing a new geometry, effective solutions can be achieved. The space between the more regular layout and the actual boundaries is best occupied by screen planting. While actual usable space may be reduced, the resulting garden will feel larger and rest easier on the eye.

For other small gardens, it may be extreme or dramatic level changes, high boundary walls, or tight, restricted dimensions that create awkward spaces. The design responses to such extremes may be idiosyncratic but achievable and often clever. Design is about problem solving and often the greatest problems produce the most successful and imaginative solutions. Designers will be able to highlight issues and potential solutions effectively.

Red and Black Pool

VLADIMIR SITTA / MAREN PARRY – TERRAGRAM PTY LTD

DIMENSIONS 11 x 9m (36 x 30ft)

SOIL sandy

ASPECT south-west facing (in southern hemisphere)

KEY FEATURES existing pool

The swimming pool was already in place in this garden, although it needed complete renovation. There was a steep slope from the house down to the pool and direct access was not possible. The owners wanted to link the garden to the inside of the house and to screen a neighbouring house. Incorporating primary colours was a very important feature of the brief.

The pool was refurbished and retiled in black, with the surrounding area tiled in bright red, randomly laid tiles. A retaining wall built to raise the level of the lawn was rendered and painted. Inset into the wall are several niches suitable for a glass of wine or things that need protection from the water.

At the higher level, a lawn is punctuated by a single pear tree for shade and to enhance privacy. A decked area runs along the back of the house to form a sitting area. To emphasize the change of level, the retaining wall is topped by a water channel tiled in yellow mosaic and with green pebbles scattered along the bottom. A curving path and steps of reclaimed bluestone links the house, upper garden, and pool, and planting along the perimeter is of very tall bamboos for privacy.

above To emphasize the change of level in the higher part of the garden a retaining wall is topped by a water channel tiled in yellow mosaic with green pebbles scattered along the bottom.

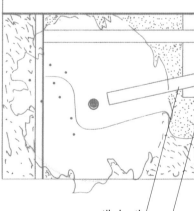

tiled path

bluestone paving

left Although the swimming pool was already in place it needed refurbishing and retiling – the palette reflects the owner's preference for primary colours.

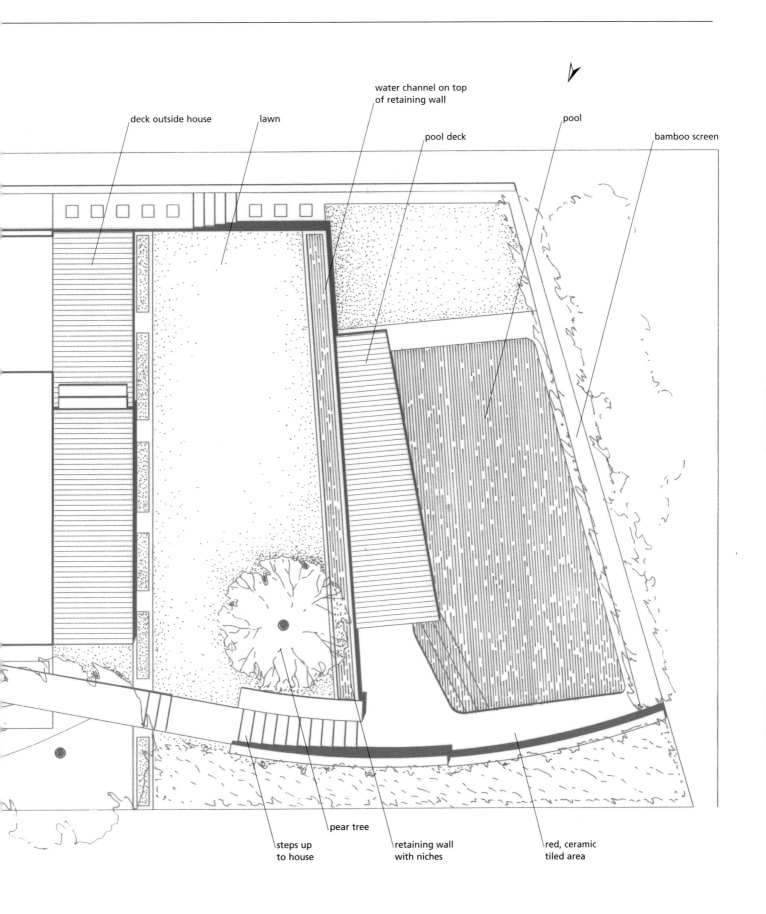

deck outside house

lawn

water channel on top
of retaining wall

pool deck

pool

bamboo screen

pear tree

steps up
to house

retaining wall
with niches

red, ceramic
tiled area

Basalt and Black Pebbles

CLEVE WEST

DIMENSIONS 8.5 x 5m (26 x 16ft)

SOIL medium loam

ASPECT south-east facing

KEY FEATURES bush-hammered basalt

This garden was presented to its owners as a ready-made, designed garden to go with their new-build house. They wanted a simple space, leaving plenty of room to satisfy their need to garden.

To create privacy, a line of pleached hornbeams screens the bottom of the garden and an *Amelanchier* gives structure. A simple, butt-jointed terrace of mint limestone links the sitting space under the existing arbour with the rest of the garden. As the garden slopes away from the house, a retaining wall of bush-hammered basalt crosses it, forming a step down on the path to the garage as well as a link to the square pool. Basalt coping continues the edging of the pool and forms bands across the limestone path. The small pool is constructed using a box-welded butyl liner, which is then covered in a bed of black pebbles. Paving to access the side of the house is of mint limestone slabs set through black pebbles.

Planting includes *Myrtus communis* as well as *Iris* 'Deep Black', *Miscanathus nepalensis, Astrantia major,* and *Libertia formosa.*

left *The long-flowering perennial* Astrantia major *was on the list of planting for this newly built house.*

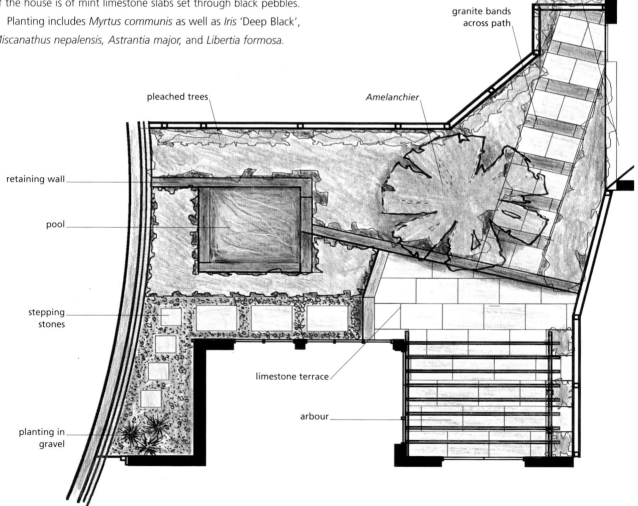

pleached trees

Amelanchier

garage

granite bands across path

retaining wall

pool

stepping stones

limestone terrace

arbour

planting in gravel

Candlelit Relaxation

CLAIRE MEE DESIGNS

DIMENSIONS 5 x 5m (16 x 16ft)

SOIL clay

ASPECT south facing

KEY FEATURES decorative block wall with candles and decking

This small garden was very dark and uninviting. The owners wanted a light, functional space that seemed larger. Two areas of seating were required: one for relaxing and one for dining and entertaining.

Retaining the existing change of level, the garden is divided into two parts. A decked area leads directly out from the house. The decking is set widthways to increase the impression of size. Each boundary is planted with tall standard trees to give height. Between each tree, a mirror on the wall gives an illusion of space.

At the higher level, a sitting area is furnished with two built-in benches, each with a pergola over the top for climbers. At the back, a large, freestanding wall of decorative blocks can be lit at night by candles set into the pattern created by the blocks.

above A key feature of this garden was the decorative block wall, shown here with one of the seating areas and pergolas.

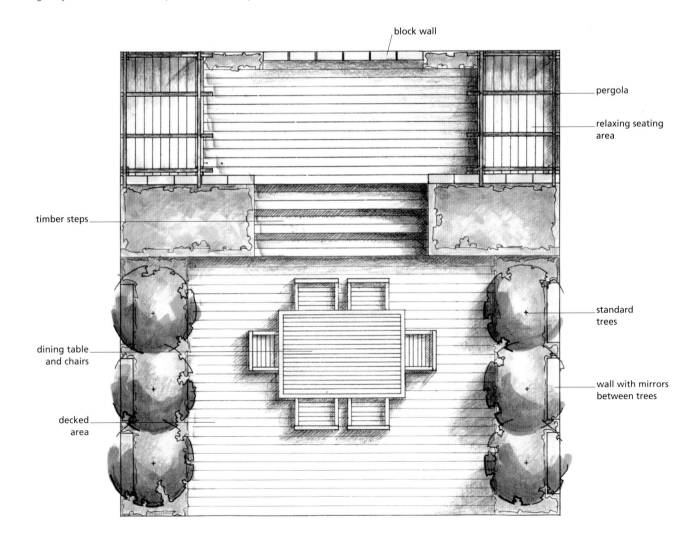

block wall

pergola

relaxing seating area

timber steps

standard trees

dining table and chairs

wall with mirrors between trees

decked area

Oriental Feel

FISHER TOMLIN

DIMENSIONS 16 x 7.3m (53 x 23ft) and 20 x 5.5m (60 x 17ft)
SOIL slightly sandy, well draining
ASPECT north and east facing
KEY FEATURES Japanese detailing

Having just returned from Japan, the owners were keen to bring a sense of oriental design into this garden. The two areas form a side access pathway and, at the back of the house, a long, narrow garden for sitting out and entertaining.

The first garden is primarily for walking through on large, rounded, flat stepping stones. To one side is a small woodland stream that needed to be fenced off from children. Gates using authentic Japanese detailing are set at each end of the path and

woodland planting is included to either side. To manage the level change with the house, a raised bed was built of wood, again in keeping with the theme. At the end of the path and through the second gateway, a small play area is paved in granite setts and a bench is incorporated into the retaining wall for the comfort of adults supervising children.

Steps built of bricks to match the house, inset with granite setts, lead up to the main part of the garden. Here a granite sett path leads through gravel planted with bamboos, specimen maples, and witch hazels. A cloud tree (*Ilex crenata*) is set at the focal point of this space. A long, low, oak bench provides seating, and standing posts of green oak with black walnut inlays mark the ends of the path.

Garden for walking through

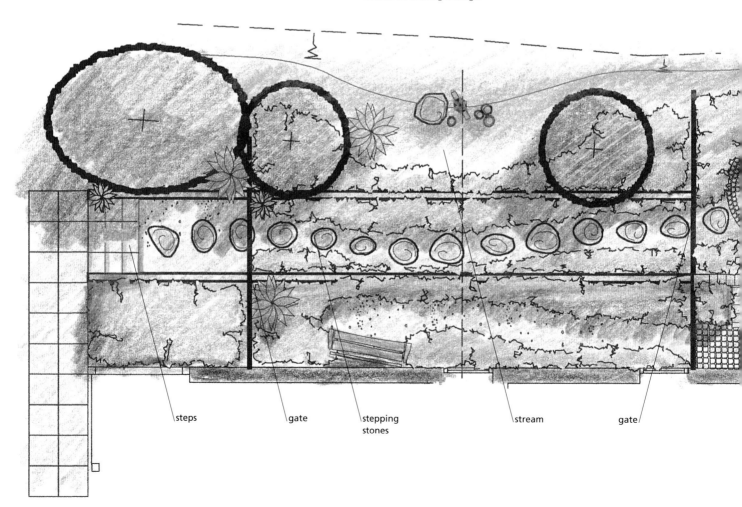

steps   gate   stepping   stream   gate
                             stones

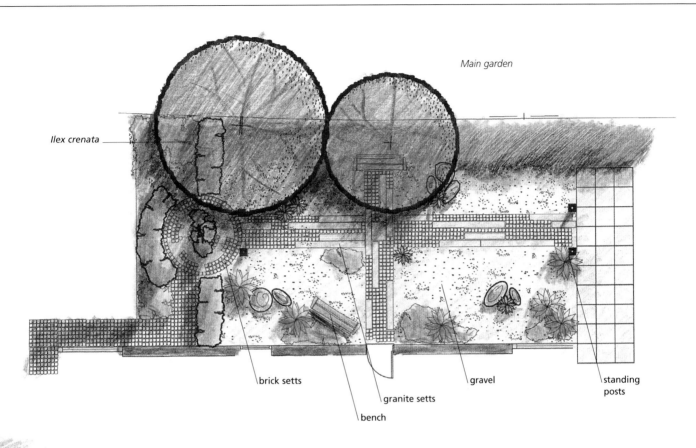

Main garden

Ilex crenata

brick setts

granite setts

bench

gravel

standing posts

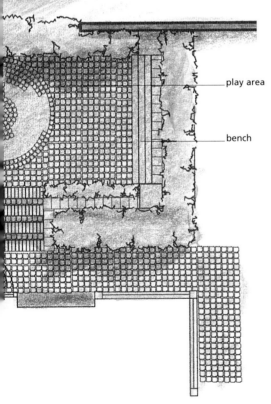

play area

bench

above *The oriential design for this garden included the large stepping stones in the "walk-through" area.*

Curves and Circles

DOUGLAS COLTART – VIRIDARIUM DESIGN STUDIO

DIMENSIONS 10.5 x 11m (35 x 36ft)

SOIL loam

ASPECT north-west facing

KEY FEATURES millstone bubble fountain

right The blue oat grass Helictotrichon sempervirens is an evergreen perennial – the designer used the graceful curves of grasses such as this to distract from the shape of the garden boundaries.

The owners of this garden wanted to transform a very awkwardly shaped, small space into an interesting and restful area for entertaining. Apart from the paving near to the house, curves and circles are used in the design to distract from the shape of the garden's boundaries.

A curving path leads across the lawn to the circular, paved patio area. The narrowing of the path helps to give the impression that the garden is larger than it actually is. On the patio, there is a small, millstone bubble fountain surrounded by pebbles to enliven the garden with the sound and sight of water. A timber bench gives a focal point to this part of the space. An area of curved, timber decking gives movement and has a *Prunus serrula* growing through it. There are a number of pots on the decking to allow seasonal planting to be incorporated.

In the most awkward part of the garden, around the paved terrace, an area of gravel, rocks, and pebbles is planted with grasses *Festuca glauca, Helictotrichon sempervirens,* and *Pennisetum alopecuroides, Hostas* 'Halcyon' and 'Frances Williams', and alpines. The garden also contains a multi-stemmed *Betula utilis* var. *jacquemontii* to provide height and for its white stems.

right The perspective shows the garden space in its wider context, in which the curved shapes and forms hold the attention.

Douglas Coltart

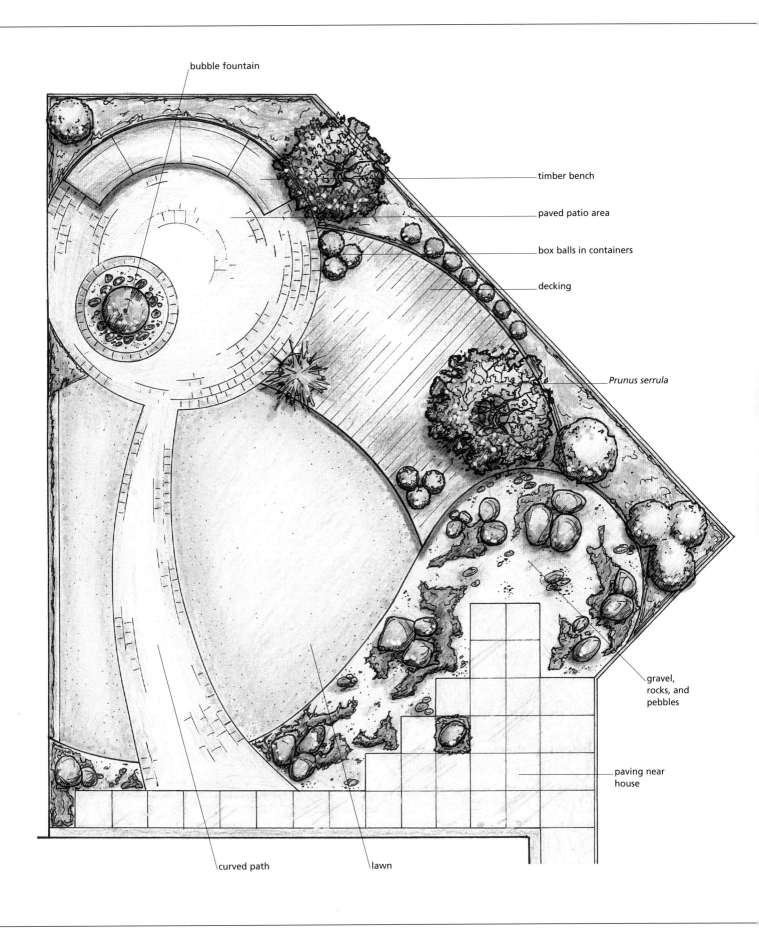

bubble fountain

timber bench

paved patio area

box balls in containers

decking

Prunus serrula

gravel,
rocks, and
pebbles

paving near
house

curved path

lawn

Tree House in an Old Yew

ANDREW WILSON ASSOCIATES

DIMENSIONS 22 x 15m (70 x 50ft) maximum

SOIL shallow over chalk

ASPECT south facing

KEY FEATURES level change and listed yew tree

This south-facing garden forms an "L" shape wrapping around the rear of the house. The brief asked for a family garden providing play opportunities for young children. The main issue was a 1m- (3ft-) high level change rising immediately at the back door, making access into the garden awkward access and creating a tight, unusable space along the rear of the house. A listed yew tree standing close to the wall created difficulties with excavation.

Initially, the wall was excavated to produce a 1m- (3ft-) wide pathway along the rear elevation. This opens out into "L"-shaped brick steps that give easier access to the main garden. The paving of the main terrace is in York stone with brick strips crossing the garden to emphasize the width of the space and to tie the paving into the wall and to the house itself.

The tight space alongside the house and close to the road is used for a children's swing and a raised deck was constructed as a free-standing "tree house" around the yew tree. Elsewhere, lawn and cottage planting is introduced to complement the architecture of the house. An informal, stone pathway runs through the lawn to the gate, which provides the main access to the house.

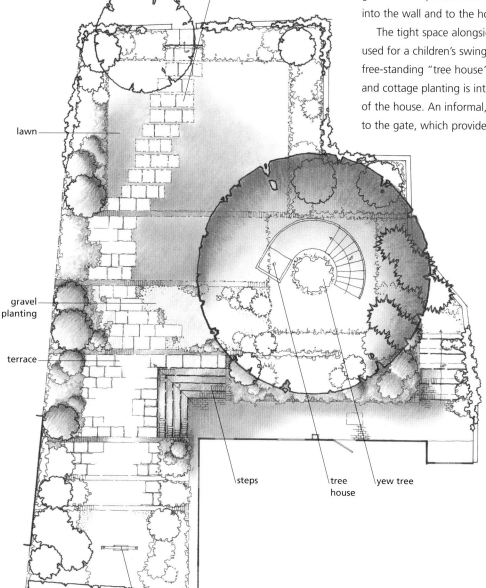

stepping stone path

lawn

gravel planting

terrace

steps

tree house

yew tree

swing

above *Bronze fennel was one of the herbs used within the loose gravel garden planting close to the main terrace.*

Offset Angles

NIGEL FULLER

DIMENSIONS 9 x 7m (30 x 23ft)

SOIL neutral

ASPECT south facing

KEY FEATURES paved circle and a gravel garden

The awkward shape and complex levels in this garden provided a challenge to the designer. An existing swimming pool was to be removed, which allowed clearing and opening up of the space without concern about disposal costs.

Attached to the house, an angled pergola gives shade and sets up the angles for the rest of the garden. Paving on this first level is of square, cut stone inlaid with panels of brick in soldier pattern. Trellis on a retaining wall obscures much of the garden at first sight. Steps lead up to a circular sitting area with a pergola over it for shade and height interest. A curved pool, fed by a waterspout, cuts in to the terrace, giving the sight and sound of water in the garden. From the terrace, stepping stones cross the pool and lead to a secluded gravel garden. Within the gravel, paving stones lead to a bench set against a wall to catch the evening sun. Relaxed planting in the gravel gives a soft feel to this part of the garden. On the opposite side of the garden, a small shed is incorporated into the design but well hidden by the angles used.

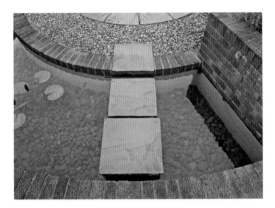

above *Replacing a swimming pool as a water feature, this curved pool fed by a waterspout cuts into the terrace.*

above *The elevation shows the view up into the higher level and pergola as seen from the house.*

pool with stepping stones

bench

paving stones

steps

paved first level

angled pergola

house

circular gravel garden

pergola

Tiny Courtyard with Glass Butterflies

ALEX JOHNSON LANDSCAPE DESIGN

DIMENSIONS 3.8 x 3.4m (12 x 11ft)
SOIL imported alkaline loam
ASPECT south-west facing
KEY FEATURES slate shelf water feature

The view from the kitchen window of this property was important to the clients, as was the opportunity to use this tiny courtyard space as much as possible. Water, seating, lighting, and a space for bins were among their main requirements. The owners were looking especially for frivolity and surprises.

The main focus of the courtyard is the slate shelf waterfall that provides strong visual and aural impact and is visible through the kitchen window. Built-in seating is arranged around the boundaries using timber lengths and incorporating glow lighting to illuminate the garden gently at night. Under one of the seats, a bin store has been constructed. Planting is predominantly on the walls (*Clematis flammula*) and in bottomless planters in the corners of the garden. Paving is in slate for simplicity and unity.

For colour and decoration, the entry gate has a stained-glass "port hole"; the glass is used again for a table. Glass butterflies and dragonflies hang from the wall near the waterfall to bring the sky into the garden. Originally, a glass owl was considered because the house is a converted barn but this proved too heavy to use so the plan was revised to incoporate lighter decorations.

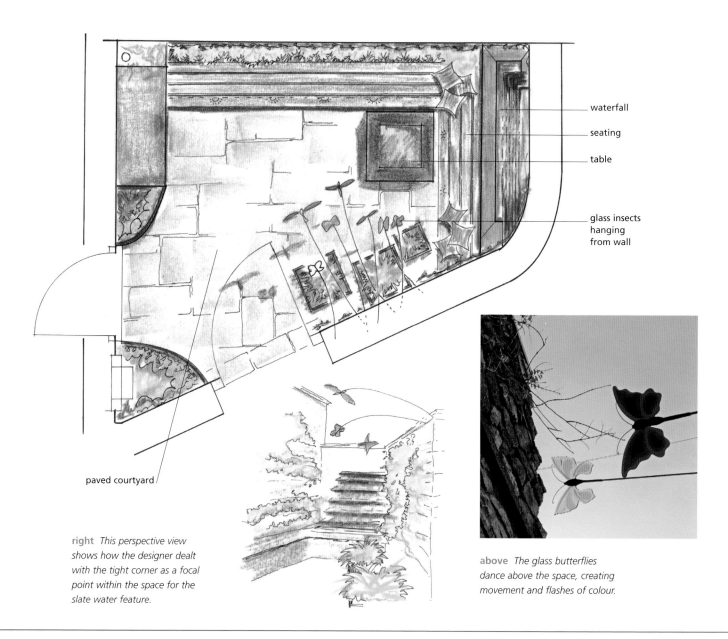

waterfall

seating

table

glass insects hanging from wall

paved courtyard

right *This perspective view shows how the designer dealt with the tight corner as a focal point within the space for the slate water feature.*

above *The glass butterflies dance above the space, creating movement and flashes of colour.*

Light and Shade

ARABELLA LENNOX-BOYD

DIMENSIONS 330 sq m (3,530 sq ft)

SOIL neutral

ASPECT east facing

KEY FEATURES informal circuit, seat around horse chestnut

This garden is characterized by the deep summer shade cast by a huge horse chestnut. The owner wanted an informal yet sophisticated garden with a sense of enclosure and privacy. The garden also needed to offer a place for children to play.

The design is influenced by the idea of a woodland glade with pools of light emerging at the outer edges of deep shade, and the need to soften hard lines within the space. A loose circuit around the garden of York stone paving links the house with a rustic pavilion, a rose arch with a seat, and a brick terrace beside the house. This returns finally to a formal lawn outside the garden room of the house. A woven willow tree seat surrounds the horse chestnut. The "living" areas of the garden are situated in the sun and complex and varied planting gives each area its character. As the light and shade within the garden varies according to the tree canopy and the seasons, different key plants perform, providing constant variety. All the plants are soft so that the children can hide among them, and many grasses have been used to give a gentle, informal, country feel.

Natural materials have been used for the key elements: trellises are of natural oak, the willow seat under the tree, and the pavilion, helping to provide a "country" style for the garden.

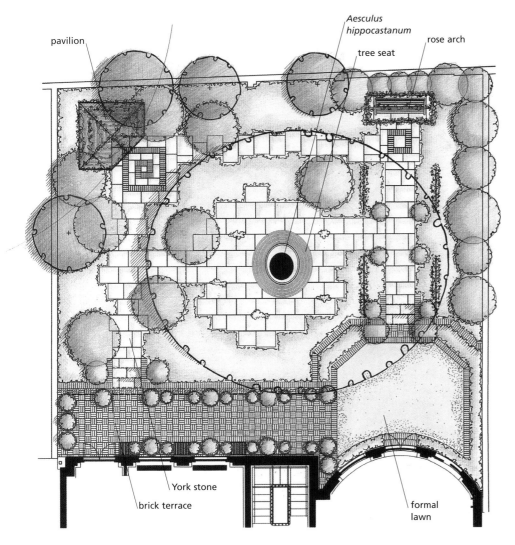

above *Mature horse chestnuts (Aesculus hippocastanum), such as the one growing in this garden, can grow to approximately 25m (80ft) high. These horse chestnuts are shown in flower.*

Dealing with Changes in Levels

BARNES WALKER LTD

DIMENSIONS 9 x 12.5m (30 X 42FT)

SOIL sandy loam

ASPECT north-west facing

KEY FEATURES decking

This site, on the edge of a steep hillside, needed level areas to be constructed to make the garden usable. A garden with year-round interest and easy maintenance was requested.

In the higher part of the garden, near to the house, a small area of lawn is bordered by stone paving and planted borders. Architectural shrubs are combined with thrusting spikes and fronds alongside feathery grasses and outrageously vibrant colours to contrast the backdrop of natural materials. From the house, a low box hedge at the end of the lawn focuses the eye to the far decked area and the view.

Farther away from the house, where the levels drop away, a timber deck is built out to extend the size of the garden at the upper level and a dining space has views out over the countryside. In the west corner of the garden, steps lead down to a lower deck and a storage area under the higher decked area. Tree ferns and cordylines in pots emphasize the textural planting.

above The photograph shows the higher part of this garden with a small lawn, planted borders, and a decked seating area.

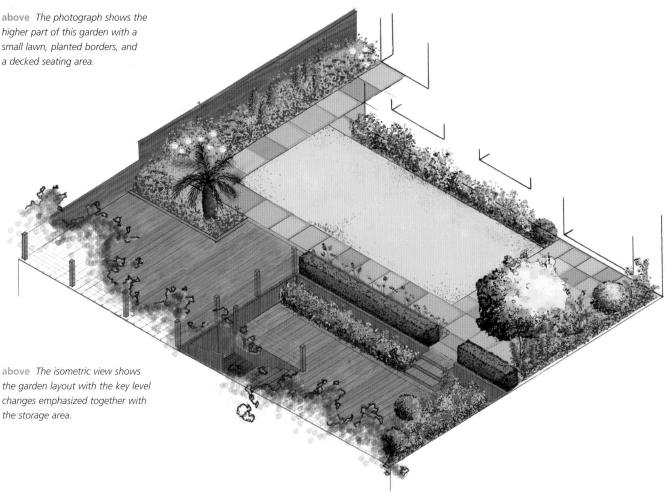

above The isometric view shows the garden layout with the key level changes emphasized together with the storage area.

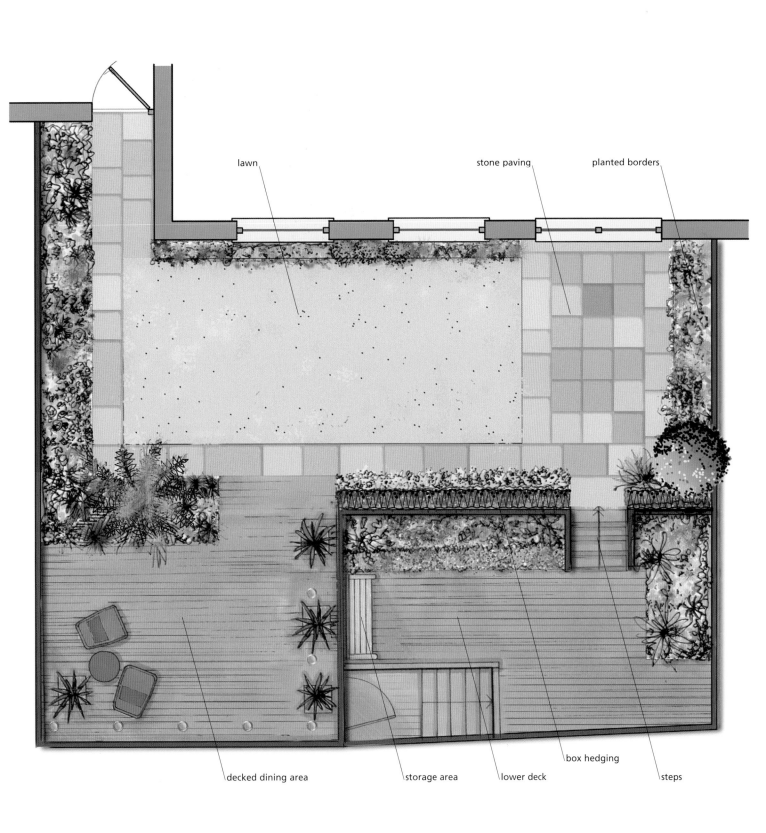

lawn

stone paving

planted borders

decked dining area

storage area

lower deck

box hedging

steps

Long, Thin Garden

GAVIN McWILLIAM – BEDROCK LTD

DIMENSIONS 25 x 2.75m (80 x 9ft)

SOIL neutral, improved with organic compost

ASPECT north-east facing

KEY FEATURES serpentine pathway of Cotswold stone

The site was very overgrown with vigorous weeds and self-seeded sycamores. Everything was removed, with the exception of a ceanothus that was retained to give the design an immediate sense of establishment while also acting as a divider between the two sections of garden. The main design constraint was obviously the extreme length of the garden in relation to its width.

The resulting design solution is a pathway of Cotswold stone meandering down the length of the garden, widening out in parts and then constricting again, giving a sense of movement. Circles of cropped granite setts are interspersed in the stone, adding interest to what would otherwise be a large area of the same colour and texture of paving. At the far end of the garden, the largest circle forms a place to rest and catch any available sun.

Planting is predominantly of grasses and bamboos used for their acoustic properties and movement; perennials are chosen for fragrance, foliage, and colour, using a palette of blues and purples. Along the length of the garden, the fencing is painted in cream to reflect all available light into the space and to unify it. Climbers are trained onto tensioned wires against the fence.

above *A pathway of Cotswold stone, inset with circles of cropped granite setts, meanders down the length of this garden.*

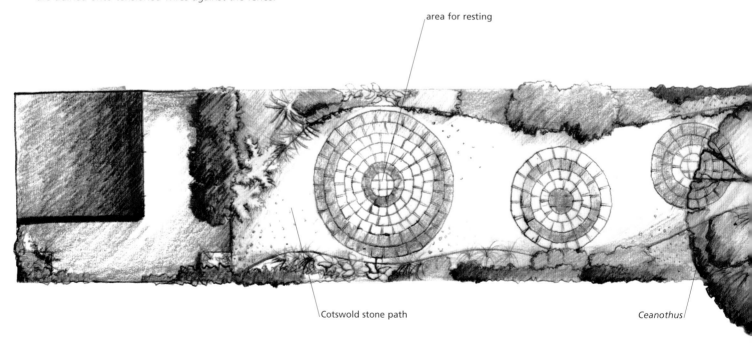

area for resting

Cotswold stone path

Ceanothus

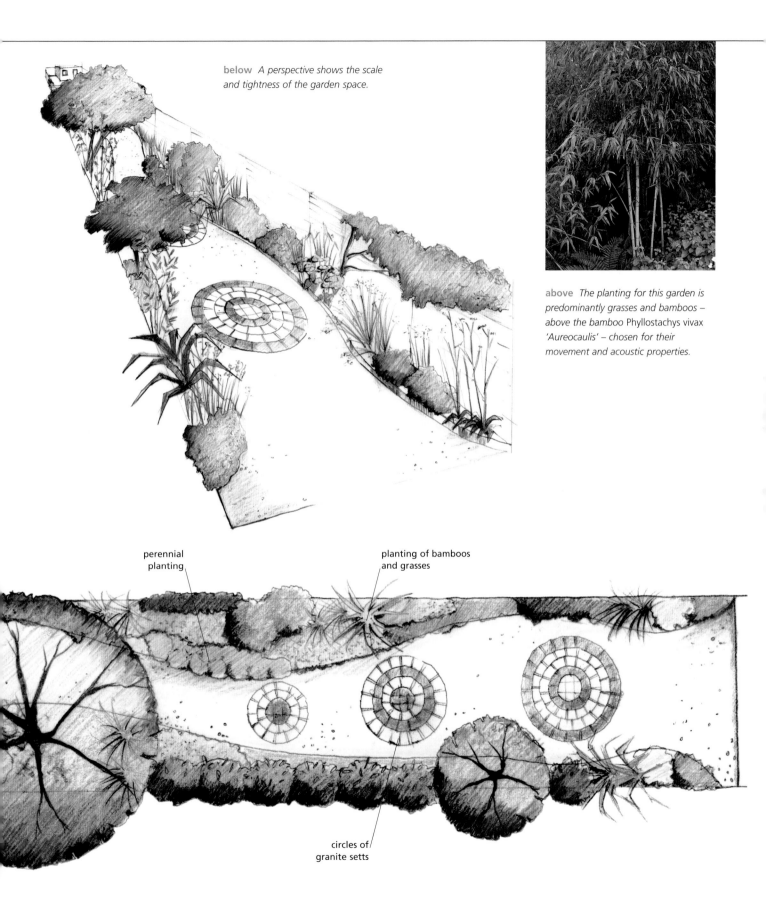

below *A perspective shows the scale and tightness of the garden space.*

above *The planting for this garden is predominantly grasses and bamboos – above the bamboo* Phyllostachys vivax *'Aureocaulis' – chosen for their movement and acoustic properties.*

perennial planting

planting of bamboos and grasses

circles of granite setts

Contemporary and Stylish Basement

DANIEL McCARTHY – WOODHAMS LANDSCAPES

DIMENSIONS 16 x 5m (53 x 16ft)

SOIL clay loam

ASPECT south-east facing

KEY FEATURES dry-stone columns

This awkward space, surrounded by high walls, presented a challenge to the designer. The brief was to create a classical contemporary garden space that was cohesive with the interior decoration. Seating was required and exterior heaters were needed to extend the season of garden usage.

Scale and proportion are important elements in balancing the design. This is achieved using tall, slender, dry-stone columns to create a dramatic feature in the garden. A stylized water feature is located between one dry-stone column and a block-work rendered plinth to create a focal point visible from the front door of the house. When fully grown climbers clothe the walls around the plinths, they will bring a private and secluded feel to the space.

Planting is in raised beds with olive trees used as specimens and grouped together to form a screen. Other plants are chosen to complement the texture and colour of the olive trees and include *Magnolia grandiflora*, evergreen clematis, and mixed herbs. Paving is enhanced by the inclusion of a stone insert into the diagonal slab pattern, leading the eye across the space. Steps lead up to a simple decked sitting area, where the most can be made of the sun.

above *Clematis cirrhosa, one of the few evergreen clematis, has cream flowers early in the year but year-round slightly bronze-green leaves.*

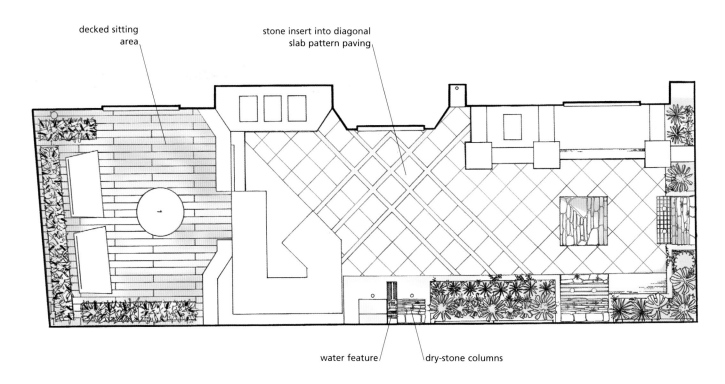

decked sitting area

stone insert into diagonal slab pattern paving

water feature

dry-stone columns

Streamside Sitting

CHRISTOPHER MAGUIRE

DIMENSIONS 150sq m (1,600sq ft)

SOIL neutral to alkaline

ASPECT south facing

KEY FEATURES deck out over the river bank

This is an awkward site with a small river running down one boundary and an irregularly shaped garden in the other dimensions. The owners wanted to remove old, uninteresting features, enlarge the sitting area, and make the most of the potential. The river is very small and has steep banks but provides sparkle and a wildlife habitat. Safety for small children was paramount and permission from the UK's Environment Agency was needed for anything that might affect the stream.

The main solution was to construct a large, square deck cantilevered at one corner over the river bank. Fixed seating along two sides of the deck performs the function of a traditional ship's bridge, giving views along the water in both directions. The seats also form part of the river's edge fencing for safety. The terrace in the garden was enlarged and two pergolas, one either side of the terrace, provide screening from neighbours and effect a transition from the new garden to the other parts of the garden. Planting gives shape to the rest of the area. A *Gleditsia triacanthos* 'Sunburst' gives height and colour in the summer, and other shrubs are architectural and chosen to give colour and texture.

above *Height and colour during the summer is provided by the deciduous honey locust tree Gleditsia triacanthos.*

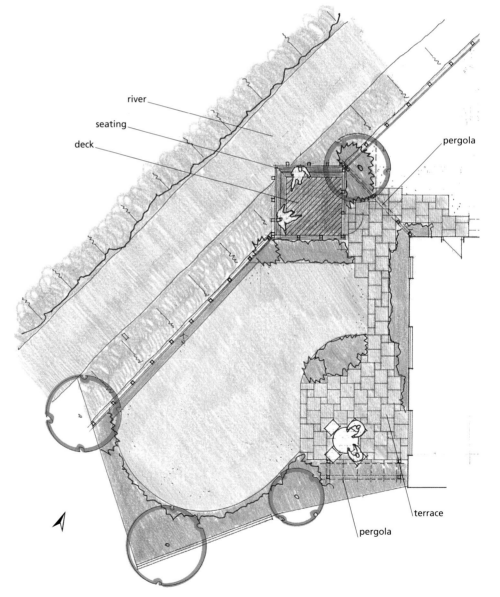

Two Terrace Areas

CHARLOTTE ROWE

DIMENSIONS 12 x 5m (40 x 16ft)
SOIL clay
ASPECT south-west facing
KEY FEATURES limestone stepping-stone water feature

Renovation of the owners' house using limestone, simple white walls, and hardwood finishes provided the inspiration for this garden. The existing space was overgrown and claustrophobic-feeling, with the upper level very close to the house. The owners didn't have time for maintenance and wanted planting with a light, Mediterranean feel to reflect their own backgrounds.

The upper level of the garden was pushed back to create two good-sized, spacious terrace areas. Paving is in Portuguese limestone and the walls are lime-washed and topped by simple bespoke trellis. The central focus of the garden is a limestone stepping-stone water feature filled with black pebbles and fed by a simple copper water spout. To complement this, a narrow planted "rill" of polished pebbles and *Soleirolia soleirolii* runs through the garden. Limestone steps lead to the higher level, where a hardwood bench is set against the wall to catch the sun.

The planting is a simple combination of shrubs and perennials using a green, blue, and white palette. Mediterranean specimens include clear-stemmed olive trees, rosemary, and lavender. Structure is provided using clipped *Prunus lusitanica* and *Cornus alba L.* with additional colour from *Geranium* 'Johnson's Blue' and *Allium sphaerocephalon*.

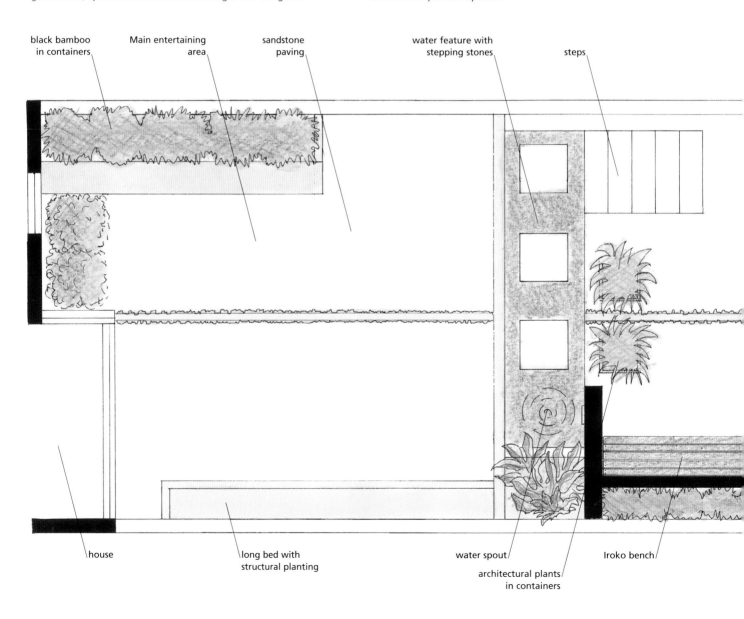

black bamboo in containers

Main entertaining area

sandstone paving

water feature with stepping stones

steps

house

long bed with structural planting

water spout

architectural plants in containers

Iroko bench

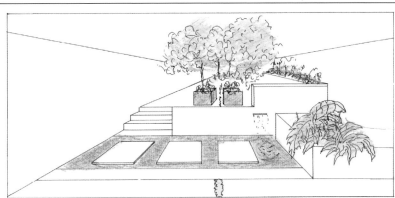

right The perspective view concentrates on the change of level and the pool as the central features of the garden.

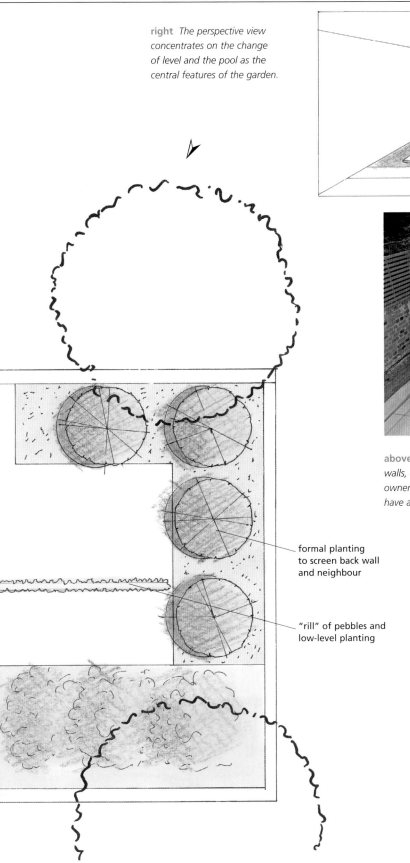

formal planting
to screen back wall
and neighbour

"rill" of pebbles and
low-level planting

above The limestone paving, white walls, and simple planting fulfil the owner's request for this garden to have a light, Mediterranean feel.

below The limestone stepping stone stone water feature is particularly effective when lit up at night.

New Courtyard

CHRISTOPHER MAGUIRE

DIMENSIONS 300sq m (3,210sq ft)

SOIL neutral

ASPECT south facing

KEY FEATURES new courtyard for sitting near the house

above *Fencing, walls, and climbers effectively divide this courtyard garden from the parking space nearby.*

A radical change was requested by these owners. The front door to their house was dominated by a large area of gravel and a few paving slabs near. Drivers were unsure where to park their cars and the overall appearance was unwelcoming. In addition, the main garden was some distance from the house and there was no sunny area for sitting out close to the house.

To separate the cars from the approach to the house, a courtyard garden with 2.2m- (7ft-) high brick walls has been created. It has a southerly aspect and the walls produce a private, secluded space perfect for dining or sitting out. The newly created garden includes a paved terrace, and gravel and planting. Climbers (*Clematis armandii, Rosa* 'Madame Alfred Carrière', and *Solanum crispum* 'Glasnevin') clothe the walls and sun-loving shrubs (*Artemisia* 'Powis Castle', *Cytisus battandieri,* and *Hibiscus syriacus*) and perennials (sisyrinchium, stachys, and hostas) colonize the beds and gravel area. Entrance to the walled garden is under a large pergola spanning a gap in the enclosing wall and the brick wall is curved to reflect the sweep of cars into their new parking space.

parking area

pergola

gravel and planting

York stone terrace

existing gravel

brick wall

"Moon Gate" Garden

DAVID STEVENS

DIMENSIONS 16 x 4.5m (53 x 14ft)

SOIL slightly acid

ASPECT north facing

KEY FEATURES "moon gate" and stainless-steel waterwall

For this tiny, walled courtyard fronting a fine Victorian villa, the brief was for an unashamedly modern composition that would act as a foil to the older house and offer room for dining and sitting.

An old conservatory that linked the pedestrian gate to the front door was demolished, and this allowed the space to be opened up so that the whole garden could work as a single entity. To the right of the front door, the slight change of level suggested a step up to the main dining area and here the whole angle of paving is changed to set up a striking positive dynamic of its own. Bands of dark, slate paving contrast with courses of pale, pre-cast concrete, the slate forming the step, with a single band perpendicular to this thrusting across the path to the front door.

To the left, a further step drops down to the quiet sitting area, paved with randomly sized sawn York stone for a more relaxed feel. Here there are two facing seats, accessed by passing through a contemporary "moon gate" made of galvanized mesh, and a stainless-steel water wall that acts as a stunning focal point.

above *The elevation of the "moon gate" shows how it divides the garden spaces while providing emphasis to the view.*

left *Bands of dark slate paving, similar to that shown here, were contrasted with courses of pale pre-cast concrete.*

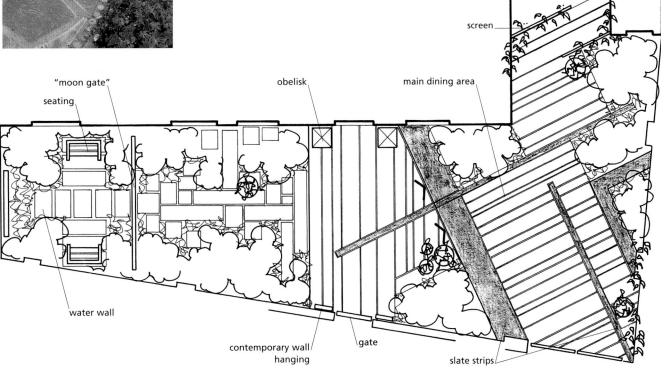

seating

"moon gate"

obelisk

main dining area

screen

water wall

contemporary wall hanging

gate

slate strips

Enclosed Seating Area

SARAH EBERLE – HILLIER LANDSCAPES / ANDREW HERRING – HERRING HOMES

DIMENSIONS 35 x 22m (116 x 70ft) tapering to 4m (13ft) at the end of the garden

SOIL neutral

ASPECT west facing

KEY FEATURES sculpted earthworks

above The space on one side of the house is planted with drifts of groundcover echoing the character of the surrounding countryside.

This property is on the edge of farmland and the owners wanted their garden to reflect the character of that location. They wished to maximize the awkward shape of the space and minimize the impact of an existing golden coniferous hedge along the north boundary.

In order to disguise the pinched shape to the best advantage, an enclosed sitting area is placed in front of the house, sheltered by a tapering, curved wall. It is planted inside with *Miscanthus sinensis 'Gracillimus',* allowing only limited views down the garden and access to the rest of the garden to the south. To increase the sense of enclosure in this terrace area, a multi-stemmed birch (*Betula*) is planted in this entrance. To lessen the dominance of the conifer hedge while increasing the sense of depth in the garden, sinuously moulded banks on both boundaries are incorporated. To increase movement and unity between the mown grass walk and the banks, a prairie-style planting is used. *Deschampsia* 'Bronzeschleier' forms the base planting with *Aquilegia vulgaris* 'Woodside Blue' and *Astrantia major* for spring interest, and *Rudbeckia fulgida* var. *sullivantii* 'Goldsturm' and *Aster* x *frickartii* 'Mönch' for late-season interest.

The small space to the south of the house is planted with drifts of groundcover among strategically placed boulders. Planting includes *Liriope muscari* 'Monroe White', *Dryopteris affinis* 'Cristata', and *Bergenia* 'Silberlicht'. A Japanese maple provides height and contrast.

right Above the enclosed seating area on the terrace in front of the house are plantings of the grass Miscanthus sinensis 'Gracillimus'.

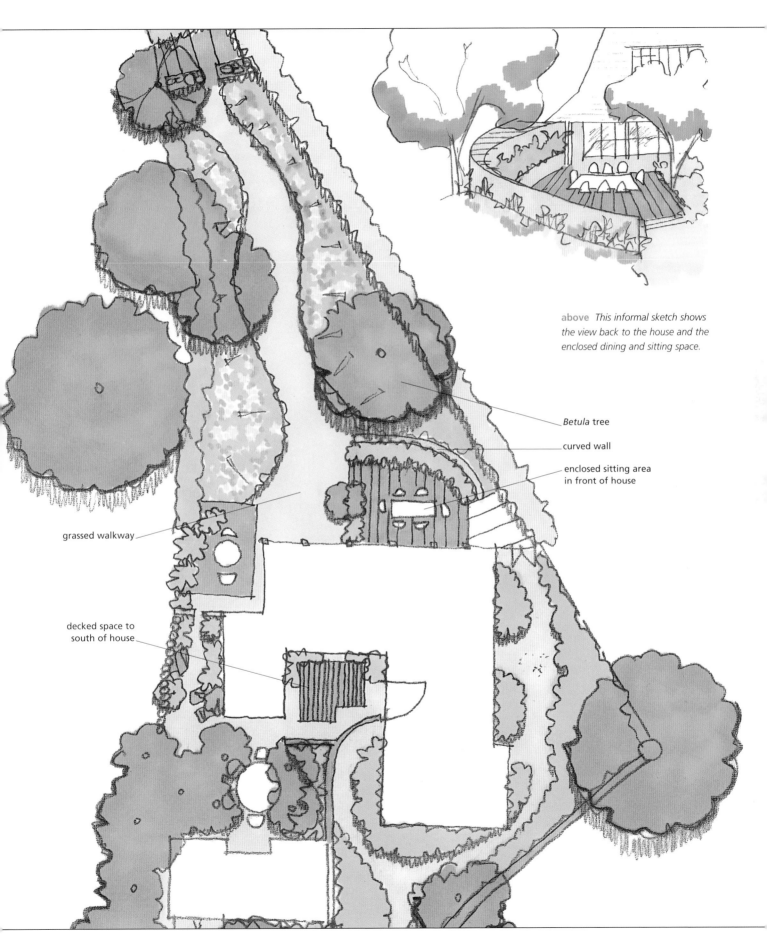

above *This informal sketch shows the view back to the house and the enclosed dining and sitting space.*

Betula tree

curved wall

enclosed sitting area
in front of house

grassed walkway

decked space to
south of house

Basalt Courtyard

JAMES LEE

DIMENSIONS 5.8 x 5m (18 x 16ft) with 2m (6ft) change in levels

SOIL clay

ASPECT north-east facing

KEY FEATURES contemporary trellis, basalt, and a glass screen

The brief was to create useable space from a very uninviting, dark, and grimy space. Access into the garden from the basement level of the house was difficult, involving climbing narrow steps with small treads. The garden also needed to be contemporary, to reflect the interior style of the house, and be child friendly. Building regulations needed to be complied with in relation to a barrier between the upper and lower levels of the garden.

A stylized, horizontal trellis of western red cedar contains the space and provides privacy. Cedar is also used for the decking steps leading out from the house at ground level. The main paving is in Italian basalt, which is also used to form a table and for treads on the steps up from the basement. The restrained use of materials helps to unify the garden and makes it restful to the eye.

The glass screen that acts as a safety boundary between the upper and lower levels is set at 1.1m (3ft) from ground level in the upper garden; it continues on the same horizontal plane all around the edge, meaning that it rises 3.2m (10ft) above the lower level and thus creates a feature of this detail.

Planting is restricted to four species only: *Phyllostachys nigra, Ophiopogon planiscapus,* and *Soleirolia soleirolii,* planted in the strip across the basalt paving, and *Muehlenbeckia complexa.*

above *An overview of this contemporary garden showing the strip of the perennial* Soleirolia soleirolii *running across the basalt paving.*

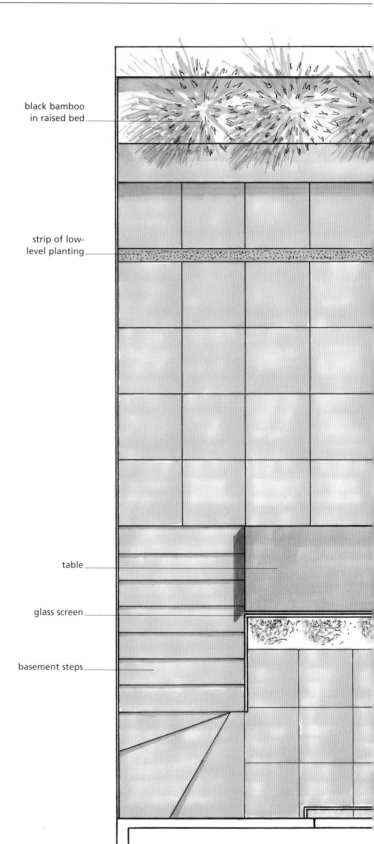

black bamboo in raised bed

strip of low-level planting

table

glass screen

basement steps

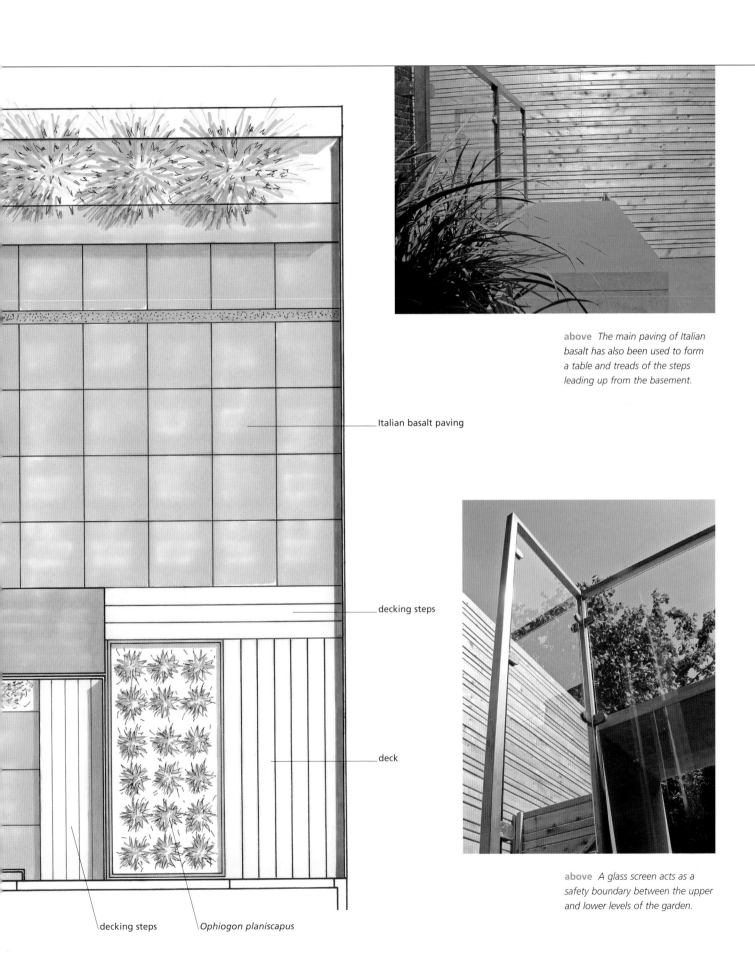

above *The main paving of Italian basalt has also been used to form a table and treads of the steps leading up from the basement.*

Italian basalt paving

decking steps

deck

decking steps   *Ophiogon planiscapus*

above *A glass screen acts as a safety boundary between the upper and lower levels of the garden.*

Sunken Parterre

NAILA GREEN GARDEN DESIGN

DIMENSIONS 10 x 20m (33 x 60ft)

SOIL heavy clay shale

ASPECT west-facing

KEY FEATURES strong "S"-shaped spine of yew

This small and extremely challenging site was the garden to a new house, with a slope from the house down to the north-west boundary of 1:4. The owners were moving from a much larger, traditional garden and were looking for a more easily managed space for pottering about. The new garden was often to be viewed from an upstairs balcony.

To resolve the slope, four new terraces were constructed, linked and separated by a strong "S"-shaped spine of yew hedging running right across the plot. From a small deck, the terraces change shape from rectangles to a sweeping curve. From the top terrace, a custom-made water feature with three glass dishes feeds water into a three-quarter-circle pool on the level below, forming the centrepiece of the garden. A curved lawn and paved sitting area are contained by a curve of yew hedging against which borders of herbaceous perennials, bulbs, ferns, and grasses sit.

Steps lead down from the curved lawn to the lowest level of the garden, where a woodland walk leads through an informal grove of trees and underplanting of ferns and other shade-loving plants to a secret, sunken parterre, again surrounded by yew hedging and with a small wrought-iron pavilion for sitting.

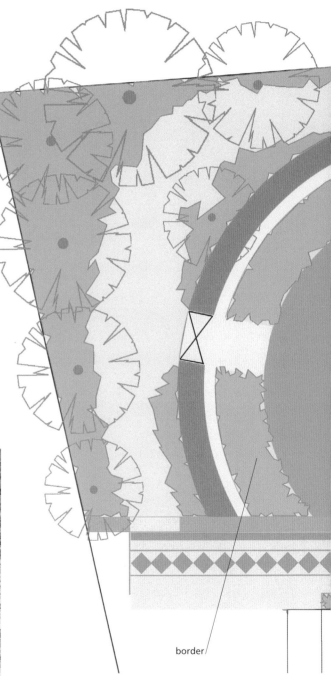

border

left The main feature of the lowest level of the garden is a sunken parterre surrounded by yew hedging.

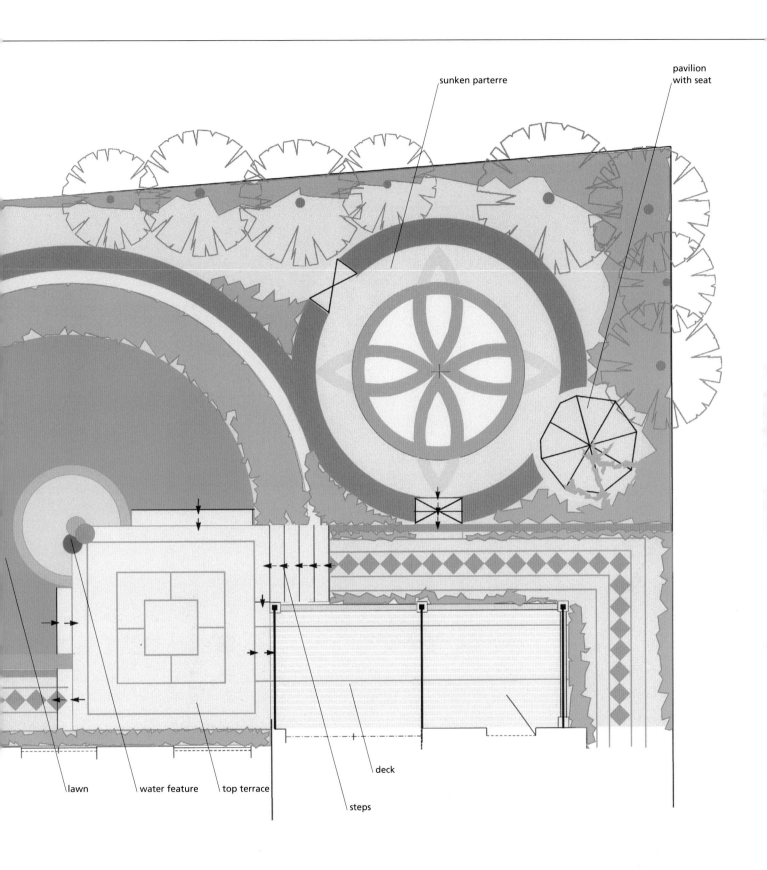

sunken parterre

pavilion
with seat

lawn   water feature   top terrace

deck

steps

Triangles and Curves

DANIEL LOBB

DIMENSIONS 22 x 22m (70 x 70ft) at the longest boundaries

SOIL chalk

ASPECT south facing

KEY FEATURES sweeping curves and water rill

As a corner triangular site with a level difference of about 1.2m (4ft) between different areas, this garden presented a large number of challenges to the designer. The owners wanted a choice of sitting areas, a secure play space for young children, and privacy from the overlooking pavement and neighbouring houses.

The design solution lay in creating arcs that radiate from a single point. This unifies the space and means that the awkward corners can be used for planting. Several of the other issues are resolved by re-contouring the ground. By carving a level sitting area along the west wall of the house and moving the resulting soil into a more gradual rise as a planting bed towards the north-western corner of the garden, privacy is increased. A sitting area emerges and the balance of the spoil is used to fill in a hollow in the front garden and to build up a level lawn at the back of the house. The higher bed is then planted with three *Betula utilis* var. jacquemontii in front of a new yew (*Taxus baccata*) hedge for contrast of the trunks against the dark green hedge.

A pergola links the side and rear gardens and gives a sitting area for supervision of children in either space as well as privacy from overlooking neighbours. A small, stepped water rill runs through planting, making the most of the slope.

above *The perspective shows the main terrace and the way in which the garden wraps around the house.*

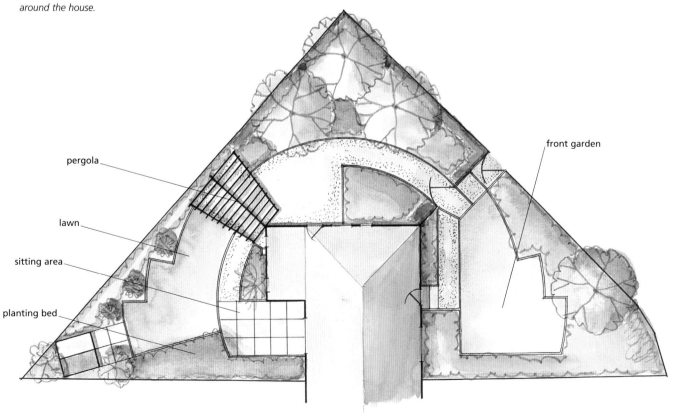

pergola

lawn

sitting area

planting bed

front garden

Inspired by Ammonites

SALLY COURT – COURTYARD GARDEN DESIGN

DIMENSIONS 15 x 7.5m (50 x 25ft) at the widest point

SOIL neutral

ASPECT south-east facing

KEY FEATURES stone path to form an ammonite shape

The owner had a collection of ammonites and this, together with two large trees that had to remain, formed the inspiration for the garden design. The site was to be "artistic" and textural with splashes of colour.

The predominant feature garden is a curving pathway of slate and Indian sandstone set on edge. This pathway borders a terraced area just outside the house laid in random, rectangular pattern of black Indian sand stone, and then continues into an ammonite shape around the existing hornbeam, graded in size so that the path appears to wrap around the tree.

Planting is in drifts and is mainly of grasses, including *Imperata cylindrica* 'Rubra', *Calamagrostis* x *acutiflora* 'Karl Foerster' (Feather reed grass), *Pennisetum alopecuroides* 'Hameln' (Chinese Fountain grass), and *Miscanthus sinensis* 'Kleine Silberspinne', with *Ophiopogon planscapus* 'Nigrescens' planted in drifts through the other grasses.

At the end of the garden, the other existing tree is a robinia. Drifts of *Liriope muscari* and *Eupatorium purpureum* (Joe Pye Weed) are planted to lead the eye down to this focal point.

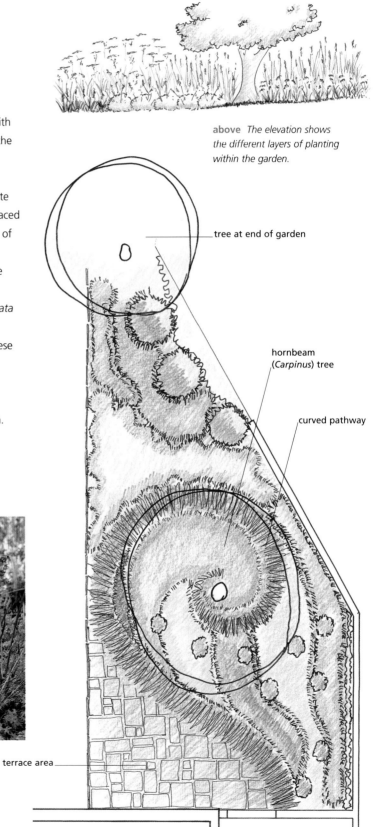

above *The elevation shows the different layers of planting within the garden.*

tree at end of garden

hornbeam (*Carpinus*) tree

curved pathway

terrace area

above *The verticals of* Imperata cylindrica *'Rubra' provide drama and colour change as the season progresses.*

Georgian Façade

XA TOLLEMACHE LANDSCAPE AND GARDEN DESIGN

DIMENSIONS 11 x 11m (36 x 36ft) and 8 x 4.5m (25 x 15ft)

SOIL neutral

ASPECT south and west facing

KEY FEATURES lavender edging and formality

The brief was to lead the visitor through a densely planted garden around the side of the house to arrive at the pleasing Georgian façade, distracting the eye from the front of the house, where a door is the focal point. The west-facing side of the garden overlooks a lawn, which was required for a children's play area, but with generous borders wrapping around it.

At the entrance to the densely planted path, a brick pathway, punctuated by brick circles and edged in lavender, leads towards the lawn and a focal planting of an acacia tree. The beds are planted with groups of clipped box balls for structure and the planting is predominantly in grey, green, creamy whites, and pink, moving through to dark reds, blues, and purples.

At the last circle on the brick path, the paving material changes to random York stone to match the terrace outside the Georgian façade. From this level, curving, stone steps lead down into the garden. Seats are placed at strategic areas and a focal point is placed in the planting bed on the east side of the garden to be viewed from the house.

above *A view of the densely planted garden at the side of the house. The path is punctuated by brick circles and edged in lavender.*

left *In this part of the garden stone steps lead from a brick path down onto a path of random York stone paving. Seats are placed at strategic points around the main garden.*

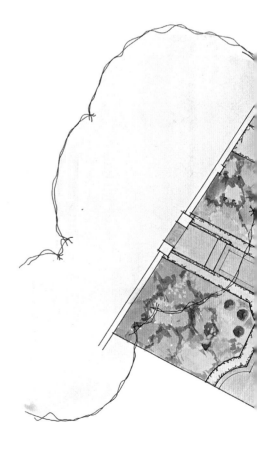

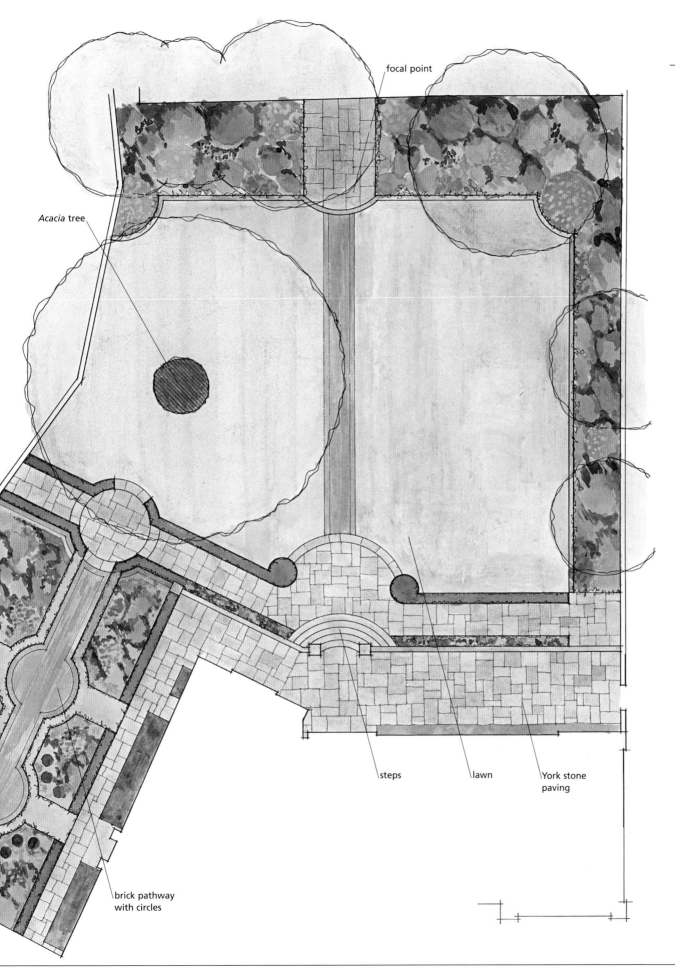

focal point

Acacia tree

brick pathway
with circles

steps

lawn

York stone
paving

Sunken Garden

JAN KING LANDSCAPE & GARDEN DESIGN

DIMENSIONS 20 x 5m (60 x 16ft) and 7 x 5m (23 x 16ft)

SOIL poor but friable loam

ASPECT north and west facing

KEY FEATURES sunny balcony and stainless-steel water feature

This sunken garden is reached by a flight of steps and is surrounded by very high brick walls. There is an architect-designed steel gantry already in place against the northern wall of the garden, reached by a spiral staircase. This area is sunny for most of the day. The garden leads directly off the owners' new kitchen and they were looking for an outdoor eating and entertaining space using complementary materials and unfussy contemporary planting.

Paving in the new garden is in green, Indian sandstone to match the colour of the flooring in the kitchen. Sawn squares 600 x 600mm (24 x 24in) give a crisp, minimalist appearance and are edged with smaller units of 100 x 100mm (4 x 4in). The slabs are laid at a 45-degree angle to unify the site by "flowing" the paving between the two arms of the garden. The lawn is edged in stainless steel to pick up a detail in the kitchen. A stainless-steel "Lazy S" fountain is placed exactly opposite the corner of the kitchen, differentiating the dining area from the rest of the garden.

Leaf form is important in the planting and large numbers of one type of plant are used to keep the contemporary look. The colour palette is restricted to silver, red, white, and green, and bamboos give height against the tall walls.

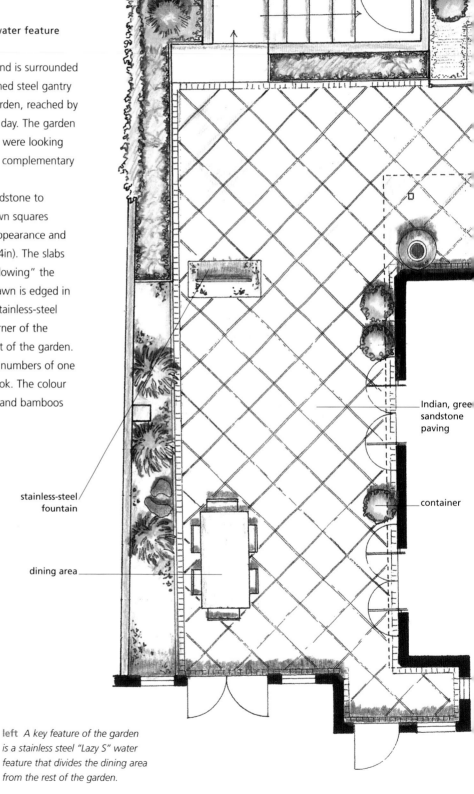

Indian, green sandstone paving

container

stainless-steel fountain

dining area

left *A key feature of the garden is a stainless steel "Lazy S" water feature that divides the dining area from the rest of the garden.*

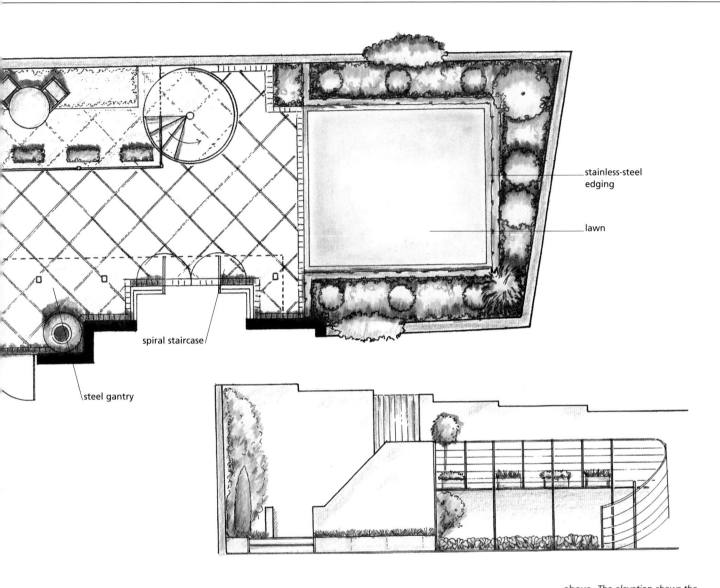

stainless-steel
edging

lawn

spiral staircase

steel gantry

above *The elevation shows the dramatic level differences between the gantry and the lower or sunken garden space, reached by the spiral staircase.*

left *This sunken garden is reached by a spiral staircase. The corkscrew topiary shrubs in containers contrast well with the more informal planting elsewhere in the garden.*

Glittery Paving for a Party Space

ANNIE GUILFOYLE – CREATIVE LANDSCAPES

DIMENSIONS upper 4 x 4m (13 x 13ft); lower 3.8 x 1.7m (13 x 6ft)

SOIL sandy neutral

ASPECT south-east facing

KEY FEATURES terrazzo, gabions, and water feature

The owners had contrasting expectations from the garden space: one wanted a quiet area for contemplation and growing herbs, and the other sought a bright, lively party area. Colour requirements ranged from muted blues and purples to loud and clashing. Both wanted architectural plants to be a framework for the garden. Existing steps up from the lower level were to be retained because of cost constraints.

Paving throughout the garden is a terrazzo made to the designer's specifications using a mix of Cornish granite and chips of heather- and blue-coloured glass and small flecks of stainless-steel to provide a sparkly and interesting base. Containers on the lower level are all custom-made in brushed aluminium. A sculptural panel was also designed to hang on the wall opposite the kitchen window to provide a focal point for interest while doing the washing-up. Another panel acts as a safety rail along the wall above the steps.

Attracting the visitor into the upper garden is a water feature of a 1.8m- (6ft) high, stainless-steel "wave", which drizzles water and acts as a focal point from the sitting room. The shape of the garden is offset to maximize the space and the raised planting beds are retained with gabions filled with pebbles. Seats are made of slatted hardwood (Iroko) tops fixed to the gabions. For added sparkle, a string of lights is threaded through the gabions.

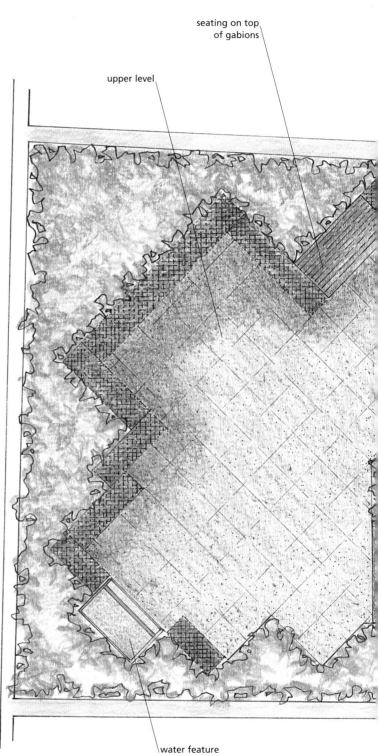

seating on top of gabions

upper level

water feature

left A sculptural panel in the lower level of the garden makes an arresting feature when viewed from the kitchen window of the house.

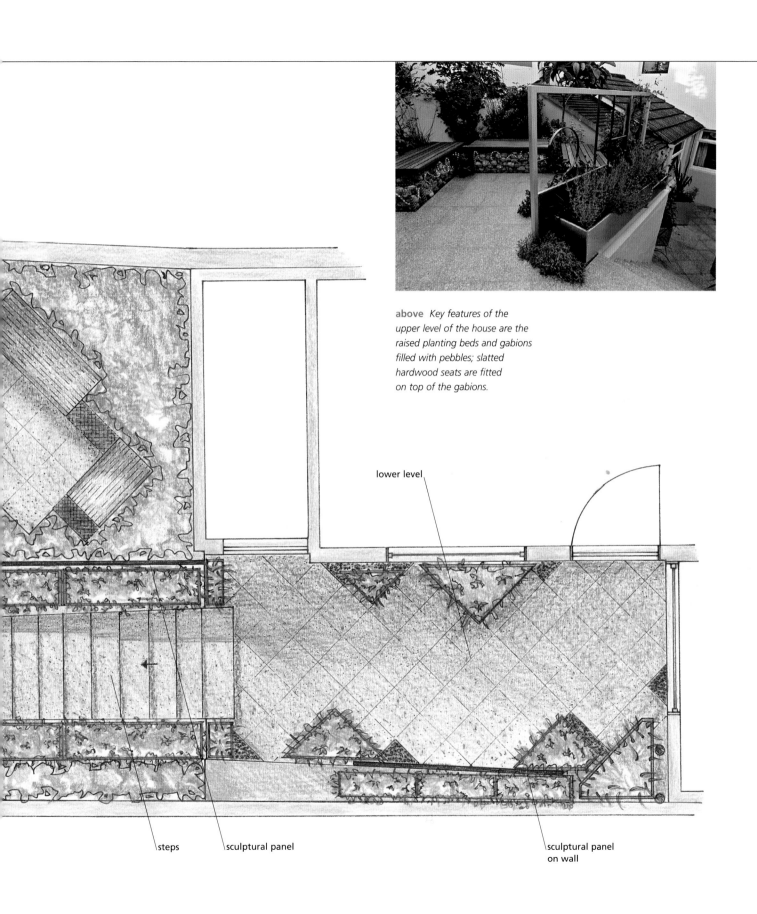

above *Key features of the upper level of the house are the raised planting beds and gabions filled with pebbles; slatted hardwood seats are fitted on top of the gabions.*

lower level

steps

sculptural panel

sculptural panel on wall

Awkward Slope

DAVID STEVENS

DIMENSIONS 10 x 15m (33 x 50ft)

SOIL neutral topsoil (after the builders' rubble had been excavated)

ASPECT north facing

KEY FEATURES gravel terraces

This was an extremely awkward site with a sharp, diagonal slope leading up into the right-hand corner, which was more than 2m (6ft) higher than the area immediately outside the house.

Leading out from the French doors, the design provides ample room for sitting and dining, the irregular widths of paving, laid with expressed joints, occupying the only existing level area of ground.

Moving away from the main sitting area, the design is turned to 45 degrees from the house, to allow the steps and radiating brick walls to climb the diagonal slope more easily. The retaining wall allows the slope to be terraced, the intermediate spaces being floored with gravel and planting, the latter naturally spilling from level to level. The highest level is given over to a deck that naturally sits comfortably over the slope and catches the afternoon and evening sun. Overhead wires are strung across it for climbers and a specimen *Sorbus cashmiriana* 'Hedl'. is planted behind.

Planting is important in this garden, to soften the positive underlying hard landscape structure and also to help screen another house to the east on higher ground.

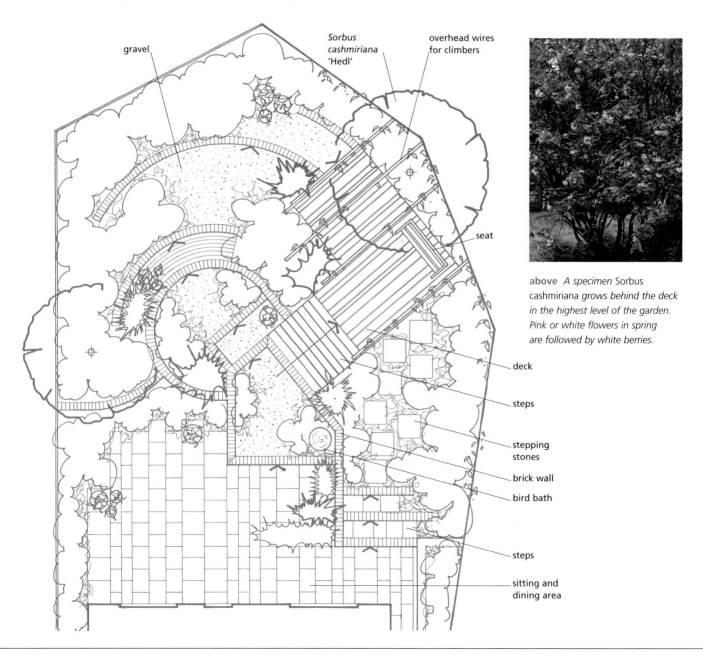

gravel

Sorbus cashmiriana 'Hedl'

overhead wires for climbers

seat

deck

steps

stepping stones

brick wall

bird bath

steps

sitting and dining area

above *A specimen* Sorbus cashmiriana *grows behind the deck in the highest level of the garden. Pink or white flowers in spring are followed by white berries.*

Moroccan Courtyard

JAMES ALDRIDGE GARDENS

DIMENSIONS 4 x 2m (13 x 6ft)

SOIL loam

ASPECT south facing

KEY FEATURES Moorish fountain

This very small courtyard was to be given a simple Moroccan theme with moving water and interesting planting.

Colour is very important in this design, with the paving of terra cotta, tumbled marble squares laid on the diagonal for maximum visual impact. The walls are rendered with lime plaster containing a natural red pigment to produce a faded, warm pink finish. On the shortest wall, a raised pool was built of rendered block work and a water spout juts out from a shaped area tiled in Moroccan jade-green and blue-green tiles laid diagonally. A seat was built of the same materials with a terra cotta tiled sitting surface. A large specimen Queen Palm (*Syagrus romanzoffiana*) was planted opposite the seat to give shade and overhead greenery. Other planting is of *Trachelospermum jasminoides* and *Rosa banksiae* 'Alba Plena' trained on to wires on the walls.

The tiny, upper terrace is paved in the same terra cotta tiles and six planters containing *Cupressus sempervirens* in formal lines give interest and structure. The garden is lit by soft ambient lights and with an uplighter in the pool for emphasis. Jade-green and turquoise jars containing candles are hung from metal rings fixed to the wall.

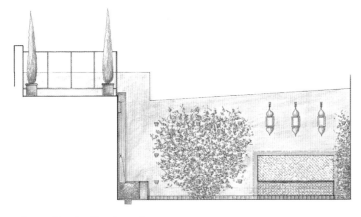

above *The elevation shows the contrast in levels that makes the water cascade possible as a focal point in the garden.*

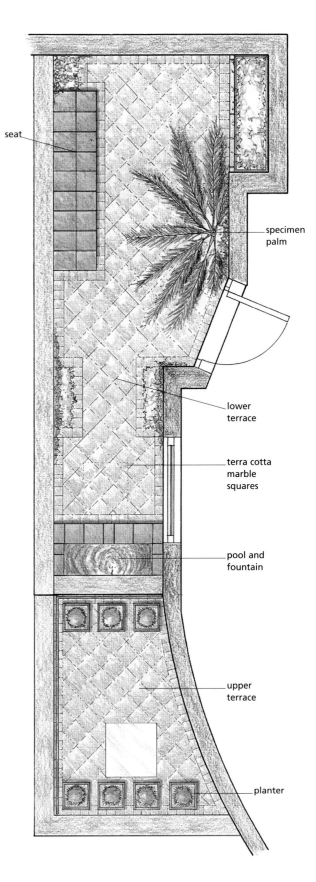

seat

specimen palm

lower terrace

terra cotta marble squares

pool and fountain

upper terrace

planter

Oriental Style

SARAH LAYTON

DIMENSIONS 10 x 9m (33 x 30ft) plus return to house of 9m (30ft)
SOIL clay
ASPECT south facing
KEY FEATURES decking

Having three small children, the owners wanted a garden that was useable all year and very easy to keep. They wanted an oriental feel to the space and for the garden to be interesting and stimulating for the children. The site is overlooked on all sides by tall houses, so planting needed to be tall and dense.

The return from the house to the garden was used to introduce a decked walkway through low planting leading to the main garden space. From the door, a 45-degree angle to make the space appear bigger is introduced into the pathway and again to lead into a small enclosed dining area. Outside the main doors from the house, a paved terrace, replete with loungers, leads to decked steps going up to a large dining deck. A table sits beside built-in benches, giving generous sitting space. Granite boulders form a safe water feature and a focus for the garden. The space surrounding the hard surfaces is densely planted with trees, including *Betula albosinensis* Burkill, and tall shrubs for screening. Other planting includes *Phormium tenax, Miscanthus, Sinensis, Nandina domestica, Heuchera* 'Chocolate Ruffles', *Pennisetum alopecuroides,* and *Helloborus* varieties.

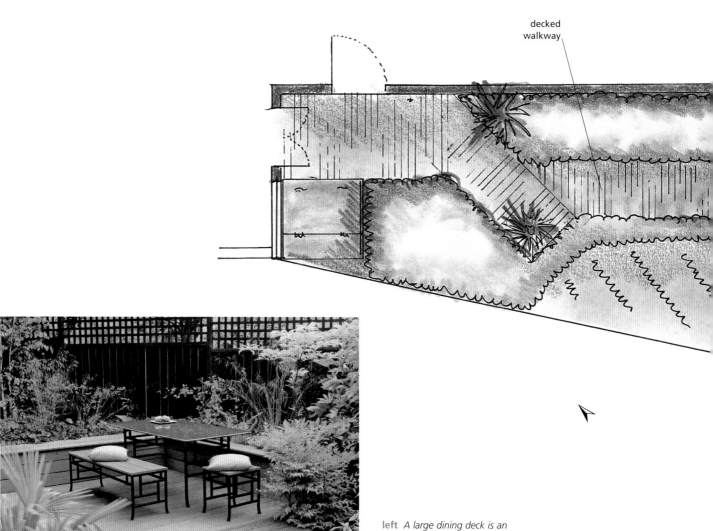

decked walkway

left *A large dining deck is an important feature of this garden. Generous seating is provided by movable and built-in benches.*

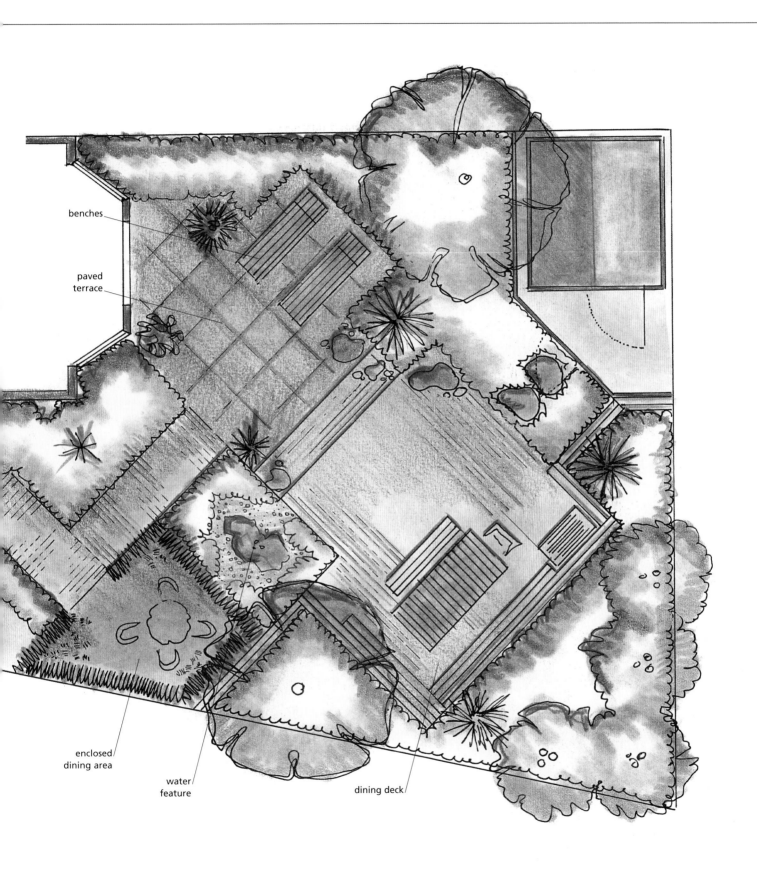

benches

paved
terrace

enclosed
dining area

water
feature

dining deck

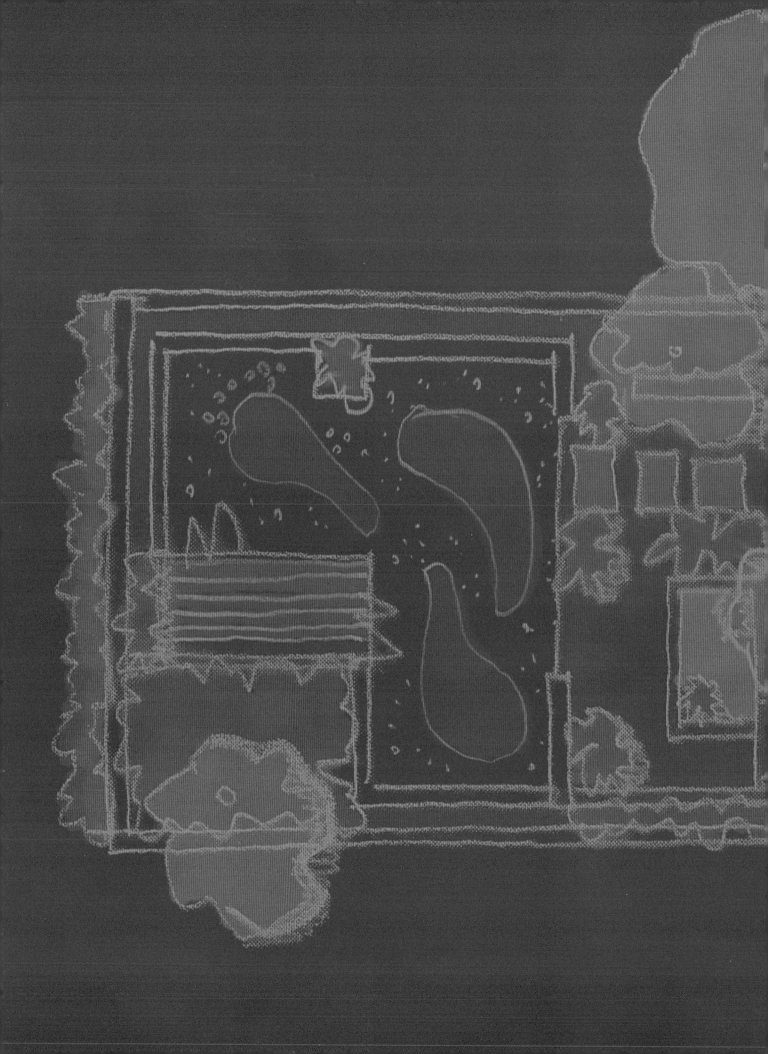

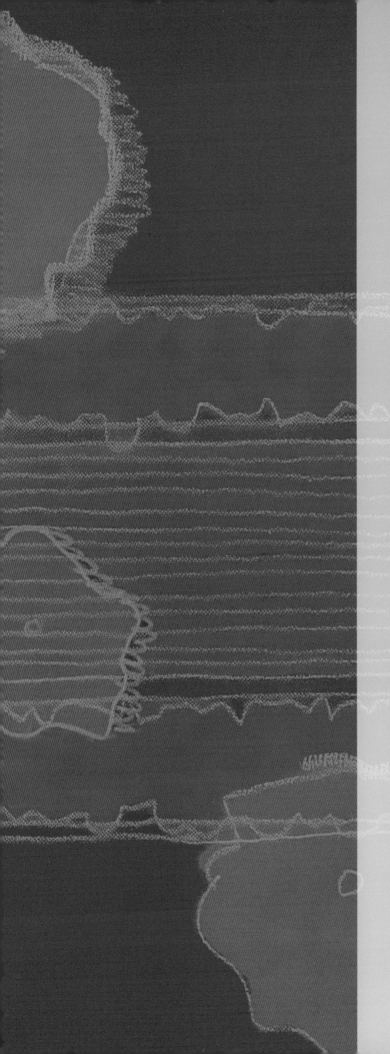

GARDENROOMS

Some gardens may be small but allow more than one space to be defined within them. Long, narrow gardens fall into this category, or those that wrap around a property, providing a series of spaces. These are referred to as garden "rooms".

There are two approaches to these gardens: to treat each space in a different way, or to relate them together. The former relies on contrast and the element of surprise; the latter relies on a harmonious approach in which changes are subtle and the entire garden feels coherent. The spaces need to be created using walls, trellis, or hedges. This allows views to be restricted, which is especially important if each space is to be different. Pathways and openings can even be staggered to limit views. In using contrasting treatments, one still needs to consider the sequence in which the moods will be experienced. Colour themes, whether painted or in flower or foliage, could increase the sense of contrast. Consider complementary colours in adjacent spaces or intense flower colour followed by green foliage or white flower. If the spaces can be seen from indoors, the themes could relate to the interior treatments. Paving materials can provide a common theme to each space, and the planting changes or important and significant plants can be repeated in each space, creating a visual rhythm or a connection between the garden "rooms".

Batchelor Pad

FISHER TOMLIN

DIMENSIONS 12.5 x 6.5m (41 x 21ft)
SOIL neutral loam
ASPECT west facing
KEY FEATURES sunbathing deck and fire pit

Creating a batchelor pad garden for entertaining, sun bathing, and holding parties was the brief for this plan. An existing large horse chestnut tree in the corner farthest from the house needed to be incorporated.

The design solution creates a sequence of spaces through which the visitor passes, each with a different character and use. Nearest the house is a decked eating area designed to accommodate the owner's existing table and chairs. Planting is structural and in pots.

From this point, a change in the direction of decking indicates a route through the garden. At the rear of the house, a large, square decked area is designed for sunbathing and is large enough for several loungers. Again, the changed direction of the decking up the steps indicates movement through the garden, and these steps lead to a square sandstone terrace laid in regular square pattern. A fire pit is placed centrally and long, green oak benches are placed on the three closed sides of the square. This forms the main focal party point at the end of the garden on the higher level.

Two specimen trees are planted, *Prunus* 'Accolade' and *Magnolia* 'Susan', the walls are clothed in climbers including *Clematis armandii* and *Trachelospermum jasminoides,* and under the large tree there is an area of ferns.

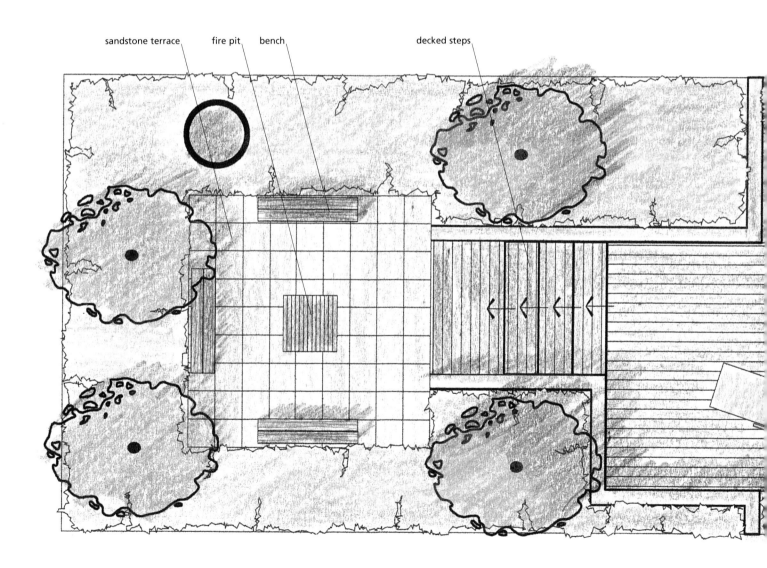

sandstone terrace   fire pit   bench   decked steps

right *The two specimen trees are* Prunus *'Accolade' and, shown here,* Magnolia *'Susan'. This deciduous shrub or tree bears fragrant flowers in spring that are purple red on the outside but paler inside.*

left *Among the climbers found in this garden are clematis and, shown here, trachelospermum. This woody evergreen climber produces white flowers in mid and late summer.*

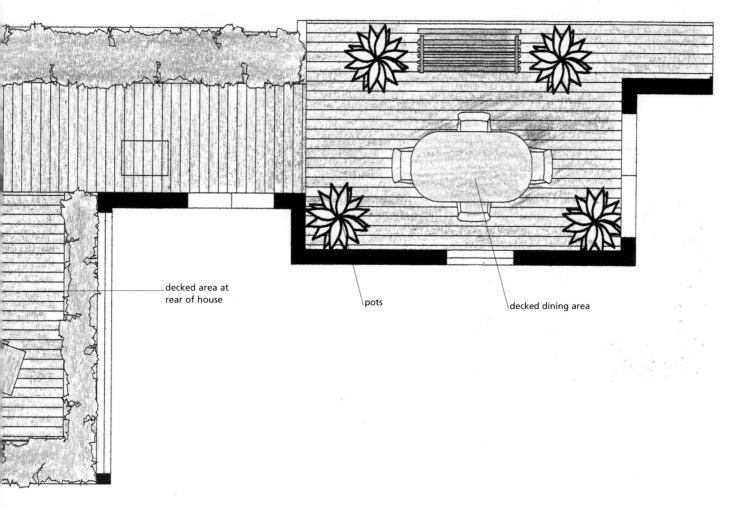

decked area at
rear of house

pots

decked dining area

Tropical Oasis

IAN SMITH – ACRES WILD

DIMENSIONS 10 x 22m (33 by 70ft) and 6 x 16m (20 x 53ft)

SOIL chalk

ASPECT rear garden south-east facing; side north-east facing

KEY FEATURES "totally tropical" deck

above *Acanthus are vigorous architectural perennials originally native to the Mediterranean area.*

above *A luxuriant feeling was added to this garden by such plantings as gunnera. The leaves of these large-leaved perennials can reach 2m (6ft).*

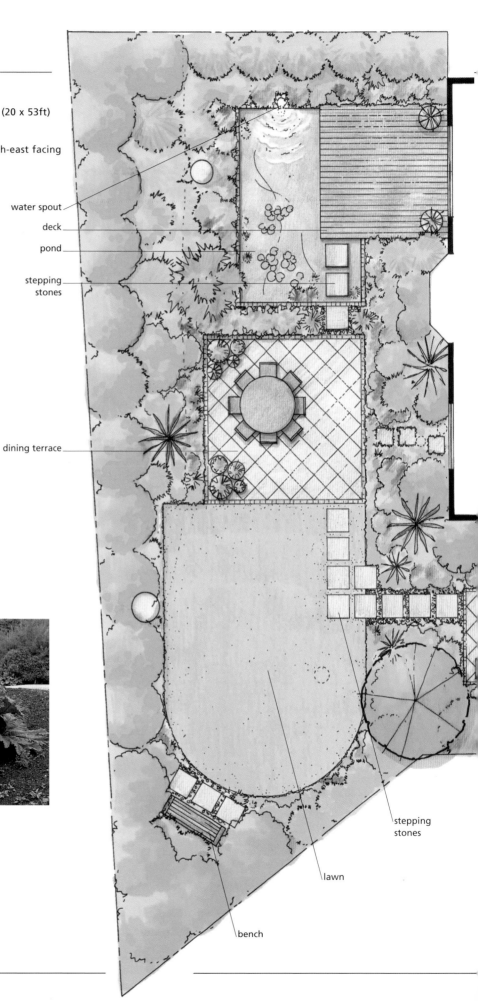

water spout

deck

pond

stepping stones

dining terrace

stepping stones

lawn

bench

The owners of this garden wanted a space to remind them of favourite holidays taken in Hawaii, Thailand, and the Orient. They wanted a calm, green, almost tropical oasis but with a feeling of space and openness and with different places to visit at different times of the day. The garden also had to look good from inside, especially from the sitting room.

To fulfil these requirements a "totally tropical" deck was installed leading off the timber-floored sitting room to extend the living space outside. A formal pond, surrounded by large, tropical planting and with a water spout, gives seclusion and the sound of water. Sandstone stepping stones lead through the garden, across the Indian Sandstone dining terrace and on to the lawn. The grass acts as a foil to the lush planting and is shaped to detract from the pointed corner of the garden. The stepping stones then continue across the grass and lead to a secluded "G&T" spot outside the kitchen to catch the evening sun. There is a utility space in the shady north-western corner of the garden, behind the garage.

Planting is lush and luxuriant to create a tropical ambiance. The boundaries are screened by bamboos and large evergreens to give maximum privacy. Within the garden, *Trachycarpus fortunei*, *Chamaerops humilis*, cordylines, gunnera, and fatsia give the tropical feel desired, and cannas, acanthus, and croscosmia add to the luxuriant feel.

above *The view from the entrance to the deck shows how the garden intriguingly opens out across the pool and stepping stones.*

secluded area
with bench

utility space

Two Connected Gardens

MARK LUTYENS ASSOCIATES

DIMENSIONS garden 1 42 x 19m (140 x 59ft); garden 2 42 x 9m
(140 x 30ft)

SOIL thin gravel with lots of rubble

ASPECT south-east facing

KEY FEATURES linking hornbeam hedge

These are neighbouring properties. The first garden was designed
in the 1990s for owners who wanted a very strong structure and
plenty of scope for planting. Space was required for a writer's
summerhouse and views of the garden from the upstairs windows
were very important. To make the most of the afternoon sun, the
garden needed to have sitting space at the far end. The second
garden was designed much more recently, for owners whose brief
was, "We like what you did next door, but could you make it
low maintenance, please."

In each garden, the space is divided into three areas: a paved
area near the house, a lawn, and then a more secluded area for
sitting. In the first garden, footings to an old stable were found and
these were turned into a canal. To bring interest and division to
each of the gardens, a pleached hornbeam hedge crosses both,
screening the last third of each and linking the two gardens when
they are viewed from above. In each garden this hedge forms
a colonnade under which visitors pass to access the last outdoor
room. The owners of the first garden are keen gardeners and
requested a vegetable garden, espalier fruit trees, and an interesting
collection of rare plants. The second garden has more robust
planting to ensure that it is easy to maintain.

*below The two elevations show
the way in which the garden spaces
are formed by hedges. Pools and
steps can also be clearly seen.*

pleached
hedge

deck

vegetable
garden

bench

lawn

paved
area

Garden 1

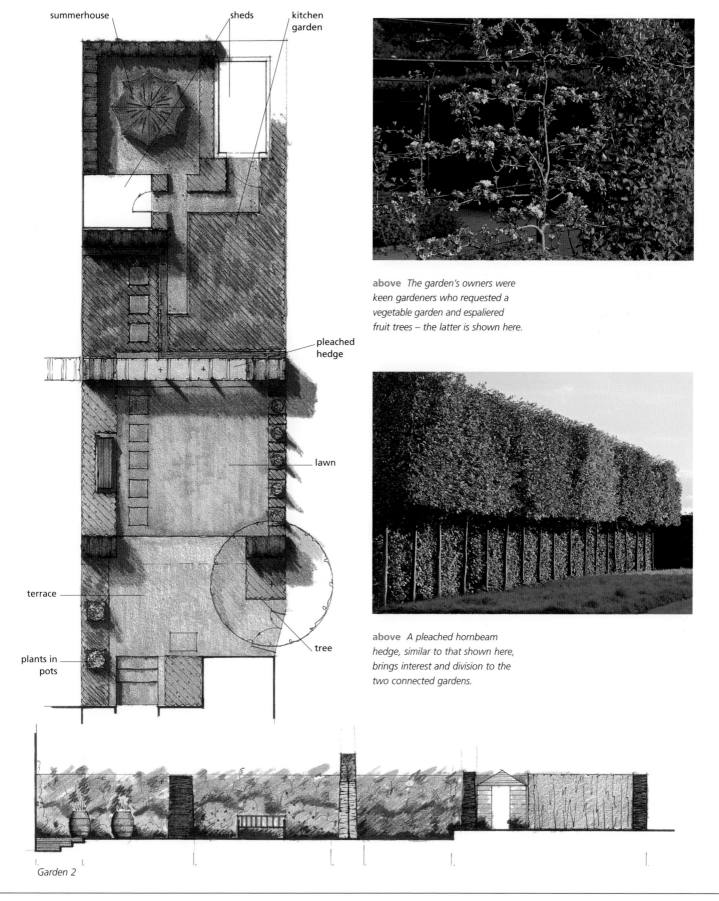

summerhouse

sheds

kitchen garden

pleached hedge

lawn

terrace

plants in pots

tree

above *The garden's owners were keen gardeners who requested a vegetable garden and espaliered fruit trees – the latter is shown here.*

above *A pleached hornbeam hedge, similar to that shown here, brings interest and division to the two connected gardens.*

Garden 2

Integrating a Jungle

JULIE TOLL

DIMENSIONS 28 x 6m (92 x 20ft)

SOIL clay loam mix

ASPECT west facing

KEY FEATURES barbecue area and jungle.

The owner had already begun transformation of this long, thin garden but had found it a challenge. The arbour and jungle at the far end were already in place but they needed integrating into the rest of the garden. Other requirements were for a lawn and strong division of the space to create interest. The owner was very interested in being involved in maintaining the garden and liked large architectural plants and grasses.

Next to the house is a large entertaining area with a barbecue offset to one side designed like a bar with tall stools sitting up to it. Paving is of rectangular pieces of black limestone laid in a linear pattern down the garden interspersed with fine gravel. The stone also interlocks with timber decking laid in the same direction, which forms the dining area.

Beyond the screen of a high hedge, a lawn forms the next "room" of the garden. Tall planting then disguises an area with a small bubbling boulder water feature set into grey-and-white gravel. The gravel path then continues through a jungle-like area with dense, lush planting, and railway sleepers forming easy stepping places. At the far end of the garden an arbour is the final attraction. Planting includes many grasses, deschampsia, calamagrostis, and *Cortaderia selloana*.

above *In this area of the garden tall planting surrounds a small bubbling boulder water feature set into grey and white gravel.*

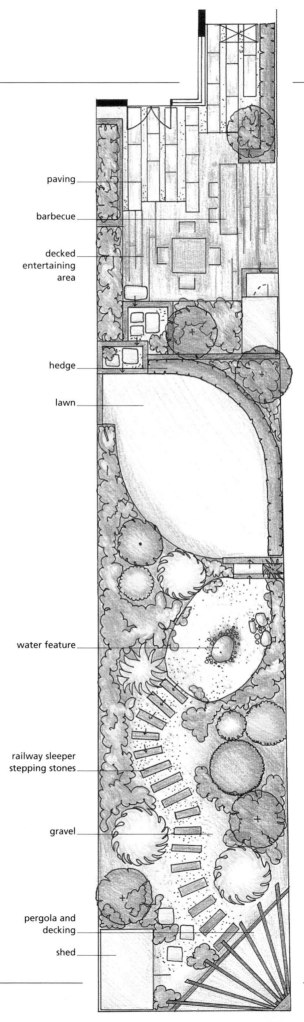

paving

barbecue

decked entertaining area

hedge

lawn

water feature

railway sleeper stepping stones

gravel

pergola and decking

shed

Cool, Sophisticated Planting

SARAH EBERLE – HILLIER LANDSCAPES / ANDREW HERRING – HERRING HOMES

DIMENSIONS 28 x 10m (92 x 33ft)
SOIL neutral loam
ASPECT north-east facing
KEY FEATURES large, timber deck

Levels in the rear garden meant that the space felt overlooked by neighbours and visually separated from the basement kitchen area. A new contemporary space for entertaining was required together with easy access to an office building at the bottom of the garden.

The central feature of this design is a large deck, 9.5m (31ft) long by 4.5m (14ft) wide, which is sunk into the garden with low retaining walls to either side for occasional sitting. This makes the space feel visually protected and more "secure". Set into the deck is a multi-stemmed *Prunus serrula*. A small raised pool at the edge of the deck is a feature from both the office and the deck. Paving elsewhere in the garden is of cut York stone in large regular linear sections that reflect the scale and size of the deck.

Planting is predominantly for foliage interest with colour overlay limited to white and blue. This produces a cool, sophisticated and unified scheme. Grasses include *Miscanthus sinensis* 'Gracillimus' and *Carex pendula* 'Moonraker'. Other plants chosen for foliage texture are *Hydrangea arborescens* 'Annabelle', *Potentilla fruiticosa* 'Abbotswood', *Heuchera cylindrica* and *Angelica archangelica*. A variety of ferns also bring interesting texture and *Geranium* 'Jolly Bee' adds a good blue.

right *This perspective sketch shows the central deck space used for dining beneath the tree canopy.*

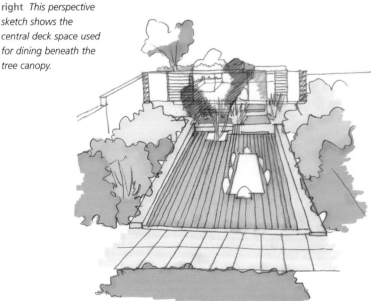

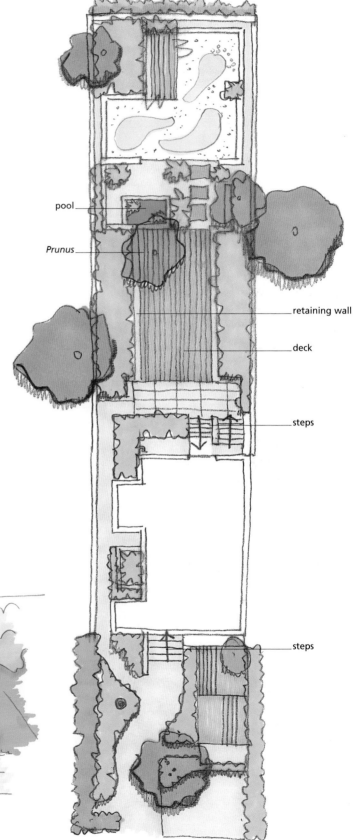

pool

Prunus

retaining wall

deck

steps

steps

Steel and Glass

PHILIP NASH DESIGN LTD

DIMENSIONS upper area 3.5 x 11.5m (11 x 39ft); lower area
3.5 x 8m (11 x 25ft)

SOIL alkaline chalky clay

ASPECT north-west facing

KEY FEATURES glass benches and cantilevered deck

A transformation from building site to an exciting and original
garden was the aim for these owners. The site was on several
levels with lots of sharp corners and limited access, and the brief
was to use contemporary materials to bring strong design to the
space and to make it more enticing to use.

Outside the house, a cedar deck is set at the level of internal
floors so that the garden flows out of the house. Kiln-formed
glass benches and a table appear to float above the deck and are
under-planted with ferns, giving a lush and tropical feel. A tall
Trachycarpus fortunei is planted through the decking, bringing height
and a further hint of the tropics. A large (6 x 1.2m / 20 x 4ft) pool
accents the change of level and adds the reflective quality of water
to the design. A solid 125mm- (5in-) thick, kiln-formed glass stepping
stone across the pool leads to stone steps up to the middle terrace.

With white, painted walls and large, architectural planting, this
stone terraced area brings light and space into the garden and leads
again, via decked steps, up to a cantilevered top deck, which gets the
last of the evening sun. Again planting grows up through the deck
and under a glass table and benches. A remote-control LED lighting
system illuminates the garden, particularly the pool and the glass step.

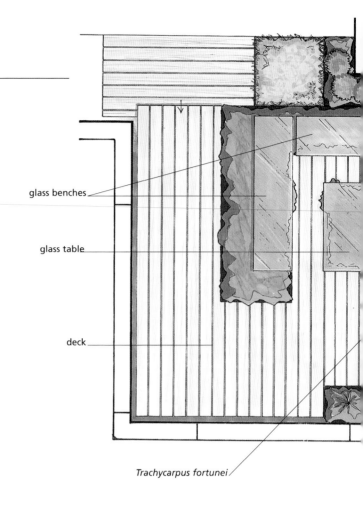

glass benches

glass table

deck

Trachycarpus fortunei

above *An LED system has a dramatic effect
as it illuminates the pool area and the
contemporary glass seating and table.*

above *In daylight the tropical architectural
planting is as much of a feature on the cedar
deck as the glass table and chairs.*

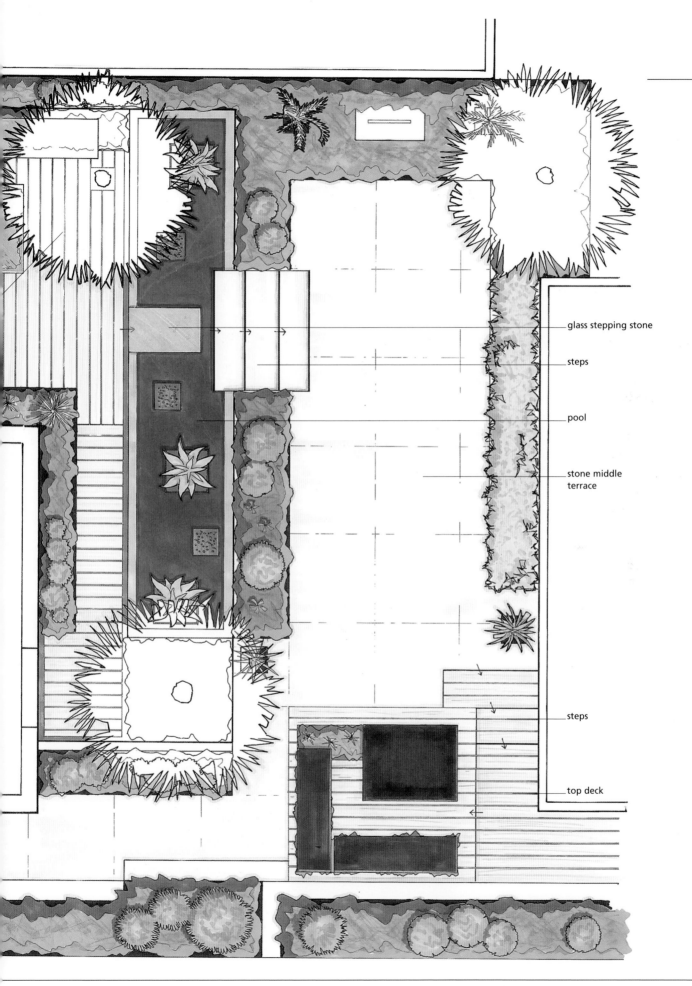

glass stepping stone

steps

pool

stone middle terrace

steps

top deck

Garden of Rooms

CARO OLDROYD – CLIFTON NURSERIES

DIMENSIONS 23 x 5.2m (71 x 16ft)

SOIL neutral over clay

ASPECT north-west facing

KEY FEATURES rooms divided by hedges and decking

Views down the garden from a new, glass extension were requested, but the owner didn't want the whole space revealed at first glance. A series of rooms was suggested but also that the whole should work together, especially when viewed from the upper floor of the house.

The garden is broken up by three hedges; nearest to the house, a low, yew hedge gives enclosure of the Indian sandstone terrace for dining. Passing between two *Acer palmatum* 'Bloodgood' (to be maintained at 1.8m (6ft) in a tiered umbrella shape), another yew hedge, slightly higher, leads onto a further garden area. At ground level there is also a threshold of timber decking, which reinforces the sense of progression between garden "rooms". This area is densely planted into raised beds created from new oak sleepers set on edge. These beds help improve drainage and light levels for planting and play with heights for interest and privacy.

The final "garden" is obscured by a high beech hedge, chosen for its copper colour during the winter months, and again the decking defines the space on the ground. An existing summerhouse is repaired and painted in a light colour to act as a focal point for the garden. Key plants offer a mix of evergreen and deciduous, herbaceous, and perennial, with good winter structure and evergreens to carry the garden through the winter.

above *A view of the final part of the garden includes the high beech hedge and the summerhouse that acts as a final focal point.*

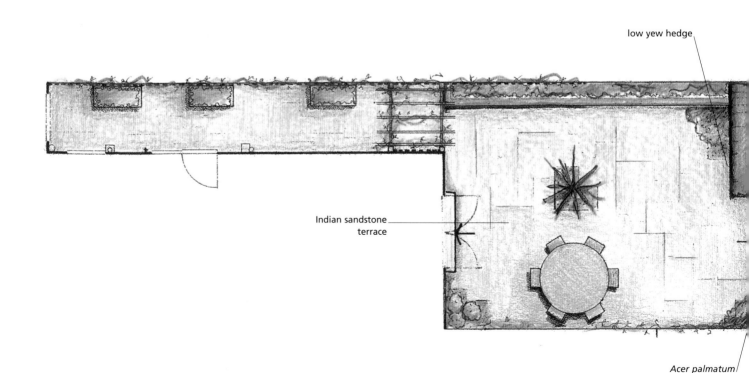

low yew hedge

Indian sandstone terrace

Acer palmatum 'Bloodgood'

above The perspective view shows
how the hedges provide partial
but effective screening, retaining
the tantalizing central view.

above This picture of beech
hedging shows how stunning
its colour can be during the
drab winter months.

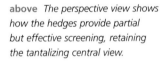

timber decking
threshold

high beech
hedge

raised bed

decking

summer
house

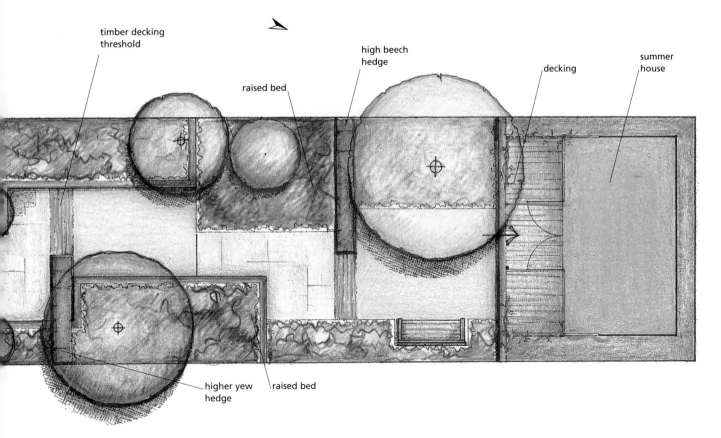

higher yew
hedge

raised bed

View to the Hills

KEITH PULLAN GARDEN DESIGN

DIMENSIONS 25 x 17m (80 x 55ft)

SOIL neutral to alkaline

ASPECT east facing; 300m (1,000ft) elevation and superb views

KEY FEATURES undulating dry-stone wall and rill through garden

This space wraps around the house to form a shallow garden mainly concentrated around the east and north of the house. The site was very exposed to wind but wonderful views out over surrounding hills meant that the owners did not want to enclose and protect the space. Some structural height was requested but not at the expense of the views. The main terrace was already in place and additional paving materials needed to match it because the budget was limited.

To ensure that the garden relates to both the character of the building and its surroundings, a dry-stone wall is used to flow through the garden. The undulating shape of this wall echoes the surrounding hills and provides interest and movement through the garden. Water is used as a central element, visible from the house and near the main seating areas. A rill falls from a stone trough and moves gently across the garden, crossing the dry-stone wall twice before falling into an informal pond.

Geometry is very strong, with square paving slabs laid in gravel forming sitting areas and paths throughout the space, giving a unified look and an air of formality. Clipped box balls and a glade of silver birch trees on the north side of the house also enhance this aspect of the garden, while other planting softens the effect.

below *The perspective drawing shows the expansive view and the relationship of the garden to the house and pergola.*

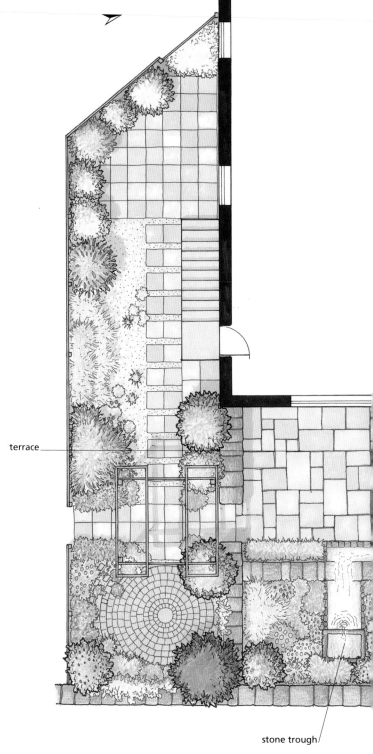

terrace

stone trough

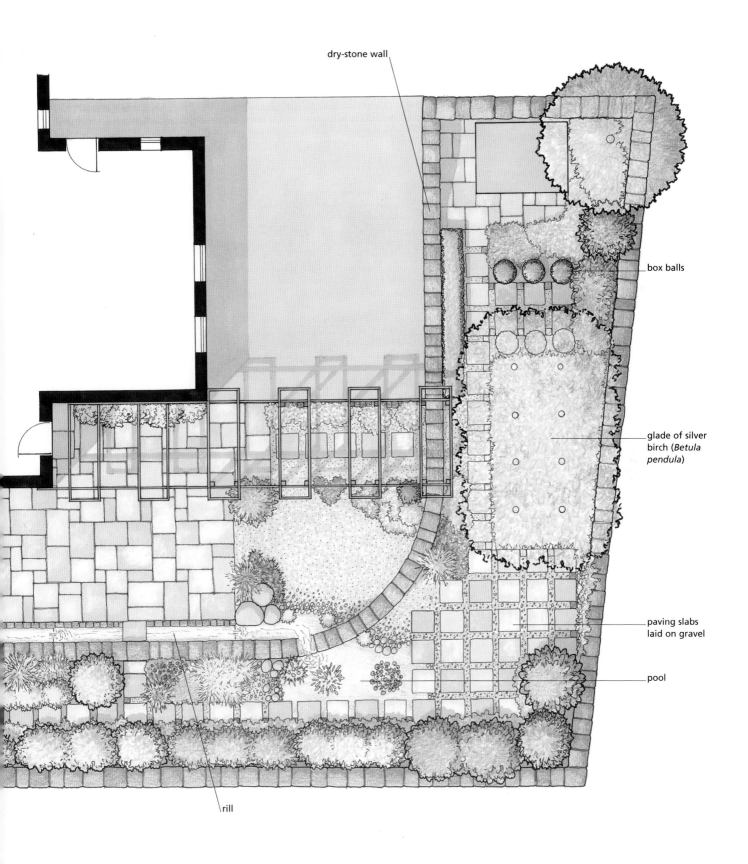

dry-stone wall

box balls

glade of silver
birch (*Betula
pendula*)

paving slabs
laid on gravel

pool

rill

Contemporary Plantsman's Garden

MICHAEL DAY

DIMENSIONS front 7 x 14m (23 x 47ft); rear 13 x 16m (43 x 53ft)

SOIL thin alkaline

ASPECT front south-west facing; rear north-east facing

KEY FEATURES strong simple lines softened by "billowy" planting

The owner of this site is a keen gardener and the brief was to provide as many planting opportunities as possible, exploiting the level changes within the garden. She was looking for a soft, contemporary style with strong geometry softened by masses of planting. The rear of the garden needed screening from neighbours and to provide a sheltered micro-climate for the plants.

The garden slopes gently away from the house and the level changes are managed one step at a time using railway sleepers, which then continue to define the different areas of the garden. The eastern side of the garden is set aside as a work area and vegetable garden, with raised beds and bark paths to allow easy working access. Within the main part of the garden, a polished, granite fountain feeds water into a stone-edged rill and then into the pond, keeping the water moving and fresh. The pond is planted with water lilies to encourage wildlife. A gravel garden is made up of light-coloured pebbles with grey-and-white boulders, and is planted with *Sedum telephium* 'Matrona', *Phlomis russeliana,* and lavenders.

A timber walkway and stepping stones across the pond allow movement through the garden, and a sunny seating area looks back to the house along the length of the rill. Three screens (two in the gravel garden and one behind the bench) divide the garden, creating an element of surprise.

above *Stepping stones across the pond and a timber walkway give a sense of movement through the garden.*

above *This axonometric view shows how the complex spaces and structural elements relate together.*

left *Near the house a pond is fed from a polished granite fountain that feeds water into a stone edged rill.*

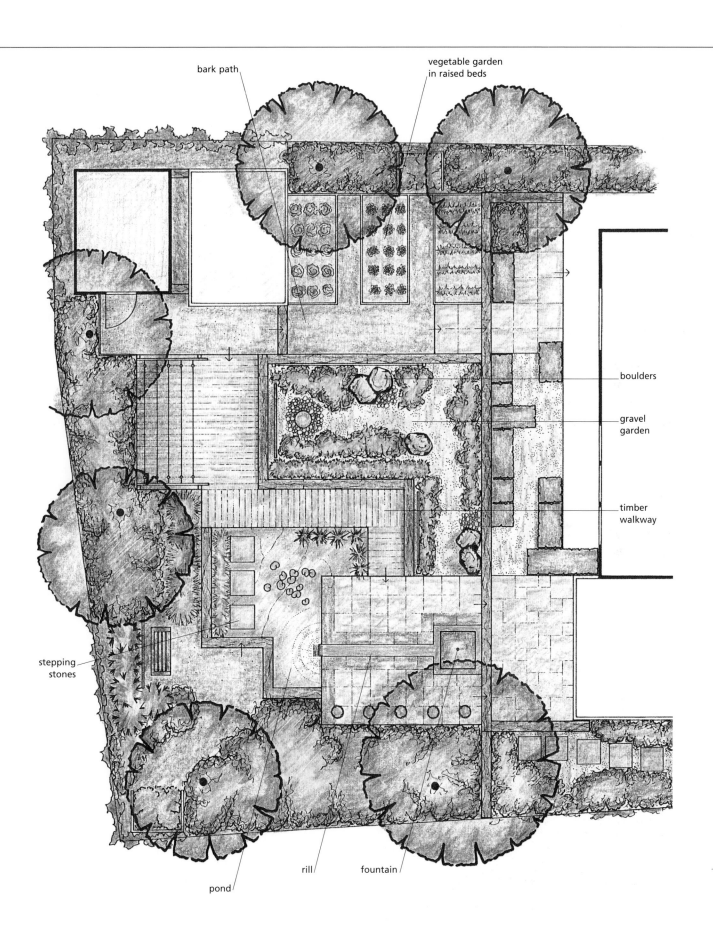

bark path

vegetable garden
in raised beds

boulders

gravel
garden

timber
walkway

stepping
stones

pond

rill

fountain

VERYSMALLGARDENS

As towns and cities become more densely populated, outside space becomes smaller but more precious. Our tendency is often to overcrowd these spaces or to miniaturize the features, when what is really needed is one big idea. Dense planting can work well, creating shade, foliage, or stem pattern, and an escape from the harsh realities of urban life. Simple paving can be a foil to luxuriant planting; there is also room for smaller-scale elements such as cobbles and setts, mosaic and paving patterns. The joints and crevices between them encourage moss or tiny, groundcovering species to grow in the shade, creating miniature landscapes and restful corners.

For more minimal solutions, the quality of detail and the use of interesting paving are essential: poor workmanship and bad combinations of materials and surfaces are easily noticed. Fossil-heavy limestone, riven slate, or sediment-patterned sandstone create intricate patterns that give depth to the space. Decks can create elegant and scale-enhancing surfaces, and stainless steel will gleam and sparkle, perhaps along with the movement and sound of trickling water. Bold foliage or architectural planting create drama.

Even if space is so tight that only one statement can be made, make it big, bold, and adventurous. Sculpture, wall hangings, furniture, and ornaments add style, colour, and life to even the tiniest garden.

Simplicity is Style

ARABELLA LENNOX-BOYD

DIMENSIONS 142sq m (1,520sq ft)

SOIL neutral

ASPECT north-east facing

KEY FEATURES play lawn, shallow steps, and vine tunnel

From the modern façade of the house, the clients wanted to create a contemporary, low-maintenance garden with maximum space for children to play. The garden is entered from a car parking space through a subtle gate that opens onto a vine tunnel, an arched metal pergola cloaked with vines that allow dappled sun to reach the slim border of hostas, saxifrages, and acanthus below. The tunnel and pale, limestone path that runs through it add mystery to the garden while subtly obscuring the adjacent boundary wall. The path terminates in a mass of textural bamboo and a terra cotta pot planted with an architectural hosta.

On the north boundary of the garden, a wall of water flows into a pool planted with *Zantedeschia aethiopica* 'Crowborough'. There is a small, square lawn edged with a limestone trim and this leads to shallow, limestone steps down to a limestone terrace outside the house. Borders are narrow but boldly planted for maximum impact, allowing space for children's play. On the terrace, French clay pots are planted with box or white agapanthus to add colour and interest to the steps. The terrace provides a restful spot to dine alfresco in the summer or simply to enjoy the garden.

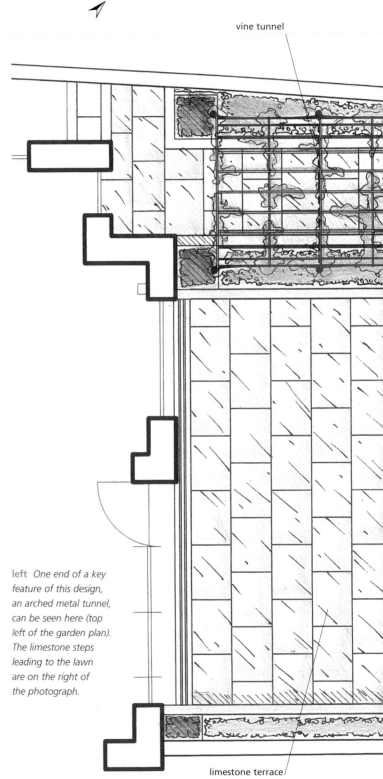

vine tunnel

left *One end of a key feature of this design, an arched metal tunnel, can be seen here (top left of the garden plan). The limestone steps leading to the lawn are on the right of the photograph.*

limestone terrace

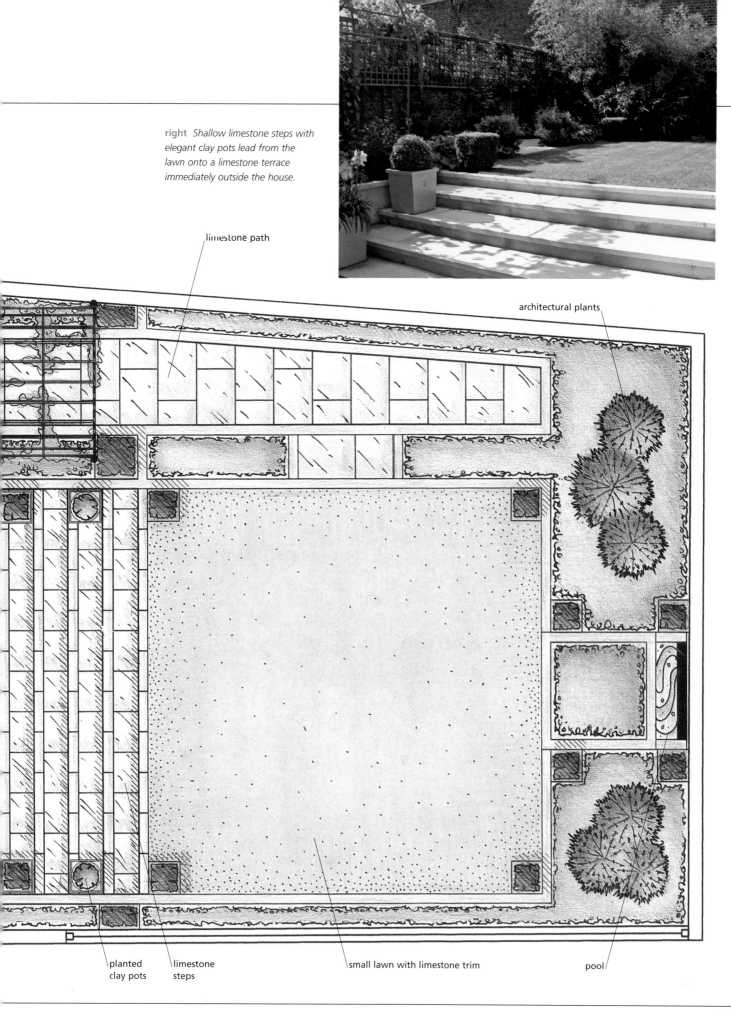

right *Shallow limestone steps with elegant clay pots lead from the lawn onto a limestone terrace immediately outside the house.*

limestone path

architectural plants

planted clay pots

limestone steps

small lawn with limestone trim

pool

Tiny Sandstone Courtyard

CLEVE WEST

DIMENSIONS 5.6 x 3.9m (19 x 13ft)

SOIL sandy loam

ASPECT west facing

KEY FEATURES sandstone paving

The owner of this tiny, paved terrace wanted something more interesting and inviting to encourage use of the garden. The space leads onto a communal garden so it was not possible to enclose it completely. Drainage was also an important consideration.

To increase the feeling of space and to introduce an element of movement, the paving is offset at different angles. The smaller area of paving is set slightly higher than the main area. Sandstone paving of various dimensions and textures has been used, with one large sandstone boulder and smaller stones forming a step between the two areas. Smaller stones bleed off from the larger ones and grade down to sandstone mulch around the plants. The planting is kept minimal to give a strong sense of unity, with use of *Calamagrostis* x *acutiflora* 'Karl Foerster', *Molinia caerulea* subsp. *caerulea* 'Variegata', and *Eryngium bougatii* for structure. A mass planting of *Agapanthus* 'Midnight Blue' separates the two areas of paving and defines the level change.

left A major planting of the clump forming perennial Agapanthus *'Midnight Blue' separates the two areas of paving in this garden.*

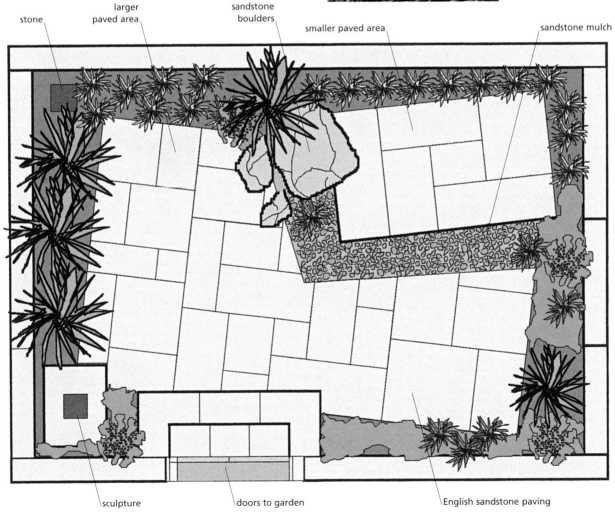

stone

larger paved area

sandstone boulders

smaller paved area

sandstone mulch

sculpture

doors to garden

English sandstone paving

Sun Throughout the Day

DOUGLAS COLTART – VIRIDARIUM DESIGN STUDIO

DIMENSIONS 10.7 x 11m (35 x 35ft)

SOIL loam

ASPECT south-east facing

KEY FEATURES small light-reflecting pool

The owners wanted a low maintenance garden with places to sit out to capture the sun throughout the day. The design has used the slight level changes within the garden to emphasize the different sitting areas. Near the house, the paving is widthways across the garden but it is bisected by the pathway leading from the house, which has slabs laid in the direction of travel leading toward the two sitting areas. The lower area is a paved, circular patio with a small reflecting pool of water offset to one side to reflect sunlight into the space. To the east of the garden is a small summerhouse with a circular, decked area in front. From the central path this is at a raised level and steps lead up to it. The planting beds in the garden are at the higher level and are contained by curved retaining walls flowing from the area nearest the house out and around the lower circular patio.

Planting includes a multi-stemmed birch (*Betula utilis* var. *jacquemontii*) and two *Betula pendula,* as well as *Viburnum plicatum* f. *tomentosum* 'Mariesii', roses, and sedums. Yuccas and phormiums give structure and eremurus add height in the summer.

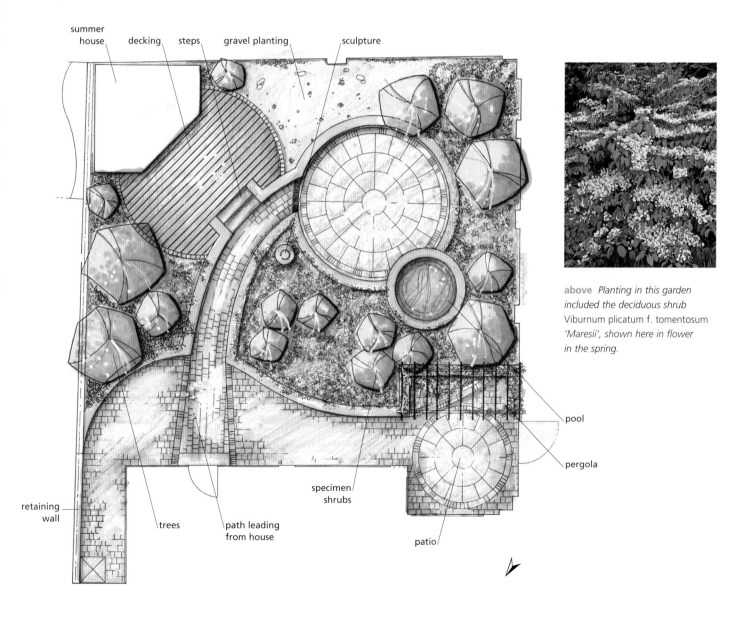

above *Planting in this garden included the deciduous shrub* Viburnum plicatum f. tomentosum *'Maresii', shown here in flower in the spring.*

Small Wildlife Garden

CHERYL CUMMINGS GARDEN DESIGN

DIMENSIONS 38sq m (407sq ft)
SOIL very free-draining loam
ASPECT south-east and south-west facing
KEY FEATURES illuminated steel column water feature

The owner of this small town garden wanted an oasis in which to sit outside with some privacy. Providing a haven for wildlife and including a moving water feature were also priorities. Because the house is listed and in a conservation area, screening the garden from the outside world could be done only with lush planting, which was problematic because, at its widest, the garden is only 4m (13ft) across.

A small pond with a tall steel column water feature provides the focal point. This gives height and movement, and at night the column is lit to give a tranquil atmosphere. As a result of the sheltered micro climate in the garden, an olive tree was planted to give height and an under storey of densely planted shrubs, grasses, and perennials gives a luxuriant and private feeling. A small paved sitting area is provided, with space for a couple of chairs. A glass-topped table is positioned over the pool to maximize space.

A soft contemporary style is used for the garden, enhanced by the choice of simple decoration. Two ceramic spheres adorn the terrace, and to encourage birds a large ceramic plate has been used as a bird bath on the terrace.

above Although this garden was tiny it was important for the owners to have a paved area with enough room for some seating.

left A pond with a tall steel column water feature is the focal point of this garden. A glass topped table is positioned over the pond to maximize space.

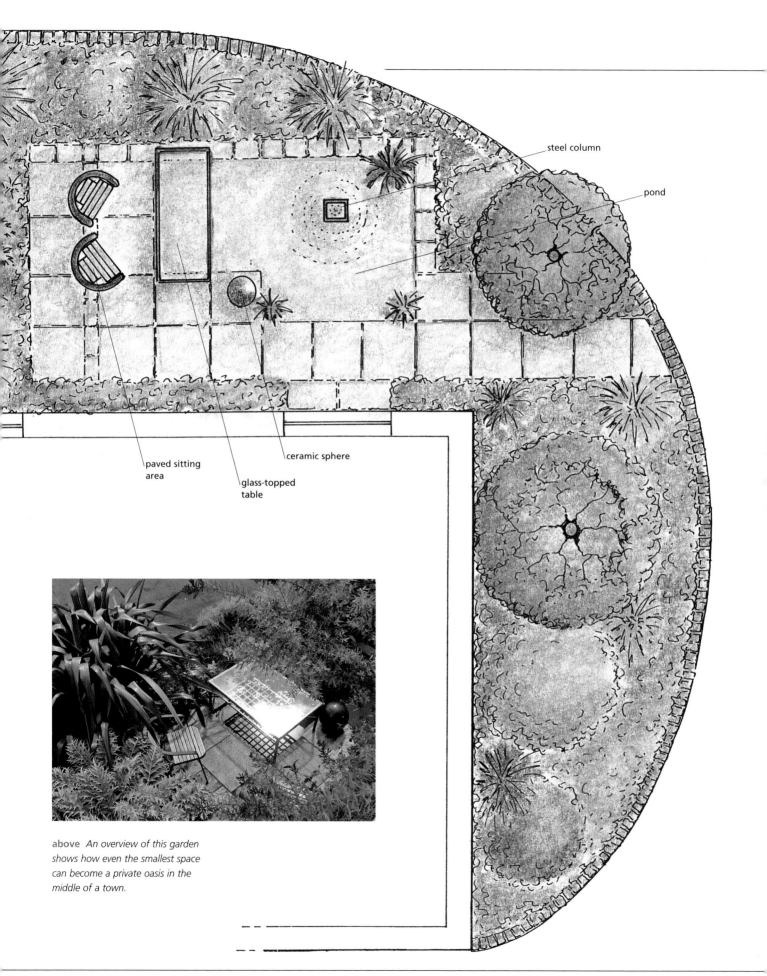

steel column

pond

ceramic sphere

paved sitting
area

glass-topped
table

above *An overview of this garden
shows how even the smallest space
can become a private oasis in the
middle of a town.*

Contemporary Walled Courtyard

PAUL DRACOTT

DIMENSIONS 5.5 x 4.5m (18 x 15ft)

SOIL sandy loam

ASPECT south facing

KEY FEATURES York stone retaining wall with LED lighting strip

This town centre cottage has a contemporary glass sun room that looks over the enclosed, walled courtyard, and a garage at the far end of the garden. The owners wanted to improve steep steps down from the house and to create a dining space as a secluded "external room".

The design creates one simple, open space surrounded by raised beds. The steps from the sun room are extended across the width of the courtyard and the gradient is made more generous. The paving is of diamond-cut York stone flagstones 50mm (2in) thick laid in a simple grid pattern. The raised beds are built from lengths of the same thickness of York stone stuck together with epoxy resin adhesive. The lack of a bedding joint gives the impression that the stone pieces are stacked and gives a clean contemporary look. This is enhanced by incorporating a central strip of ten pieces of 5mm- (¼in-) thick glass stuck together with adhesive and backed with blue LED strip lights. The resulting lighting effect washes the garden in low-level blue light delineating the perimeter of the seating area.

The garage is screened by three *Phyllostachys nigra* in black rectangular pots that create a back drop for the garden. A multi-stemmed *Amelanchier lamarckii* gives height and structure to the space, and the raised beds are planted with *Hosta sieboldiana*, ligularia, and grasses. In the shaded areas, *Acanthus mollis* and more hostas are used

above *The planting in the raised beds includes hostas, grasses, and, shown here, the large, clump-forming perennial* Ligularia.

steps from
sun room

below *This perspective sketch provides an effective view of the small enclosed space.*

Amelanchier lamarckii

raised beds

York stone flagstones

Phillostachys nigra in pots

Bright, Clean Courtyard

FISHER TOMLIN

DIMENSIONS 6.5 x 6.5m (22 x 22ft)

SOIL new topsoil/compost mix

ASPECT south facing and very hot

KEY FEATURES rendered pool

The owners of this small space wanted a bright, clean courtyard with simple lines and possibly a central focus but nothing too traditional. The garden needed to be brought up to the level of the house interior and access was very restricted.

The result is a testament to simplicity and restraint in design. This formal and symmetrical solution uses traditional materials in a clean and modern way. A grid square of bricks on edge forms the framework to the design, with the majority of the paving being irregularly sized York stone. Regularly spaced specimen *Amelanchier* x *grandiflora* 'Ballerina' trees set into *Buxus* cube "planters" complete the garden's structure. On the rear wall there is a raised rendered pool with a modern fish ceramic fountain spout set onto a pebble surface with an evergreen frame. On each side wall there

are built-in rendered and painted benches, which complete the symmetry. The walls, planters, and water trough are all painted a pale cream to unify the space and maximize the light available.

Other planting is very restricted and simply limited to *Trachelospermum jasminoides* and the fern *Polypodium vulgare*.

above *The view across the courtyard to the mosaic pool and spout, the central feature of the garden.*

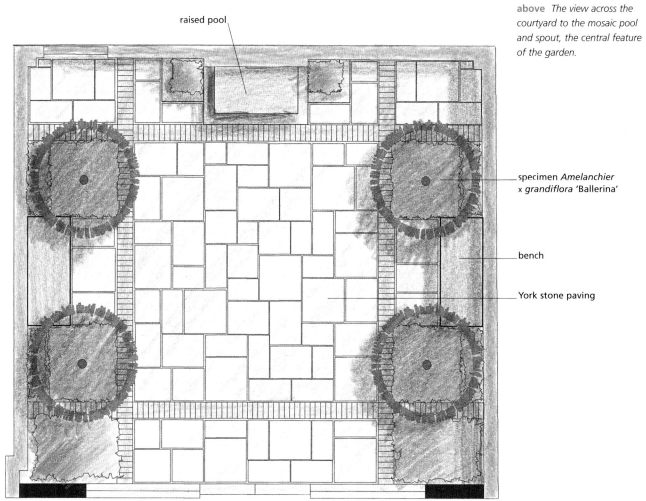

raised pool

specimen *Amelanchier* x *grandiflora* 'Ballerina'

bench

York stone paving

Canal Reflecting Pool

ANDREW WILSON ASSOCIATES

DIMENSIONS 12 x 7m (40 x 23ft)

SOIL neutral loam

ASPECT south facing

KEY FEATURES timber deck and a canal-like reflecting pool

The client originally requested a cottage garden but other requirements, including a play space for young children, storage, and outdoor dining for eight to ten people, meant that the garden became minimalist in style to maximize the usable space.

Borders are reduced to narrow, gravel-covered oblongs allowing space only for climbing plants to clothe the black-stained trellis that unifies the boundary fences. A blackberry and espaliered apple is also introduced. Black bamboo (*Phyllostachys nigra*) is used to screen the storage shed from the house.

The main features of the garden are the timber deck, which provides a substantial dining area, and a canal-like reflecting pool, both of which run across the width of the garden to emphasize scale. Large boulders sit in the water to provide a "fishing" facility for the children, and a gentle fountain ripples the water. Iris and other aquatic plants emerge from the water, disguising the edges of the canal. The lawn and stepping stones appear to float on the surface of the pool. Large, zinc planters decorate the deck, behind which up-lighters wash the climber-covered boundaries, producing subdued lighting to allow the garden to be used through the evening after darkness has fallen.

The garden walls are planted with *Vitis coignetiae* and *Clematis armandii* and, at the bottom of the garden, a birch (*Betula*) tree provides shade for a more intimate sitting space and a view back to the house.

left *The elevation shows the screening of the storage shed and the way in which the canal pool divides the garden spaces.*

boulder   zinc planter

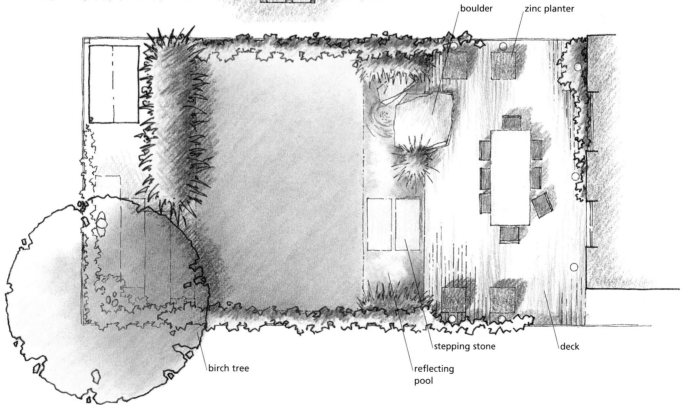

birch tree

stepping stone   deck

reflecting pool

Tiny Shady Courtyard

CLAIRE MEE DESIGNS

DIMENSIONS 3.6 x 2.8m (11 x 8ft)
SOIL not relevant
ASPECT north facing
KEY FEATURES built-in furniture and willow panels

This tiny, enclosed, and very shaded garden is attached to a very small apartment and the brief was to make the space function as an "outdoor room". The interior decoration was influenced by Japanese style and this theme was to continue into the garden using rich dark reds and dark stained wood. Minimal planting was possible because light levels were very low.

To give the best illusion of space, Yellow Balau hardwood decking is used with the angles offset to emphasize the longest dimensions available. Using these angles, a large built-in bench was set into a corner of the garden. Built as a timber frame and then clad in decking to match the ground, it gives a simple and unified look to the space.

To introduce planting into the garden, bespoke planters were made in shapes to fit each small area. These are powder-coated in ruby red to fit with the Japanese theme. The dining table, bench, and two chairs are also of timber, stained to the same colour as the other wood. Scatter cushions on the bench bring a splash of colour and softness to the space.

To screen the unsightly walls, large willow panels are mounted onto them and back-lit for a soft and moody lighting effect. Planting has a Japanese feel, using a mature *Acer palmatum* 'Sango-kaku' for its red trunk, *Trachelospermum jasminoides*, and the bamboos *Phyllostachys nigra* and *Nandina domestica*.

Acer palmatum 'Sango-kaku'

bench, table, and chairs

left *The stained timber dining furniture is a key feature in this small apartment's "outside room".*

hardwood decking

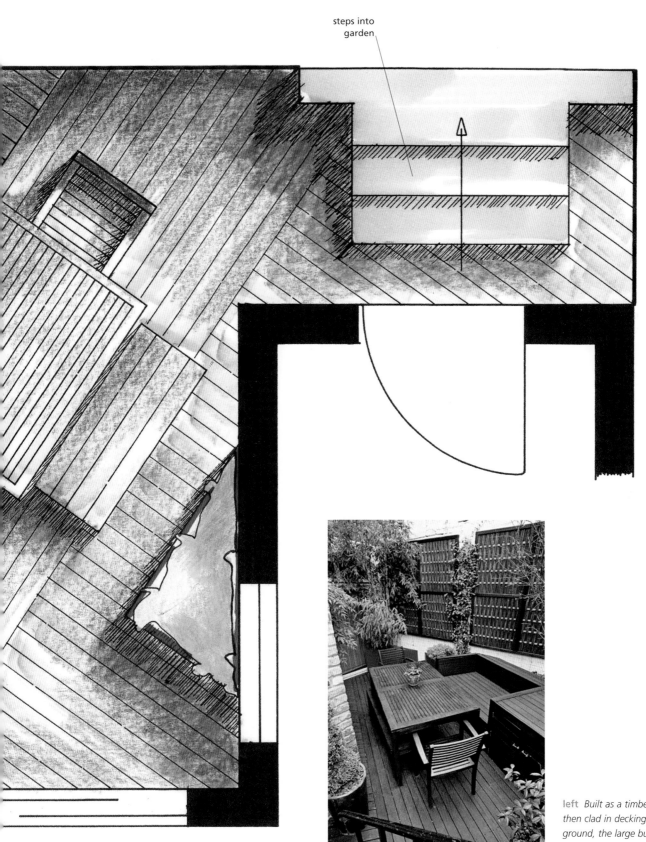

steps into
garden

left *Built as a timber frame and then clad in decking to match the ground, the large built-in bench is set into a corner of the garden.*

Bright Contemporary Space

NIGEL FULLER

DIMENSIONS lower courtyard 5 x 2m (16 x 6ft);
upper roof garden 5 x 2.6m (16 x 8ft)
SOIL neutral
ASPECT south facing
KEY FEATURES large painting by Ray Covell

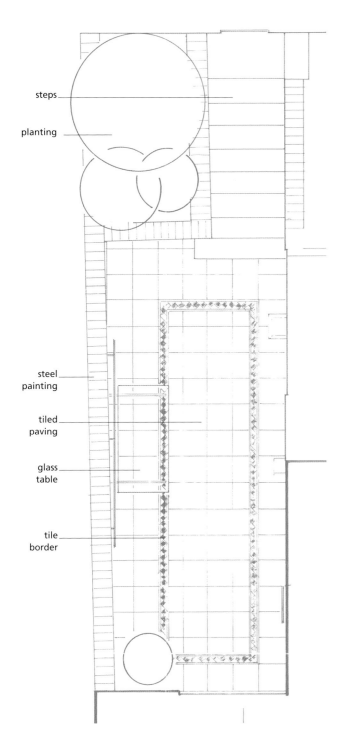

steps

planting

steel
painting

tiled
paving

glass
table

tile
border

As a dark, dismal, and utterly uninviting area at the rear of a property, this space presented an opportunity to open it up and to inject new life. Plants were not required by the owners, but they wanted brightness and colour as well as a place to sit. Minimal maintenance was crucial to success of the design. The major challenge was the 3m- (10ft-) high boundary wall.

By using very light-coloured paving and white-rendered walls, the designer has made the space light-filled and clean-looking. The tiled pattern in the paving gives definition and introduces colour. This is then carried through to the bluish glass table and the colours in the large painting hanging on the wall. This is constructed from a 2.5 x 1.2m (8 x 4ft) sheet of galvanized steel and is fixed securely to the wall. It is lit at night by fibre optic lights. Planting is restricted to pots of clipped yew balls and an olive tree.

Steps at the end of the garden lead up to a roof area that is decked and has seating at an angle for simplicity and clean lines.

above *This formerly dark, gloomy courtyard was revitalized by the use of light coloured paving, white rendered walls, and a decorative tiling pattern.*

Maintenance-Free Garden

CLAIRE MEE DESIGNS

DIMENSIONS 6 x 5m (20 x 16ft)

SOIL clay

ASPECT north-east facing

KEY FEATURES raised rill

This very small, city property was owned by a busy professional who wanted a maintenance-free garden. The interior of the house was state-of-the-art modern and the outside area was to complement this. Use of the garden was to be mainly at night, so lighting was very important.

To bring movement and interest to the space, a raised rill with a copper spout spilling water into it runs along the width of the back wall of the garden. A raised bed behind this is planted with five *Phyllostachys nigra*. The rear wall of the garden and the walls of the rill are rendered in a natural sand colour to tie in with the high London stock brick walls to either side. The water feature is topped with coping stones of polished black concrete to match the paving over the rest of the garden.

above *Because this garden was to be used mainly at night it was important that key features, such as the raised rill, were well lit.*

A small level change outside the house is managed with three steps turned sideways to the building and the level change is restricted to 600mm (24in) so that no balustrade is required.

raised bed with bamboo

dining and relaxing area

rill

copper water spout

steps

Communal Garden Space

ROBERT MYERS – ELIZABETH BANKS ASSOCIATES

DIMENSIONS 35 x 17m (117 x 55ft)

SOIL imported loam

ASPECT north-east facing

KEY FEATURES dramatic stone water wall between garden levels

The brief for this small site was to design a semi-private communal garden space for local residents as well as a small public square off the street between retail units. Ventilation units from the car park beneath the site needed to be screened and the site is next to a main railway station so noise was a potential issue.

The garden is equally divided between its two major user groups. The lower area is the more public space and is close to the road. Here, *Robinia pseudoacacia* trees are planted for colour and height, and these are set into a hardwearing base of bound gravel surrounded by York stone slabs. There is a long stone-and-timber seat and a statue, which was relocated from a previous building on the site. The garden is bisected by a dramatic stone "water wall" that is framed at the lower level by dense planting of

bamboo (*Fargesia nitida*). The moving water screens the ambient noise on the site as well as giving movement to the space and dividing the garden into its two areas.

The upper level is a more intimate space with a timber seat giving views across the garden and over the public square below. There is a central lawn, surrounded on two sides by multi-stemmed sumach (*Rhus glabra* 'Laciniata' Carrière) and underplanted with shade-loving herbaceous plants, grasses, and ferns. Against the buildings are beds filled with a mixture of box (*Buxus sempervirens*) and grasses (*Calamagrostis* x *acutiflora* 'Karl Foerster').

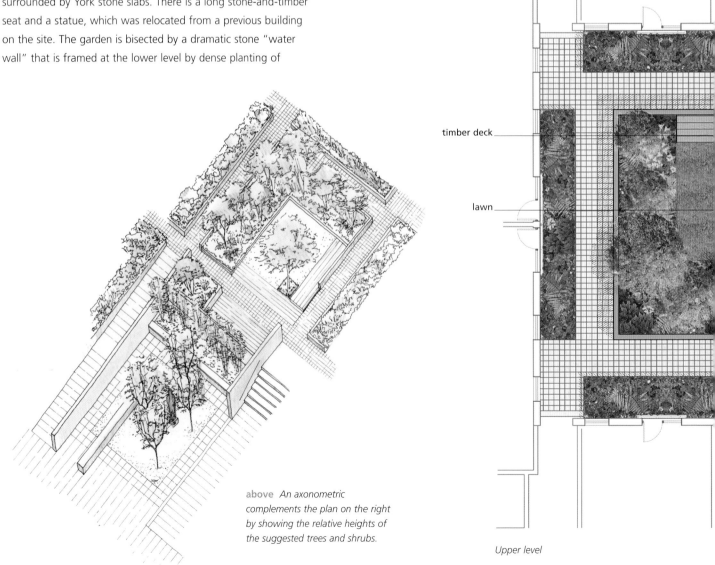

timber deck

lawn

above *An axonometric complements the plan on the right by showing the relative heights of the suggested trees and shrubs.*

Upper level

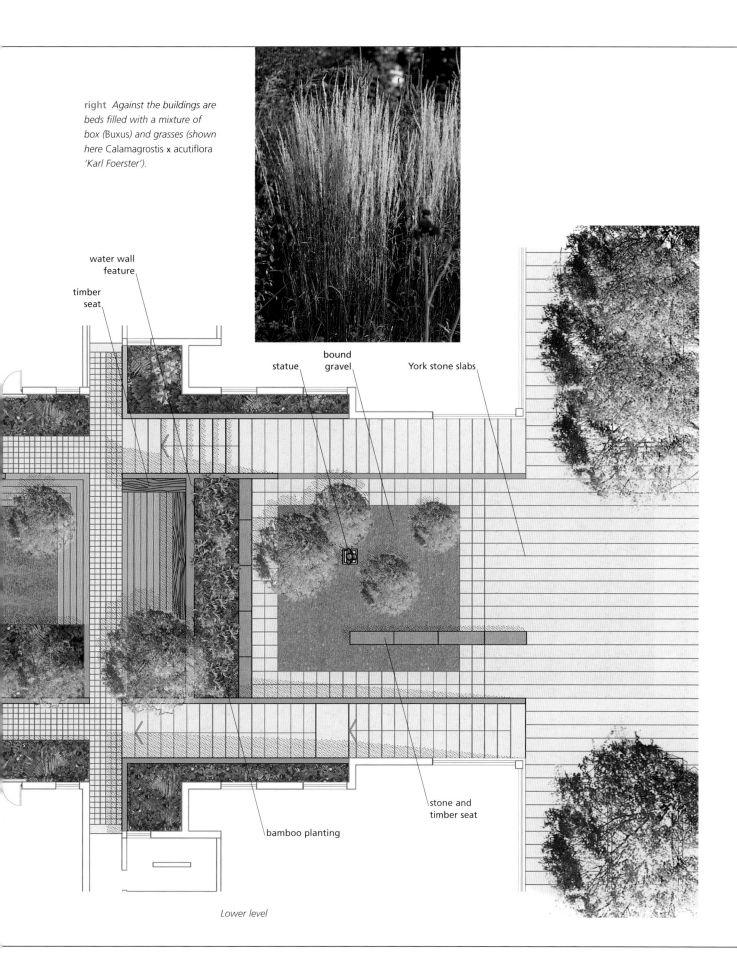

right *Against the buildings are beds filled with a mixture of box (*Buxus*) and grasses (shown here* Calamagrostis x acutiflora *'Karl Foerster').*

water wall feature

timber seat

statue

bound gravel

York stone slabs

stone and timber seat

bamboo planting

Lower level

Outside Gallery

MARCUS BARNETT AND PHILIP NIXON

DIMENSIONS 4.5 x 4.5m (15 x 15ft)

SOIL neutral

ASPECT south facing

KEY FEATURES black-and-white photographs and
a multi-stemmed *Rhus*

The designers won a gold medal at the Chelsea Flower Show in
2005 in the Chic Garden category for this design. It was created
for a collector of photography to allow the outdoor display of
part of his collection, as well as accommodating relaxation and
contemplation. The idea of contrast is conceptually important in
the theme and reflects the importance of contrast in the black-
and-white photographs on the walls.

White rendered walls with framed, profiled metal-sheet panels
on which the photographs are mounted, and an incorporated
bench, strike a contemporary note, forming an inviting corner
to sit. The photographs are lit from behind so that they can be
appreciated after dark and uplighters skim the walls for a soft
wash of light.

A polished, concrete floor, coloured to match the notional floor
of the house, provides unity of design between inside and outside,
and a stepping stone into the garden marks the entrance to the
space. When viewed from different angles, the small dark pool at
the front of the garden reflects elements of the design. Planting
continues the theme of contrasts. The multi-stemmed *Rhus typhina*
lifts the design and the visitor's eye; it also provides dappled shade.
Principal flower colours are purple and stark white, foliage is fresh
and green with contrasting leaf textures.

pool

concrete floor

stepping stone
into garden

left *An outstanding feature of this
garden was the display of black and
white photographs, shown here lit
from behind after dark.*

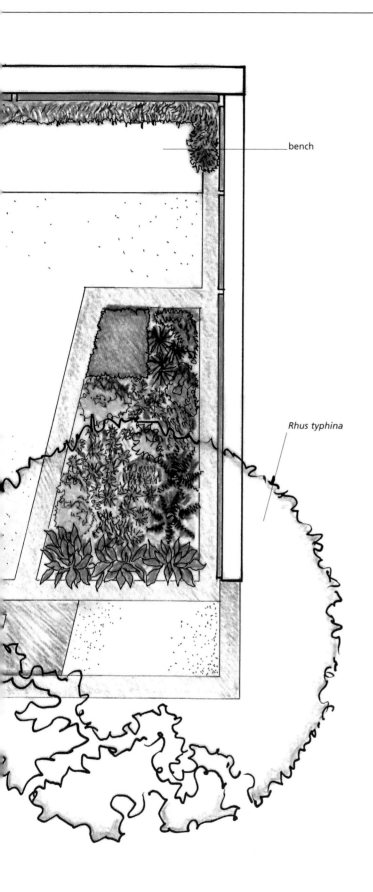

bench

Rhus typhina

above *When viewed from different angles, a small dark pool at the front of the garden reflects elements of the garden's design.*

below *A view of the garden in daylight shows how the different planting levels complement the minimalist structural design.*

Floating Terrace

PHILIP NASH DESIGN LTD

DIMENSIONS 9 x 7.5m (30 x 24ft)

SOIL neutral

ASPECT east facing

KEY FEATURES rill and a reflective pool

Having renovated their house, the owners were looking for a garden with clean lines, and to extend the living area outside. All materials had to come through the house and the new brick walls were to remain a feature.

Extending across the width of the house, an infinity pool, 7.4m (24ft) wide by 2m (6ft) across, divides the two sitting areas within the garden. There is simple bamboo planted to either side, and a Purbeck stone terrace is accessed directly from the house. After crossing the pool on "floating" stepping stones, the visitor finds a further stone terrace surrounded by water in a stainless-steel rill that feeds, on both sides, into the infinity pool. At the back of the garden, a glass water wall provides the focal point, and, during the day, its pale colour reflects light back into the space. Planting is structural and low-maintenance, including *Yucca gloriosa* in pots marking the ends of the planting beds, as well as *Olea europaea*, *Phormium tenax* 'Variegatum', and *Ligularia dentata* 'Desdemona'.

During the evening, this garden really excites, with blue LED strip lighting illuminating the pool and rills, creating a soft ambient atmosphere and highlighting the shapes of the planting.

above *An infinity pool with "floating" stepping stones is the key feature in the garden of this recently renovated house.*

right *The water feature becomes even more visually stunning at night once the blue LED strip lighting has been turned on.*

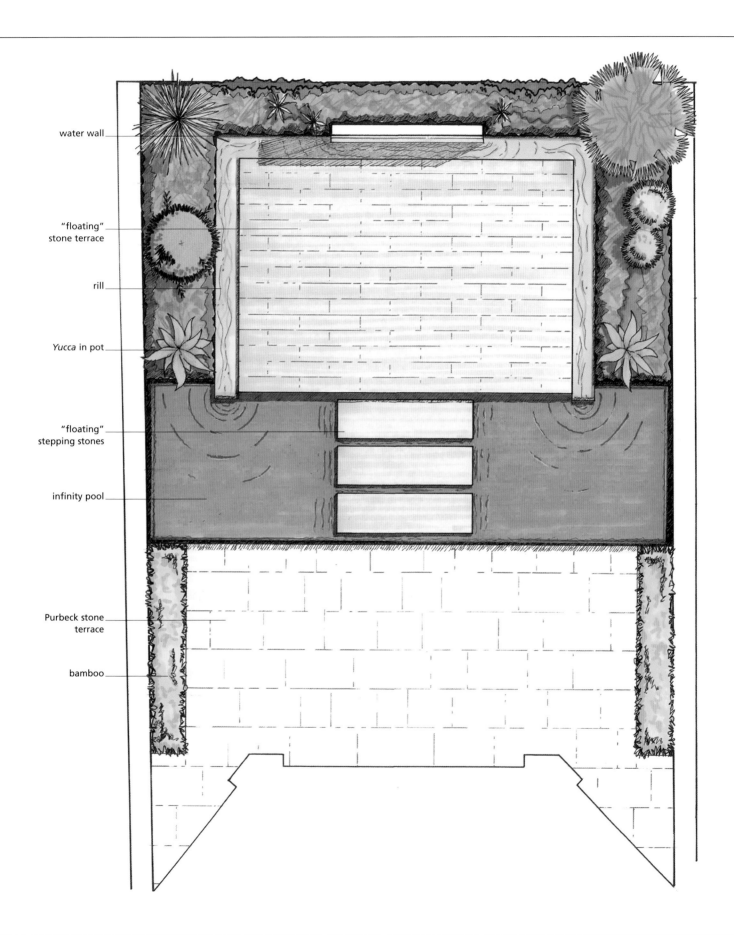

water wall

"floating"
stone terrace

rill

Yucca in pot

"floating"
stepping stones

infinity pool

Purbeck stone
terrace

bamboo

Funky Basement

PAUL DRACOTT

DIMENSIONS 8.5 x 5m (27 x 16ft)

SOIL sandy loam

ASPECT south facing

KEY FEATURES stainless-steel cascading rill

The garden of this terraced townhouse is at basement level, with access via steep, narrow steps. The brief was to create a funky garden space incorporating water, a small lawn, and coloured lighting.

The resulting design creates interlocking plateaux on different levels. These are bisected by a stainless-steel rill that drops down at the edge of each level and finally drops into a covered pool at the lowest level by the house. From the house, a western red cedar deck provides an informal entertaining space and leads to generous York stone steps up onto a diamond-cut and flame-textured York stone flagstone terrace. A small lawn is taken right to the boundaries with an edging of York stone and, at each end of the lawn, panels of concave, mirrored tiles create sculptural features. At the rear of the garden, a small terrace for more formal dining is flanked by an aubergine painted rendered retaining wall, and a panel containing a stainless water spout links the garden with the interior design style.

Jungly planting includes *Chamaerops humilis*, phormiums, *Fargesia murielae,* and *Fatsia japonica,* as well as other grasses and bamboos, to soften and add movement to the garden. The stainless-steel elements and the steps are lit with blue strip LED lights, and the mirrored panels are lit in both red and blue.

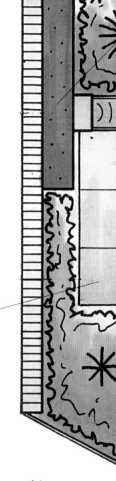

above *The interlocking plateaux on different levels in this basement garden are bisected by a stainless steel rill.*

terrace

left *At the rear of the garden an aubergine painted retaining wall is punctured by a panel containing a stainless steel water spout.*

retaining wall   rill   wall   pool

York stone edging   lawn   terrace   steps   wall   deck

above *The sketch elevation shows the location of the mirrored tiles along the boundary wall and recessed into the planting.*

Lush and Wild in the City

CHARLOTTE ROWE

DIMENSIONS 9 x 7m (30 x 23ft)
SOIL clay
ASPECT north-west facing
KEY FEATURES shade planting

The owners of this house situated in a city conservation area were keen to ensure that a new design for the garden would be in keeping with the style of the house and other local buildings. They also wanted, in what is a very small space, to create a garden journey through rich, lush planting. No hard edges were to be seen and the space needed to look organic and densely planted – a little wild if possible.

The design solution is to create a garden at 45 degrees from the house with a path that leads the eye past a water feature and to the far right-hand side, where there is a bench. This also optimizes the space and makes the garden seem much larger than it is. Paving is of reclaimed York stone edged with deep, red bricks to match the house, thereby uniting the space. To soften the hard materials, virtually every crack and gap along the path is filled with *Soleirolia soleirolii* and *Alchemilla mollis*.

Only about a third of the garden receives direct sunlight, so the planting is a mix of ferns including two *Dicksonia antarctica*, evergreen shrubs, and some shade-tolerant plants such as *Euphorbia amygdaloides* var. *robbiae* and *Persicaria polymorpha*. In the sunnier areas, there is a mix of perennials to provide seasonal colour and interest. Three pyramid-shaped bay trees provide year-round interest and structure.

above *A view across this city garden shows the York stone paving, the water feature, and the seating area.*

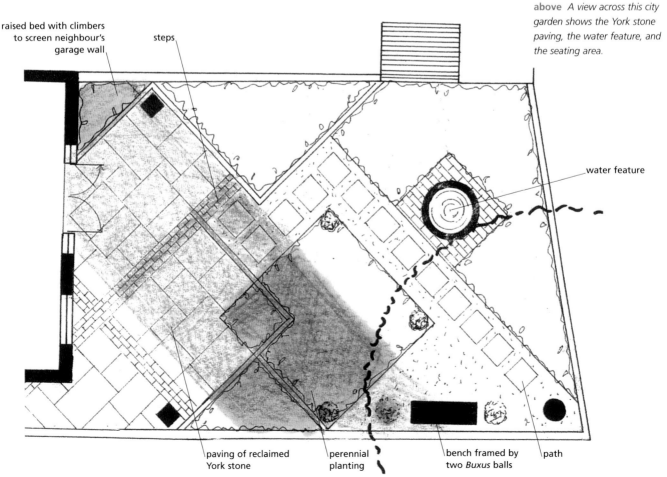

raised bed with climbers to screen neighbour's garage wall

steps

water feature

paving of reclaimed York stone

perennial planting

bench framed by two *Buxus* balls

path

Evening Garden

MICHAEL DAY

DIMENSIONS 6 x 9m (20 x 30ft)

SOIL well-drained alkaline

ASPECT south-east facing

KEY FEATURES circular seating area

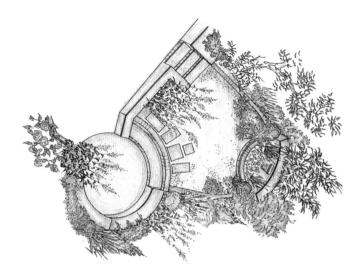

The owners wanted to sit out in this tiny garden in the evenings to make the most of the late sunshine. They wanted to have a space for entertaining and that the garden should look good from their sitting-room window. Some screening was needed to ensure privacy from neighbouring properties.

A circular seating area is set into the garden at the level of the driveway, which is slightly lower than the rest of the space. This increases the sense of enclosure and privacy. Retaining walls around the circle are stepped at various heights with a stone coping to match the paving stones, providing additional seating. From this area, steps lead up to a gravel garden with stepping stones through it and planting into the gravel to soften the overall design. In the western corner of the garden, a small water spill from a stone wall falls onto cobbles, and there is a backdrop of bamboo (*Fargesia nitida*) to enhance the water feature as well as softening the boundary. In the front corner of the garden, an *Amelanchier lamarckii* provides height, some screening from neighbours, and a full stop to the design.

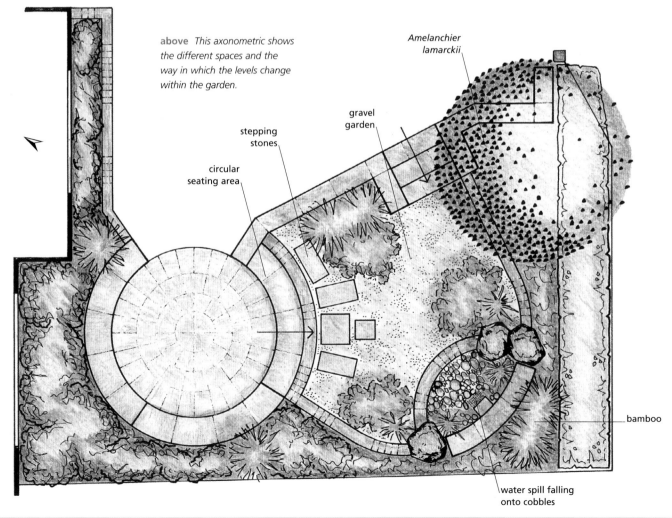

above *This axonometric shows the different spaces and the way in which the levels change within the garden.*

Amelanchier lamarckii

gravel garden

stepping stones

circular seating area

bamboo

water spill falling onto cobbles

Arches and Circles

NIGEL L. PHILIPS LANDSCAPE AND GARDEN DESIGN

DIMENSIONS 6.5 x 6.5m (22 x 22ft)

SOIL alluvial soil over chalk

ASPECT south-west facing; sheltered from prevailing winds

KEY FEATURES brick arches and a circular lawn

The owners work from home and requested that this garden look good throughout the year. In particular, the views from the kitchen and a balcony were important. An existing series of semicircular brick arches supplied the inspiration for the design theme.

The sight line for the design is across the garden from the back door of the house to give the maximum feeling of space. The small, circular lawn is contained on the house side by the same bricks as the terrace and on the planting side by 200mm (8in) raised, wooden edging. At the junctions between the two edges are stacks of wooden pillars 400 (16in), 600 (24in), and 800mm (30in) high. The brick terrace provides a generous sitting area and incorporates a herb garden planted in gaps in the paving.

The brick arches along the south-eastern side of the garden contain spiral sculptural objects that are underplanted with box edging. Along the sight line across the lawn, a raised circular, wooden platform leads to a small round pool, clad in timber and containing a fountain to bubble gently. Behind the pond, mirrors reflect back into the garden, increasing the sense of space. Planting is cottage-style, including campanulas and alchemillas, but with a strong evergreen structure.

pool

stack of wooden pillars

above *The circular design of this garden, was influenced by the existing brick arches.*

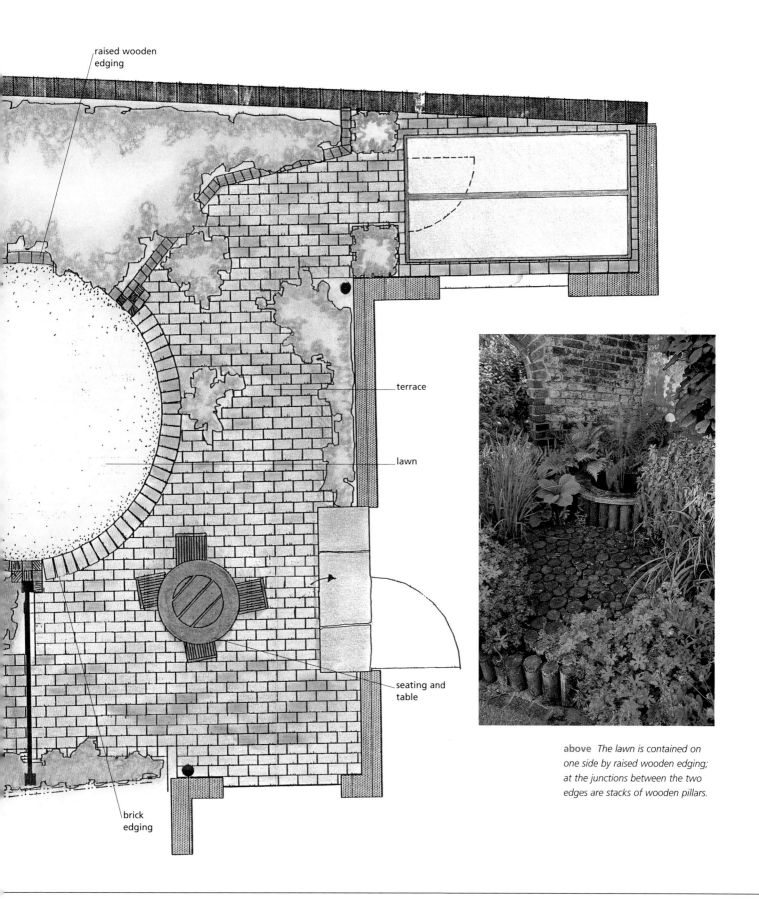

raised wooden
edging

terrace

lawn

seating and
table

brick
edging

above *The lawn is contained on
one side by raised wooden edging;
at the junctions between the two
edges are stacks of wooden pillars.*

Shot with Blue

CHARLOTTE ROWE

DIMENSIONS 5 x 4m (16 x 13ft)

SOIL clay

ASPECT east facing

KEY FEATURES built-in seating and a blue rill of light

This city courtyard needed to work hard as an extension to the house. The owners required extra living and entertaining space, even on dark winter evenings, as well as storage for bicycles and all the garden cushions but, in particular, they wanted a funky outdoor space with wow factor.

The solution was to design a series of fitted benches built of warm hardwood, integrated with a bicycle shed and a corner water feature. Cushions in a range of colours are used to make the timber benches comfortable. One of the benches doubles up as a mobile wine cooler on castors so that a larger number of people can be entertained occasionally. Rather than use classic paving, a polished poured concrete floor is used with its aggregate revealed to create an interesting, textured, and sparkling floor.

A simple dark-blue-painted pool in the corner of the garden is fed by a copper spout, bringing the sight and sound of water into the space. Planting is minimal with box balls, lavender, the grass *Stipa tenuissima,* and acid-lime-green heuchera. Fragrant climbers are used all around the walls.

More conventional up-lighting is used in the beds and water feature but, to stunning effect, a blue streak of light is incorporated within the concrete floor and follows the shape of the seating, giving the requested wow factor.

above and right *In order to provide the owners of this garden with extra living and entertaining space a series of fitted benches were fitted into this courtyard garden. A blue streak of light at ground level, incorporated into the floor, and following the shape of the seating, provides the "wow" factor.*

right *This perspective sketch shows the main seating space, storage shed, and wine cooler.*

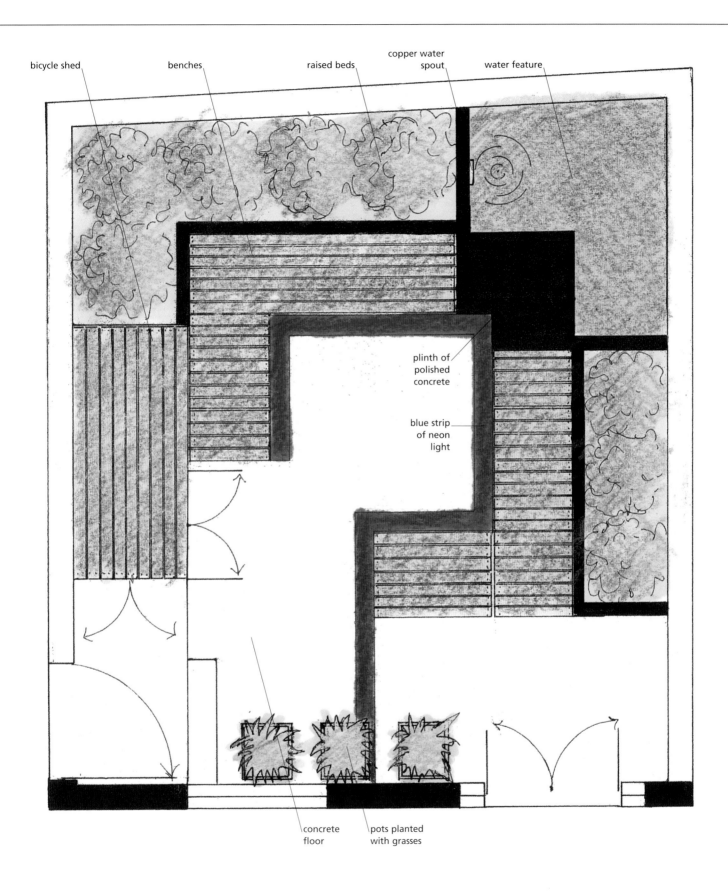

bicycle shed

benches

raised beds

copper water
spout

water feature

plinth of
polished
concrete

blue strip
of neon
light

concrete
floor

pots planted
with grasses

Flavour of "Down Under"

NATALYA SCOTT – MOOREA LANDSCAPES LTD

DIMENSIONS 12 x 4m (40 x 13ft) tapering to 2m (6ft) wide

SOIL neutral

ASPECT north facing

KEY FEATURES tree ferns

Maximizing use of this small, shaded garden was the main aim for the design. The owners needed an area for relaxing and entertaining, and wanted to have a flavour of New Zealand and Australia. An existing sunken seating area needed to remain.

The space divides into four main areas and tree ferns (*Dicksonia antarctica*) are planted throughout the garden. From the house, a small mosaic of a pond with fish, designed by the owner, gives interest in what could be a difficult area. Pots planted with architectural and exotic plants lift the space. The existing seating area is enhanced by lush planting of bamboos and ferns, including dryopteris and *Osmunda regalis*. Steps lead up to a small lawn on which to sunbathe and then to the sunniest part of the garden, which is paved in terra cotta tiles and provides a dining area. The boundaries are clad in reed panels to screen the existing fencing, except at the end of the garden where cladding is in marine plywood that is then painted cobalt blue, providing a contrast to the exotic planting.

Other planting among the tree ferns is of *Cordyline australis*, *Phormium tenax*, *Agave americana*, and *Yucca filamentosa*.

left *The owners of this tiny shaded garden wanted planting found in Australia and New Zealand – this included* Cordyline australis.

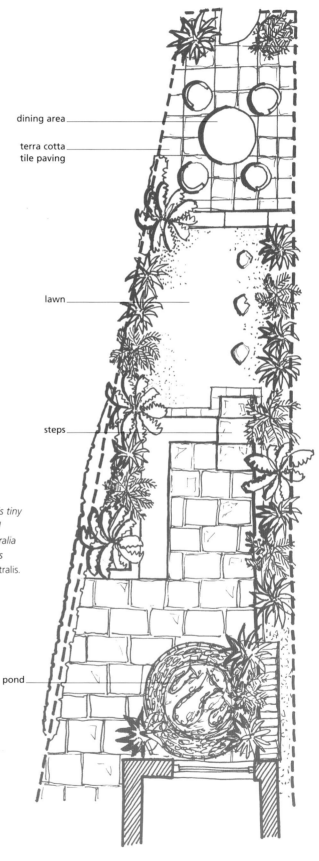

dining area

terra cotta tile paving

lawn

steps

pond

Light and Shade

CHARLOTTE KIERKEGAARD DESIGN

DIMENSIONS 7.5 x 5.5m (24 x 18ft)
SOIL loam
ASPECT north facing
KEY FEATURES raised beds topped with timber

In this tiny garden, problems were accentuated by the sunken nature of the space and the existence of a five-storey brick wall on one side. The aim was to introduce light into the garden and to plant shade-loving plants. An existing, overgrown pond needed to be removed and a 1.5m (5ft) height difference from the house to the back of the garden needed to be accommodated. Access to the site was very restricted.

The central part of the garden is paved in white concrete for its reflective qualities. By the house, a decked area conceals existing drainage points. The level change is managed by building ascending raised beds 500mm (20in) high, rendered and painted white, each topped with a timber coping so that the lower level forms seating and the second becomes a ledge for drinks or similar. In the top level a specimen *Pinus sylvestris* is planted. Other planting is of grasses, including *Deschampsia cespitosa* 'Morning Dew', junipers, and herbaceous perennials: *Hosta* 'Bressingham Blue', *Geranium himalayense*, *Anenome* x *hybrida* 'Honorine Jobert', and *Aster novi-belgii* 'Victor'.

right *This tiny axonometric shows the relationship of the small space to the towering pine.*

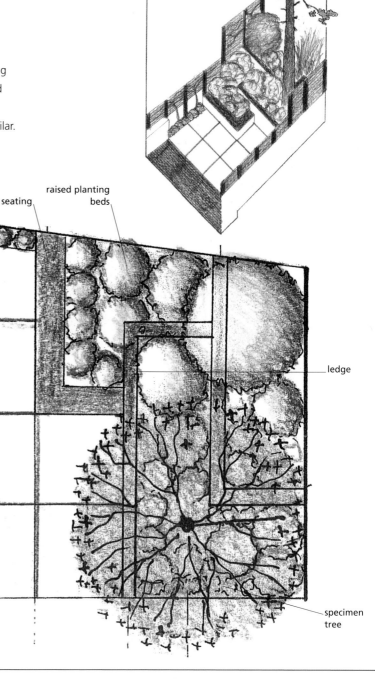

decking

white concrete paving

seating

raised planting beds

ledge

specimen tree

Venture Garden

SILK HALL GARDEN DESIGN

DIMENSIONS 6 x 4m (20 x 13ft)

SOIL fertile and neutral

ASPECT south facing

KEY FEATURES segmented mirror with each section angled differently

This Gold Medal-winning garden from 2005 is contemporary and stylish. Designed with a hint of early Islamic influence, it is not a themed garden but a calming and beautiful place to relax or to be with friends.

The garden is based around a simple raised pool with a trickle of water focusing the attention within the space. Two large palms (*Trachycarpus fortunei*) frame the entrance to the garden and set the tone for the rest of the planting, which is mostly exotic and architectural, mixed with some more familiar hardy plants. Structure is lent by *Yucca gloriosa*, *Cordyline indivisa*, *Chamaerops humilis,* and *Agave americana*. Glaucous foliage is set against deep plum foliage for contrast without the need for flower colour. Examples include *Colocasia esculenta, Canna* 'Black Knight', and *Eucomis comosa* 'Sparkling Burgundy'.

The curving lines of the low walls, which double as seating, gives a retro feel, which is emphasized by a tubular light running through the silvery, wooden flooring. Behind the pool is a polished, steel segmented mirror, with each piece angled separately to allow reflection of light and individual elements: sky, water, or leaf shapes.

above *The Islamic influence of this design is reflected in its simple lines, light colours, architectural planting, and water feature.*

right *The garden is based around a raised pool into which pours a trickle of water. A steel segmented mirror behind the pool reflects its planting.*

above *The axonometric view reveals how the main planting and architectural elements work together, providing a sense of scale.*

seating

mirror

raised pool

large
palms

tubular
lighting

wooden
flooring

Modern but not Minimalist

HELEN BILLETOP GARDEN DESIGN

DIMENSIONS 9 x 3.5m (30 x 11ft)

SOIL neutral loam

ASPECT south-west facing

KEY FEATURES galvanized-steel pergola and sett path

Reminiscent of so many tiny gardens behind Victorian cottages, this space was to be redesigned so that it would be modern without being minimal. It was also to have planting attractive to birds. The only view of it from the house is of a long, narrow side passage (not seen in the plan), so it was necessary to provide interest here and to soften the rather unwelcoming environment.

The palette of hard materials chosen for the garden reflects the owner's interior design style for the house. Stone paving for the passage and terrace is laid widthways to widen the garden's appearance. Along the passage, tall "Long Tom" planters are planted with standard bay "lollipops", and the neighbour's fence is screened with reed panels to improve the ambience.

Where the terrace opens out at the end of the house, a galvanized-steel pergola spans the whole area, defining it. Custom-made timber panels, painted a silvery-blue colour, are suspended from the pergola to provide a climbing frame for roses, clematis, wisteria, and *Trachelospermum jasminoides*.

A small step up from the terrace, a granite sett path curves to the gate at the back of the garden. An oval resting place on the path gives a sitting spot beneath an *Amelanchier* x *grandiflora* 'Robin Hill', planted for its attractiveness to birds.

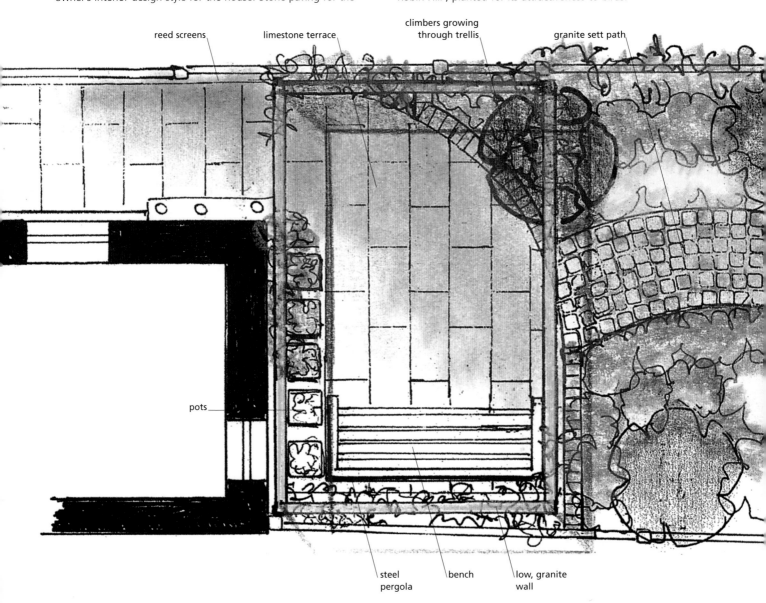

reed screens — limestone terrace — climbers growing through trellis — granite sett path — pots — steel pergola — bench — low, granite wall

left *A view of the back of the garden showing how the terrace leads up to a granite sett path with an oval resting place halfway along.*

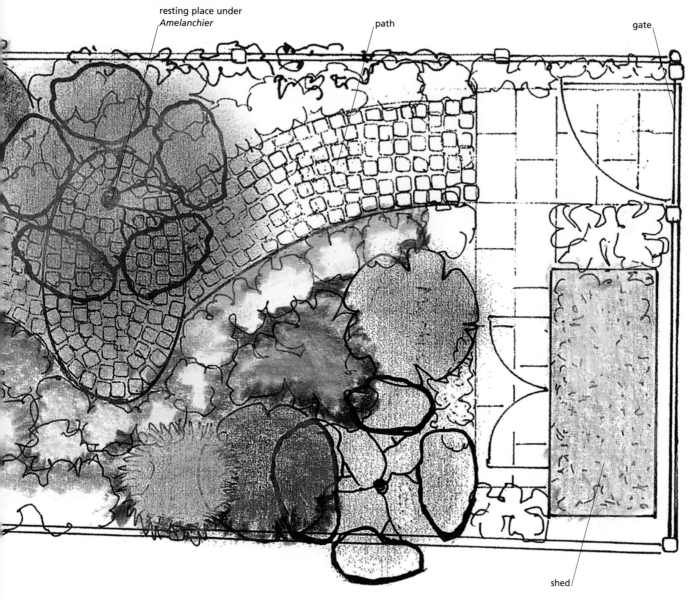

resting place under
Amelanchier

path

gate

shed

Urban Eden

CARO OLDROYD – CLIFTON NURSERIES

DIMENSIONS 7 x 5m (23 x 16ft)

SOIL not known

ASPECT not known

KEY FEATURES interesting material combinations and planting

This show garden was designed as a small urban courtyard for a discerning professional, providing a respite from the hustle and bustle of the city. A sunny aspect on entering the garden gives way to a shady and secluded sanctuary to unwind and relax.

With a contemporary layout and strong geometric lines, the planes of alternating cool-blue slate, *Soleirolia soleirolii,* and smooth pebble mosaic move in and out of the planting on either side, creating an illusion of increased width. The materials also create visual and textural interest underfoot. A hardwood bench set on large, Welsh slate blocks is semi-enclosed on three sides by bamboo for privacy, and a water feature entices the visitor to the far end of the garden. The water is in a glass tower, lit from within, creating a soft glow and with a gentle bubbling water noise. The pergola is a combination of black-stained beams and thick bamboo poles.

Planting is bold and architectural to create a lush, jungle atmosphere. The emphasis is on foliage texture punctuated with bright, tropical colour. Other key plants include tree ferns (*Dicksonia antarctica*), loquats (*Eriobotrya japonica, Pittosporum tenuifolium*), and red hot pokers (*Kniphofia*).

above *Both the materials and the planting indicate that this garden was designed as a shaded and secluded sanctuary.*

right *A further calming feature is glass tower water feature at the far end of the garden. Lit from within, it provides the sound of gently bubbling water.*

bamboo and hardwood pergola

bench

water feature

Soleirola solerolii

tree fern (*Dicksonia antarctica*)

smooth pebble mosaic

blue slate

Integrated Features

ANNIE GUILFOYLE – CREATIVE LANDSCAPES

DIMENSIONS 12 x 5.5m (40 x 18ft)

SOIL neutral

ASPECT south-east facing

KEY FEATURES pleached trees, topiary, and a water feature

An outdoor room with wow factor was what the owners of this property were after. This meant substantial lighting for evening use when entertaining friends and a water feature of note to provide a focal point in the garden. A simple, contemporary design with grasses, white flowers, and scent were also stipulated.

The lower terrace area to the south-east of the garden had to incorporate a large pad foundation integral to the building, so planting is into raised beds constructed on top of this foundation.

Pleached hornbeam trees (*Carpinus betulus*) are planted along the boundary, adding vertical structure that helps to clothe the walls and contribute winter interest to the garden. Key shrubs are selected for their shade tolerance and include *Vibernum tinus, Viburnum davidii,* and *Choisya ternata.* Box balls of varying sizes are dotted around, inter-planted with grasses and under-planted with bulbs such as *Allium hollandicum.* The clump-forming perennial *Libertia formosa* provides evergreen foliage and white flowers.

To maximize space, the steps up to the north-west are designed to wrap around the pool and are generously proportioned to make them an inviting place to sit. The pool has two levels, allowing the water to bring movement and sound to the garden.

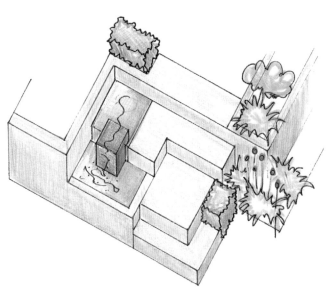

above *The axonometric view is used to explain the detail of the level change with the water cascade alongside.*

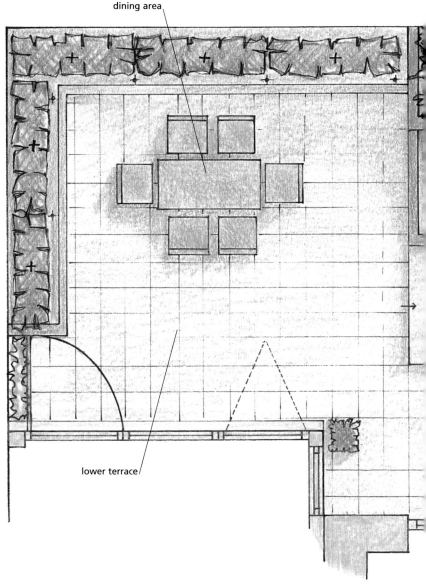

dining area

lower terrace

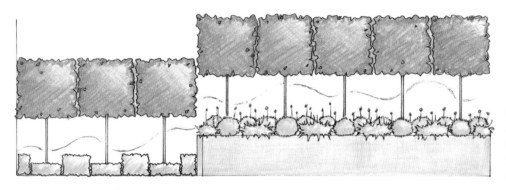

left *The elevation shows the arrangement and height of the boundary pleached hedging and the way in which the level change is repeated in the planting.*

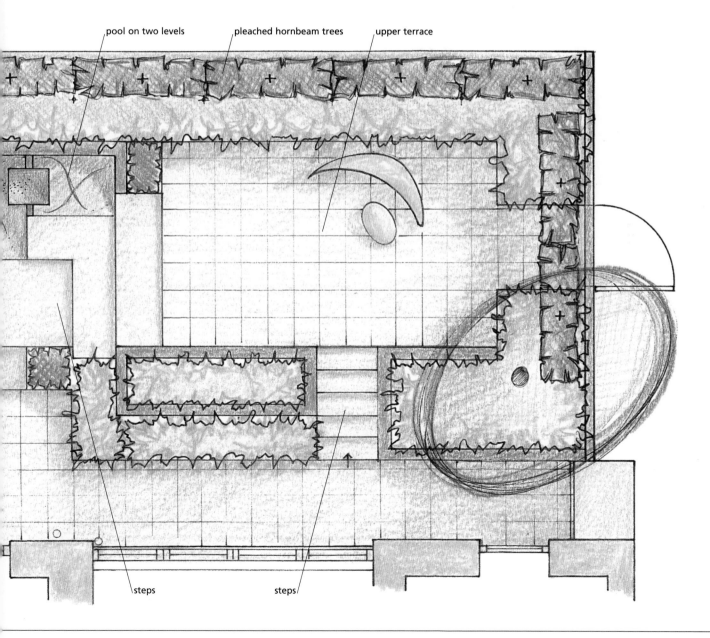

pool on two levels   pleached hornbeam trees   upper terrace

steps   steps

Turf and Heathers

NIGEL FULLER

DIMENSIONS 6 x 6m (20 x 20ft)

SOIL not known

ASPECT south facing

KEY FEATURES curved turf seat

This design was for a show garden, so there was no owner's brief to meet and the plan results entirely from the designer's imagination. The outcome featured a huge curved turf seat with massive brick "arms" at either end. This bench reached 1.2m (4ft) in height. At the front of the garden, new railway sleepers gave a strong, horizontal entrance to the design, which was carried through into the planting at the front of the stand. This was of heathers to create a coloured ribbon effect, mulched with charcoal. Tegular paving was used for the circular area in front of the turf seat, and a tall narrow tree gave height and softness to the overall look of the garden.

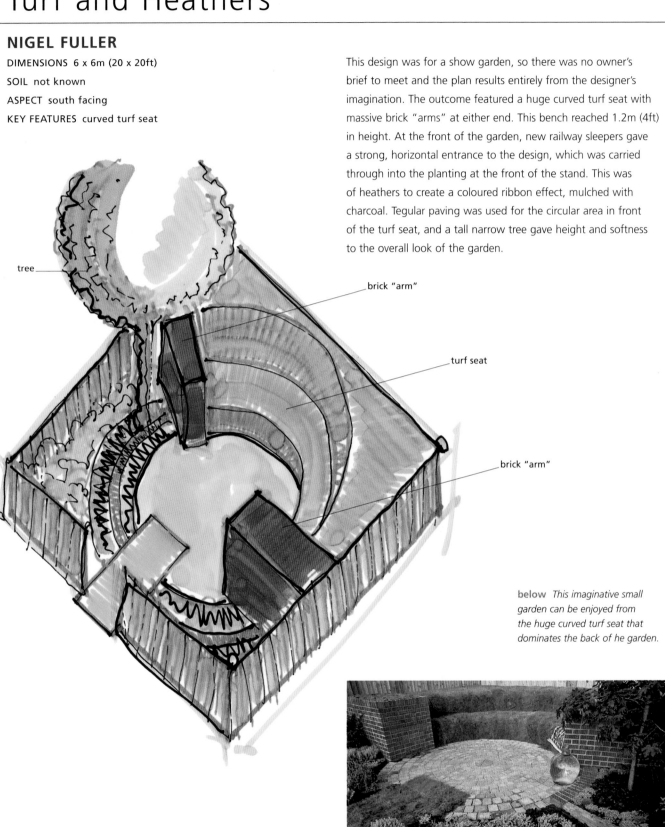

tree

brick "arm"

turf seat

brick "arm"

below *This imaginative small garden can be enjoyed from the huge curved turf seat that dominates the back of he garden.*

Bright and Modern Courtyard

SALLY COURT – COURTYARD GARDEN DESIGN

DIMENSIONS 5.5 x 3.5m (17 x 11ft)

SOIL no soil

ASPECT north-east facing

KEY FEATURES sail-style awning and tensile screening

left *An elevation view of the narrowing corner showing the printed tensile screen that suggests a view beyond.*

The owner had already had some work done in this small courtyard, including installation of a deck, a raised plinth along the northern wall, and a small amount of lighting. She now realized that more design input was needed to achieve a finished look so that the garden was ready for entertaining. The space was overlooked by neighbouring flats and the rear of another building with very ugly windows.

The main solution was to install a tensile screen fixed to an aluminium frame with a printed photograph of a path leading through an avenue of lavender and olives, which covers the entire length of the unsightly window at the rear of the garden. The screen is back-lit so that its effect continues during the evening. All the walls have been re-rendered and painted to match the colour of the house.

For sunny days, and when extra privacy is required, an awning can be attached to the walls to provide a "roof". Four spherical "Snowball" lights mark the corners of the garden, and additional wall lights are added to improve the ambience. Planting is very simple, with four fern palms (*Cycas revoluta*) planted in large pots.

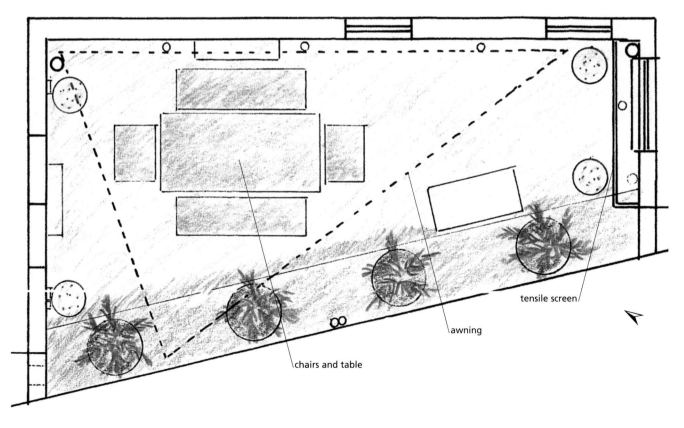

tensile screen

awning

chairs and table

Directory of Designers

Acres Wild Landscape and Garden Design
1 Helm Cottages
Nuthurst, Horsham
West Sussex RH13 6RG, UK
tel +44 (0) 1403 891084
email enquiries@acreswild.co.uk
website www.acreswild.co.uk

James Aldridge Garden Design
5 Choumert Mews
Choumert Road
London SE15 4BD, UK
tel +44 (0) 7956 159922 (mobile)
email design@jamesaldridgegardens.com
website www.jamesaldridgegardens.com

Elizabeth Banks Associates
Hergest Estate Office
Ridgebourne Road, Kington
Herefordshire HR5 3EG, UK
tel +44 (0) 1544 232035
email mail@eba.co.uk
website www.eba.co.uk

Barnes Walker Ltd
Unit 6, Longley Lane
Northenden, Manchester M22 4WT, UK
tel +44 (0) 161 946 0808
email design@barneswalker.co.uk
website www.barneswalker.co.uk

**Marcus Barnett Landscape
and Garden Design**
Studio CW8/9, The Cranewell
2 Michael Road, London SW6 2AD, UK
tel +44 (0) 20 7736 9761
email design@marcusbarnettdesign.com
website www.marcusbarnettdesign.com

Helen Billetop Garden Design
58 Northcote Road
St Margarets, Twickenham
Middlesex TW1 1PA, UK
tel +44 (0) 20 8892 3825
email helen@helenbilletop.com
website www.helenbilletop.com

Alison Brett – Hortus Design + Build Ltd
Unit 46, Dunsfold Park
Cranleigh, Surrey GU6 8TB, UK
tel +44 (0) 1483 277267
email info@hortusdesignbuild.co.uk
website www.hortusdesignbuild.co.uk

Jill Brindle – Silk Hall Garden Design
The Manse, Silk Hall
Tockholes, Darwen
Lancashire BB3 0NQ, UK
tel +44 (0) 7711 318 466 (mobile)
email jillbrindle@btinternet.com

George Carter
Silverstone Farm, North Elmham
Norfolk NR20 5EX, UK
tel +44 (0) 1362 668130
email grcarter@easynet.co.uk

**Douglas Coltart – Viridarium
Design Studio**
21 Deacons Place, Girvan
Ayrshire KA26 9BZ, UK
tel +44 (0) 1465 811118
email douglas@viridarium.co.uk
website www.viridarium.co.uk

Sally Court – Courtyard Garden Design
The Workshop, 32 Broadway Avenue
East Twickenham, Middlesex TW1 1RH, UK
tel +44 (0) 20 8892 0118
email sally.cgd@btconnect.com
website www.courtyardgardendesign.co.uk

Cheryl Cummings Garden Designer
6 Maple Drive, Monmouth
Monmouthshire NP25 5DZ, UK
tel +44 (0) 1600 719014
email cheryl@gardendesignerwales.co.uk
website www.gardendesignerwales.co.uk

Liz Davies Garden Design
Croesllanfro Farm
Rogerstone, Newport
South Wales NP10 9GP, UK
tel +44 (0) 1633 894343
email lizplants@aol.com
website www.lizplants.co.uk

Michael Day Garden Design
The Chalet, Marston Meysey
Swindon, Wiltshire SN6 6LQ, UK
tel +44 (0) 1285 810486
email info@michaeldaygardendesign.co.uk
website www.michaeldaygardendesign.co.uk

Paul Dracott – Agave
5a West Street, Comberton
Cambridge CB3 7DS, UK
tel +44 (0) 1223 264292
email info@agaveonline.com
website www.agaveonline.com

Andrew Duff
The Design Studio, 33 Douglas Road
Surbiton, Surrey KT6 7RZ, UK
tel +44 (0) 20 8972 1020
email andrew@landscape.freeserve.co.uk

Sarah Eberle – Hillier Landscapes
Ampfield House, Ampfield, Romsey
Hampshire SO51 9PA, UK
tel +44 (0) 1794 368733 / 368855
email hillierlandscapes@btinternet.com
website www.hillier-landscpaes.co.uk

Susanna Edwards Garden Design
9 Kings Road, Richmond
Surrey TW10 6NN, UK
tel +44 (0) 20 8940 2270
email skedwards@btopenworld.com

Fisher Tomlin
74 Sydney Road, Wimbledon
London SW20 8EF, UK
tel +44 (0) 20 8542 0683
email info@fishertomlin.com
website www.fishertomlin.com

Nigel Fuller Garden Design
7 North Street
Crewkerne
Somerset TA18 7AJ, UK
tel +44 (0) 1460 76281
email nigel.fuller2@btopenworld.com
website www.nigelfullergardendesign.com

Naila Green Garden Design
Highover, Lady's Mile
Exeter Road, Dawlish
Devon EX7 0AX, UK
tel +44 (0) 1626 888598
email naila@corporate-gardens.co.uk
website www.nailagreen.com

Annie Guilfoyle – Creative Landscapes
Daisy Cottage, 40 Lutener Road
Easebourne, Midhurst
West Sussex GU29 9AT, UK
tel +44 (0) 1730 812943
email annie@creative-landscapes.com
website www.creative-landscapes.com

Alex Johnson
3rd Floor, 90 Whiteladies Road
Clifton, Bristol BS8 2QN, UK
tel +44 (0) 117 973 0023
email alex@elemental.freeserve.co.uk
website
www.elemental-landscape-architects.co.uk

Charlotte Kierkegaard Design
34 Boileau Road
Barnes, London SW13 9BL, UK
tel +44 (0) 20 8255 7633
email info@kierkegaard-design.com
website www.kierkegaard-design.com

Jan King Landscape and Garden Design
The Mill House, Lane Road
Wakes Colne, Colchester
Essex CO6 2BP, UK
tel +44 (0) 1787 222540
email jan@floralking.co.uk
website www.floralking.co.uk

Sarah Layton Garden Design
13 Purley Avenue
London NW2 1SH, UK
tel +44 (0) 20 8450 1862
email sarah@blissfulgardens.co.uk
website www.blissfulgardens.co.uk

James Lee Landscape and Garden Design
55 Barry Road
London SE22 0HR, UK
tel +44 (0) 20 8693 9391
email james@jamesleedesign.com
website www.jamesleedesign.com

Arabella Lennox-Boyd
45 Moreton Street
London SW1V 2NY, UK
tel +44 (0) 20 7931 9995
email office@arabellalennoxboyd.com
website www.arabellalennoxboyd.com

Daniel Lobb
177b Old Winton Road
Andover, Hampshire SP10 2DR, UK
tel +44 (0) 7971 223262 (mobile)
email daniellobb@hotmail.co.uk
website www.daniellobb.co.uk

Mark Lutyens Associates – Landscape Architects and Garden Consultants
Unit 10, 81 Southern Row
London W10 5AL, UK
tel +44 (0) 20 8969 4206
email mlutyens@dircon.co.uk
website www.mark-lutyens.co.uk

Christopher Maguire
15 Harston Road, Newton
Cambridge CB2 5PA, UK
tel +44 (0) 1223 872800
website www.christophermaguire.co.uk

Terry McGlade – Perennial Gardens
240 Sterling Road, Toronto
Ontario M6R 2B9, Canada
tel 001 416 513 1461
email info@perennialgardens.ca
website www.greenroofonline.com

Gavin McWilliam – Bedrock Landscape Design
The Barley Mow Centre
Chiswick, London W4 4PH, UK
tel +44 (0) 7738 109945 (mobile)
email info@bedrocklandscapes.co.uk
website www.bedrocklandscapes.co.uk

Claire Mee Garden Design
132 Harbord Street
London SW6 6PH, UK
tel +44 (0) 20 7385 8614
email garden.design@clairemee.co.uk
website www.clairemee.co.uk

Rachel Myers Garden Design
56 Marsh Road, Temple Cowley
Oxford, Oxfordshire OX4 2HH, UK
tel +44 (0) 1865 747101
email rachelmyers@btinternet.com
website www.rachelmyersgardendesign.co.uk

Philip Nash Garden Design
Churcham House
1 Bridgeman Road
Teddington, Middlesex TW11 9AJ, UK
tel +44 (0) 20 8973 4325
email philip@nashgardendesign.co.uk
website www.nashgardendesign.co.uk

Philip Nixon Design
Studio CW8/9, The Cranewell
2 Michael Road
London SW6 2AD, UK
tel +44 (0) 20 7371 0066
email info@philipnixondesign.com
website www.philipnixondesign.com

Caro Oldroyd – Square Root Garden and Landscape Design and Construction
Unit 10, 81 Southern Row
London W10 5AL, UK
tel +44 (0) 20 8960 6600
email info@squarerootgardens.co.uk
website www.squarerootgardens.co.uk

Olin Partnership
The Public Ledger Building
Suite 1123, 150 S. Independence Mall W.
Philadelphia, PA 19106, USA
tel 001 215 440 0030
website www.olinptr.com

Mary Payne
2 Old Tarnwell
Upper Stanton Drew
Bristol BS39 4EA, UK
tel +44 (0) 1275 333146
email maryjpayne@yahoo.co.uk

Nigel Philips Landscape and Garden Design
Station Studio, Cooksbridge
Lewes, East Sussex BN8 4SW, UK
tel +44 (0) 1273 400983
email post@nigelphilips.co.uk
website www.nigelphilips.co.uk

Keith Pullan Garden Design
1 Amotherby Close
Amotherby, Malton
North Yorkshire YO17 6TG, UK
tel +44 (0) 1653 693885
email keithpullan@fastmail.fm
website www.keithpullan.co.uk

Charlotte Rowe Garden Design
85 Masbro Road
London W14 0LR, UK
tel +44 (0) 20 7602 0660
email design@charlotterowe.com
website www.charlotterowe.com

Amir Schlezinger – MyLandscapes
24 Camden Mews
London NW1 9DA, UK
tel +44 (0) 20 7485 6464
email design@mylandscapes.co.uk
website www.mylandscapes.co.uk

Natalya Scott – Moorea Landscapes Ltd
7 Belmont Road, Stroud
Gloucestershire SG5 1HH, UK
tel +44 (0) 1453 808230
email natalya@moorealandscapes.co.uk

David Sisley – Garden Designs and Landscapes
Straight Mile Nursery Gardens
Ongar Road, Pilgrims Hatch
Brentwood, Essex CM15 9SA, UK
tel +44 (0) 1277 374439
website
www.gardendesignsandlandscapes.co.uk

Vladimir Sitta – Terragram Pty Ltd
3rd Floor, 15 Randle Street
Surrey Hills, NSW 2010, Australia
tel 0061 2 9211 6060
email info@terragram.com.au

David Stevens International
Well House,
60 Well Street, Buckingham,
Buckinghamshire MK18 1EN, UK
tel +44 (0) 1280 821097
email gardens@david-stevens.co.uk
website www.david-stevens.co.uk

Andy Sturgeon Garden Design
15 Clermont Road
Brighton BN1 6SG, UK
tel +44 (0) 1273 553336
email andysturgeon@btconnect.com
website www.andysturgeon.com

Tim Thoelecke – American Academy of Landscape Design LLC
1926 Waukegan Road
Glenview, Illinois 60025, USA
tel 001 847 657 7900
email tim@aaldweb.com
website www.aaldweb.com

Julie Toll Landscape and Garden Design
Business & Technology Centre
Bessemer Drive, Stevenage
Hertfordshire SG1 2DX, UK
tel +44 (0) 1438 310095
email info@julietoll.co.uk
website www.julietoll.co.uk

Xa Tollemache – Landscape and Garden Designer
Helmingham Hall, Stowmarket
Suffolk IP14 6EF, UK
tel +44 (0) 1473 890799
email xatollemache@helmingham.com
website www.xa-tollemache.co.uk

Cleve West
Navigator House, 60 High Street
Hampton Wick, Surrey KT1 4DB, UK
tel +44 (0) 20 8977 3522
email info@clevewest.com
website www.clevewest.com

Andrew Wilson Associates – Garden and Landscape Design
Laurel Cottage, 12 Bridge Road
Chertsey, Surrey KT16 8JL, UK
tel +44 (0) 1932 563293
email r.a.wilson@btconnect.com
website www.andrewwilsonassociates.co.uk

Stephen Woodhams – Woodhams Landscapes
378 Brixton Road
London SW9 7AW, UK
tel +44 (0) 20 7346 5656
email info@woodhams.co.uk
website www.woodhams.co.uk

Index

Page numbers in *italics* refer to picture captions

Acknowledgments

I would like to thank the team at Mitchell Beazley for putting their faith into a second book and all the designers who so willingly gave of their time. More particularly, I would like to make a special mention of Susanna Edwards, without whose organizational skills this project would never have happened. More personally, I would also like to thank my ever-supportive family, Barbara, Rebecca, and Naomi.

Andrew

We would like to thank Andy Bard for drawing up the Philip Nash gardens, and Audrey Daw for drawing up the Mary Payne garden.

Andrew Wilson and *Susanna Edwards*

PHOTOGRAPHIC ACKNOWLEDGMENTS

Mitchell Beazley would like to thank everyone who has so kindly supplied their plans and photographs for inclusion in this book. Additional credits are as follows.

Jacket, front, clockwise from top left: Paul Dracott/Agave, Keith Pullan Garden Design x 2, Philip Nixon Design, Annie Guilfoyle/Creative Landscapes, James Aldridge Gardens; back, Cheryl Cummings Garden Design, Andy Sturgeon Garden Design, Jan King Landscape and Garden Design.

Page 4–5 Acres Wild/Ian Smith; **7** Keith Pullan Garden Design; **10** Terence McGlade/Perennial Gardens; **11** Keith Pullan Garden Design; **12** below Charlotte Rowe Garden Design; **12** above Clive Nichols/Design Charlotte Row; **13** Tim Thoelecke/American Academy of Landscape Design LLC; **14** Philip Nash Garden Design; **14–15** Gavin McWilliam/Bedrock Landscape Design; **16** Charlotte Rowe Garden Design; **17** Acres Wild; **18–19** Philip Nash Garden Design; **22** Octopus Publishing Group; **25, 34** photo Ian Smith; **47** Andrew Lawson Photography/Torie Chugg; **52** Minitheatre Productions; **55** Andrew Lawson; **66** left and right Mark Bolton; **68** David Markson; **70** Andrew Lawson; **78, 79** courtesy J. Curry; **82** Octopus Publishing Group/Michael Boys; **84** courtesy All Weather Lighting Ltd, www.allweatherlighting.co.uk, telephone +44 (0) 1299 269246; **87** Octopus Publishing Group/Howard Rice; **90** Octopus Publishing Group; **92** Andrew Lawson; **97** Harpur Garden Library/Marcus Harpur; **104** Andrew Lawson; **110** below Marianne Majerus; **112** Andrew Lawson; **113** Photolibrary.com/Garden Picture Library/John Glover; **122** Minitheatre Productions; **123** Rod Parry; **125** above and below, **126** Andrew Lawson; **130** Marianne Majerus; **135** Andrew Lawson; **145** Garden World Images/Botanic Images Inc; **146, 152, 156** Andrew Lawson; **158** Garden World Images/K Laban; **161, 165** Andrew Lawson; **166** Natural Image/Bob Gibbons; **167** Andrew Lawson; **169** above Clive Nichols/Design Charlotte Row; **171, 179** Andrew Lawson; **182, 183** courtesy N. & C. Thomas; **186** Andrew Lawson; **188** Clive Nichols; **193** left Andrew Lawson; **193** right Photos Horticultural; **194** above Andrew Lawson; **194** below Octopus Publishing Group/James Young; **197** above and below, **203, 212, 213** Andrew Lawson; **216** Octopus Publishing Group/Jerry Harpur; **225** Andrew Lawson; **234, 235** David Markson.